Troubled Talk

Language, Power and Social Process 15

Editors
Monica Heller
Richard J. Watts

Mouton de Gruyter
Berlin · New York

Troubled Talk

Metaphorical Negotiation in Problem Discourse

by
Irit Kupferberg
David Green

Mouton de Gruyter
Berlin · New York

Mouton de Gruyter (formerly Mouton, The Hague)
is a Division of Walter de Gruyter GmbH & Co. KG, Berlin.

Library of Congress Cataloging-in-Publication Data

Kupferberg, Irit.
  Troubled talk : metaphorical negotiation in problem discourse / by Irit Kupferberg, David Green.
    p. cm. − (Language, power, and social process ; 15)
  Includes bibliographical references and index.
  ISBN 3-11-018415-X (hardcover : alk. paper) − ISBN 3-11-018416-8 (pbk. : alk. paper)
  1. Discourse analysis − Psychological aspects. 2. Discourse analysis, Narrative. 3. Narration (Rhetoric) 4. Psycholinguistics. 5. Interpersonal communication. I. Green, David, 1935− II. Title. III. Series.
  P302.8.K868 2005
  401'.41−dc22
                                                              2005010443

∞ Printed on acid-free paper which falls within the guidelines of the ANSI to ensure permanence and durability.

ISBN 3-11-018415-X hb
ISBN 3-11-018416-8 pb

Bibliographic information published by Die Deutsche Bibliothek

Die Deutsche Bibliothek lists this publication in the Deutsche Nationalbibliografie; detailed bibliographic data is available in the Internet at <http://dnb.ddb.de>.

© Copyright 2005 by Walter de Gruyter GmbH & Co. KG, D-10785 Berlin.
All rights reserved, including those of translation into foreign languages. No part of this book may be reproduced in any form or by any means, electronic or mechanical, including photocopy, recording, or any information storage and retrieval system, without permission in writing from the publisher.
Cover design: Christopher Schneider.
Printed in Germany.

To Batia and Arie

Preface

About nine years ago, we decided to collaborate by combining our discourse analytic and psychological perspectives in a study of radio, hotline and cyber talk about problems. We were curious to find out how sufferers who are in an acute emotional state negotiate the meaning of their troubled experiences with anonymous others. Guided by theoretical and practical goals, we set out on a challenging journey of exploration in the course of which we discovered a treasure comprising intriguing figurative forms we named "organizing tropes". A close examination of these salient gems showed that they often encapsulate the essence of the detailed and painful personal stories unfolded by troubled selves visiting various sites where mental help is provided. We also found out that these figurative constructions enhance the interactive discussion of solutions and prevail over the limitations characteristic of problem talk. In this book, we would like to share the insights we gained with our readers, hoping that they will be able to apply them in research and in practice in other domains of life.

Deeply felt thanks are due to Monica Heller and Richard Watts, the editors of the series and Rebecca Walter at Mouton who have supported our project from its inception until it became a full-fledged book. We have been blessed with the help of Richard Watts, who has provided us with wise and supportive observations and comments that guided us at meaningful junctions of the book production. We are grateful to the anonymous readers for their insightful comments. We know that any remaining errors are entirely our own. We express our gratitude to ERAN (The Israeli Hotline) and Izhak Gilat, its professional coordinator who collaborated with us in the writing of Chapter 5. We also thank Israel Broadcasting Authority, the Israel Defense Forces Radio and the hosts Yovav Katz and Gideon Reicher for their support. We are grateful to Tami Ronen for her ongoing support and advice. We acknowledge with gratitude the students at Levinsky College of Education and Tel Aviv University for their participation in the collection of the radio corpus and those students who participated in some of the analyses of problem talk. We are appreciative of the anonymous callers and digital writers we hosted in the book. Without them, we would have never discovered the precious organizing figurative language of problem discourse. And last but certainly not least, to Batia, David's wife and Arie, Irit's husband for their immense love and patience.

List of the troubled selves

1. "Amputating the cancerous leg": Chapter 3.
2. "I was really like a mother to him": Chapter 3.
3. "Life is like a jail": Chapter 3.
4. "This puzzle – I have to find the missing part": Chapter 3.
5. "One can talk about all kinds of subjects": Chapter 3.
6. "Like you're the world's only sucker": Chapter 3.
7. "In a big bang": Chapter 4.
8. "I don't know how to get close to my middle son": Chapter 4.
9. "Am I their floor rag?": Chapter 5.
10. "The lion and the snake": Chapter 5.
11. "My life is a story in a book": Chapter 5.
12. "Why not be ahead of my time?": Chapter 6.
13. "I was the best source of light on the market": Chapter 6.
14. "I produce a new mechanism that controls the addictive behavior": Chapter 7.
15. "That person didn't have horns and didn't have a beard": Chapter 7.
16. "Everything simply started snowballing": Chapter 8.
17. "I'm like a blender": Chapter 8.
18. "But sex was always something strong inside": Chapter 8.
19. "I'm not there today": Chapter 8
20. "He becomes a nervous wreck that drags you along": Chapter 8.
21. "She is condemned to slow and painful extinction and we live in a daily hell": Chapter 8.

Contents

Preface	vii
List of the troubled selves	ix

Part 1 Defining the boundaries for problem discourse

Chapter 1 Situating problem discourse in a postmodern landscape	3
1. The troubled self visits actual and virtual sites	3
2. Institutional discourse: Between the panopticon and the workshop room	5
Chapter 2 Theoretical and methodological frameworks	15
1. Theoretical framework	15
1.1. Functional approaches to discourse	15
1.2. Global coherence	21
1.3. Narrative evaluation	22
1.4. Worlds of discourse	25
1.5. Discourse-oriented perspective on figurative language	28
2. Methodological framework	33
2.1. Corpora	33
2.1.1. "The two of us together and each of us alone" corpus	35
2.1.2. "Night birds talk" corpus	36
2.1.3. Hotline corpus	37
2.1.4. Cyberspace corpus	38
2.2. Data collection and analysis	38
3. Overview of the book	41

Part 2 Figurative bridges in radio, hotline and cyber discourse

Chapter 3 Organizing tropes	47
1. The troubled caller makes a phone call	47
1.1. Effective interactions	47
1.2. Ineffective interactions	56
2. Summary	64
Chapter 4 Open your call with a title	69
1. Topic-focused program: "I advise you to hate your mother"	69

xii *Contents*

2. General program: "I don't know how to get close to my middle son"	82
3. Summary	90

Chapter 5 Figurative conspiracies   93

1. Hotline sufferers   93
   1.1. "Am I their floor rag?"   93
   1.2. "The lion and the snake"   99
   1.3. "My life is a story in a book"   102
2. Summary   104

Chapter 6 Cyber multilogues   107

1. Cyberspace sufferers   107
   1.1. "Why not be ahead of my time?"   107
   1.2. "I was the best source of light on the market"   120
2. Summary   126

Part 3 The discursive construction of control

Chapter 7 Negotiating the right to advertise the self   131

1. The healer: "I produce a new mechanism that controls the addictive behavior" 131
2. The lesbian: "That person didn't have horns and didn't have a beard"   136
3. Summary   139

Chapter 8 The construction of addictive disorders in discourse   141

1. Addictive behaviors and codependency   142
2. Addicted and codependent selves   144
   2.1. The love addict: "Everything simply started snowballing" 144
   2.2. The obese eater: "I'm a blender"   148
   2.3. The sex addict: "But sex was always something strong inside" 151
   2.4. The abstinent gambler: "I'm not there today"   152
   2.5. An ex-alcoholic's wife: "He becomes a nervous wreck that drags you along" 154
   2.6. The anorexic's mother: "We live in daily hell"   158
3. Summary   160

Part 4   Redefining the boundaries of problem discourse

Chapter 9   Theoretical conclusions and action-oriented
            implications   167

  1. Theoretical conclusions: Global figurative coherence
     in a multilogue   168
     1.1. Professional and lay voices reshape the boundaries of
          problem discourse   168
     1.2. Figurative trans-world journeys   172
  2. Action-oriented implications   176

Epilogue   179

Notes   181

References   193

Author index   215

Subject index   219

Part 1
Defining the boundaries for problem discourse

Chapter 1
Situating problem discourse in a postmodern landscape

1. The troubled self visits actual and virtual sites

At the outset of the twenty-first century, troubled selves[1] wander about a contemporary[2] landscape full of actual and virtual institutional sites[3] that entice them to pay a visit in order to make sense of their experience. These sites comprise various therapeutic and counseling settings such as long-term and short-term therapy, hotlines, support groups, as well as the more public radio problem discussions and cyberspace forums.

Some sufferers, like *The lion and the snake*,[4] the metaphorical name we gave the hotline caller whose problems are unfolded in Chapter 5, avail themselves of the services of several sites at the same time. Once these human beings have entered one of the sites, they publicize their private emotion-laden personal stories[5] (Macdonald 2003) and negotiate possible solutions to their pressing problems with professional or para-professional representatives of the institution.

In this book,[6] we set out to explore naturally occurring institutional telephone and cyber problem discourse[7] in order to attain theoretical and action-oriented goals. In other words, we wish to describe and interpret the meaning-making processes that take place in these sites and then present our findings to our readers. The latter may wish to further explore the domain or apply the insights gained in this book in practice.

Our corpora constitute unique empirical evidence. The participants in goal-oriented telephone and cyber problem discourse are sufferers who are frequently in an acute emotional – if not suicidal – state. As a result, they experience a pressing need to speak or write about their problems. Other participants are professional psychologists, radio hosts and para-professional hotline volunteers whose institutional[8] goal is to provide mental help.[9] This complicated discursive undertaking is accomplished in a unique speech situation. While participants are faced with demanding tasks of problem presentation and negotiation of candidate solutions (Buttny and Jensen 1995), they are often constrained by factors such as the tension between their respective goals and lack of shared knowledge and/or a time limit, which may undermine communication.

How do troubled selves fare in such sites? What do they say about them? What do the professional participants say about these sites that purport to provide mental help, but in fact do not belong to the official psychological establishment? Are the sufferers who seek help in such sites actually given mental help?

Psychology-oriented quantitative studies of telephone and cyber problem discourse in Israel provide partial answers to these questions (Raviv and Abuhav 2003) by showing that both lay and professional participants are aware of the advantages and disadvantages of these services. Raviv and Abuhav (ibid.) mention the following advantages: ample distribution of efficient psychological information and popularization and advertisement of psychological services. The disadvantages (ibid.) include time limit, which undermines the efficiency and the depth of the telephone interventions, instant solutions, and overgeneralized or erroneous conclusions regarding the caller's problems.

Macdonald (2003) foregrounds the media perspective on the therapystyle talk-shows where private experience is displayed in "its 'raw' state" (ibid.: 85). "Everything else – news, sitcoms, soap operas, prime-time drama series – everything else is scripted, orchestrated, excessively edited, performed by good-looking professional actors with great lighting, top-notch photography, background music – it's all canned" (Jerry Springer, as cited in Macdonald 2003: 86). The emotionally charged public confessions made by lay persons often empower the rating-oriented talk-show hosts, who use the dramas unfolded in their programs to advance their aims without solving the lay sufferers' problems (ibid.).

In the course of this book, we explore further the voices of suffering individuals seeking help in naturally occurring telephone and cyber sites. Following research that has shown that radio, hotline, cyber and clinical problem discourse are particularly rich in personal stories whose very engine is trouble (Bruner 1997), and using a qualitative method that we developed, we examine the narrative and figurative productions of the troubled selves presented in the book. We show

how these discursive patterns are related to each other and how self-construction is negotiated and accomplished via them.

Before we shift our attention from the sites where problems are verbalized and interpreted by actual or virtual participants to a more theoretical realm where researchers reflect on these selves and the nature of the sites they visit, we would like to show what a very troubled 15-year-old adolescent said about cyber problem discourse – one of the sites we visit in this book. Example (1) is an excerpt from a message sent by this boy. In the message, the teenager describes the contribution of the virtual forum in helping him overcome his problems (see Chapter 6):

Example (1) "The only place where I can speak about it"

1 Hi.
2 I've had these feelings for a year and a half, but only now have I
3 found my inner courage[10] and shared my thoughts with other
4 people. And I'm afraid to see the school counselor because she
5 might send me to a psychologist or something like that, and at a
6 time like this I don't think that's what I need. That's why I wrote
7 to this site because it's probably the only place where I can speak
8 about it without being afraid that some action will be taken
9 against me.

We will never know for sure if this boy opted to live or committed suicide. Our interpretation of the messages he sent and the answers he received suggest that this adolescent was saved by a spur-of-the-moment virtual rescue team whose anonymous members somehow managed to shift the boy's attention from his tormented past world to a future world where life is worth living.

2. Institutional discourse: Between the panopticon and the workshop room

Where can we locate the troubled minds visiting actual and virtual institutions on a historical axis? What are the characteristics of the postmodern landscape in which these troubled selves wander? What are the characteristics of the language that they use in the actual and virtual sites where problems are unfolded and solutions co-constructed?

In this section we will describe how current scholarship answers these questions. Then, we will position ourselves as researchers vis-à-vis this theoretical landscape.

Since antiquity, Western thinkers have attempted to explain how human beings make sense of the world when they use language.[11] The issue is succinctly formulated in the following excerpt:

> The problem of how language relates to reality and to the minds that strive to grasp that reality has long exercised the finest thinkers in the Western tradition. Everyone marvels at the power of language, especially perhaps as it is deployed in science ... Somewhere in the semantic triangle formed of mind, world, and language, we suppose, lie the relationships that constitute meaning (Overton 1994). Yet these relationships have time and again resisted the best efforts of Western thinkers to characterize them explicitly and in satisfactory fullness. (Smith 1997: 15)

Following Smith's mind-world-language triangle of meaning, we will now relate to the questions formulated at the beginning of this section. The first question focuses on the definition of the term "self" from a historical perspective. Holstein and Gubrium (2000) provide a detailed answer by tracing the saga of the modern social self in the twentieth century until it reaches postmodernity. Turning away from Descartes' classic formulation of the transcendental *self* – a philosophical position that "stands over and above everyday life" (Gubrium and Holstein 2001: v) – these authors describe the conception of an empirical social self in the works of James, Cooley, Mead, and Goffman (Cooley 1964 [1902]; Goffman 1959; James 1961 [1892]; Mead 1934), where it is located in human experience and interactive discursive processes of everyday life.

And then the social self reaches postmodernity[12] – an epoch whose most salient feature is "the crisis of confidence in Western conceptual systems" (Lather 1994: 102, as cited in Holstein and Gubrium 2000). The second question that we asked concerns the characteristics of the postmodern landscape in which troubled selves wander. Brought about by a paradigm shift[13] that has been advanced largely by Western intellectuals (Seidman 1994),[14] postmodernism is defined and compared with modernism in the following excerpt:

> Dating from the Enlightenment and Descartes, the modern paradigm is based on the belief that a cognizing self can use reason and knowledge to understand and manipulate an objectively verifiable world. The postmodern paradigm abandons the individual–world duality and makes a radical move to a socio-

Institutional discourse: Between the panopticon and the workshop room 7

linguistic frame. In the postmodern view, reality – even so called scientific reality – is woven and rewoven on shared linguistic looms. (Hoffman 1997: XII)

The definition emphasizes several dimensions of the modern and postmodern paradigms that can be elaborated on within the boundaries of the semantic mind-world-language triangle presented at the beginning of this section. As far as the modern paradigm is concerned, meaning-making processes are accomplished by a cognizing self inhabiting a human mind that is, in turn, isolated from the objective world outside the mind. As for language, it functions as a neutral medium that the mind uses to mirror (Rorty 1979) or represent (Stewart 1996) the world.

Postmodernism, as the definition shows, promotes the importance of language, one of the angles of the semantic triangle we mentioned earlier. It relocates meaning-making processes by shifting them from the isolated mind to discourse, or language that is used in a specific context (or world) and is reflexively related to it.[15] In fact, it is human beings who participate in discourse and in so doing, construct the meaning of the world and the meaning of the self that constitutes a part of the human mind. So viewed from a postmodern perspective, the mind and the world are now reflected and constructed in discourse.

A postmodern definition of self-construction is often associated with narrative discourse, "the artful yet locally structured stories that comprise the contemporary self in practice" (Holstein and Gubrium 2000: 103).[16] Such local self-constructions enable the self to express itself in dynamic processes that depend on the situations where the self is located. Sometimes, however, it has so many meanings that it becomes "saturated", to use Gergen's (1991) frequently quoted epithet, and, according to some postmodern scholars, ceases to exist.

Postmodern self-plurality is vividly described in the following excerpt:

> Postmodern individuals no longer devote themselves to one job in one workplace but rush, blur-like, from office to study to other-office, to office to home; they no longer read one book, but hyperlink from website to website to home page, with just a few minutes in between to scroll through their e-mail. The postmodern woman is no longer a mother and a housewife, but a post-feminist mother-lover-friend-colleague-partner; the postmodern man is no longer a husband and worker, but a post-new man-father-friend-confident-lover-lad. (Cooper and Rowan 1999: 1)

Clinical psychologists and psychoanalysts are engaged in actual problem discourse where they encounter flesh-and-blood clients "face-to-face in the personalized intimacy of a therapeutic relationship" (Rowan and Cooper 1999: 4; see also Anderson 1997 and Frie 2003). Seeing how troubled selves actually struggle to define the meaning of their existence, these professionals find it hard to accept the theoretical annihilation of the self (Cooper and Rowan 1999). Neither does the idea of annihilation appeal to sociologists such as Holstein and Gubrium (2000) who propose a happy ending to the story of the social self that is engaged in institutional discourse, or talk at work.[17]

Before we explore Holstein and Gubrium's idea of happy ending, we should first define institutional discourse and then answer the final question we raised at the beginning of this section, concerning the characteristics of the language that troubled selves use. Two approaches to discourse that are especially pertinent to our discussion of self-construction in institutional sites are presented below: Foucault's[18] approach and institutional conversation analysis (ICA).

In an interview in 1982, two years before his death,[19] Foucault reflected on his scientific works and emphasized that throughout his life, he had explored how the meaning of the concept self is sculpted by psychological, medical, penitential, and educational discursive practices. Foucault added that these discursive practices are related to and shaped by non-discursive historical forces. In response to the question of why he had always been interested in social outcasts, Foucault replied:

> It is one of my targets to show people that a lot of things that are a part of their landscape – that people think are universal – are the result of some very precise historical change. All my analyses are against the idea of universal necessities in human existence. They show the arbitrariness of institutions and show which space of freedom we can still enjoy and how many changes can still be made. (Martin, Gutman, and Hutton 1988: 11)

This excerpt epitomizes a tenet underlying Foucault's work: Institutional discursive practices are arbitrary and do not result from universal necessities. Therefore, Foucault thinks that human beings can attempt to use the "space of freedom" that is provided to them in order to change the given state of things. One of the discursive practices that interested Foucault was self-construction. Consistent with his interest in history, Foucault specifies that self-exploring discursive practices such as Freud's psychotherapy date from seventeenth-century confessional practices of the Catholic church (Hutton 1988: 121). In his later studies on the shaping of the self, Foucault remarks that these technologies of the self have an earlier origin in the routines of monastic life of the Christian Roman Empire of the fourth and fifth centuries (ibid.).

Although Foucault repeatedly relates to institutional discursive practices, his works do not attempt to understand the local discursive mechanisms through which human beings actually communicate. Foucault prefers to explore the historical development of discourse (Macdonald 2003). His macro-perspective on discourse is elaborated on in *Discipline and Punish* (Foucault 1977). In this work, Foucault describes the panopticon – a prison or workhouse so arranged that all parts of the interior are visible from a single point.[20] For Foucault, this architectural structure symbolizes the influence historical, cultural, and social forces exert on institutional discursive practices. Holstein and Gubrium explain how Foucault's panopticon epitomizes discursive practices where control is exercised through the participants' minds:

> For Foucault, Jeremy Bentham's plan for the Panopticon prison actualizes as well as symbolizes this form of governance, combining a new concept of power with concrete application. The Panopticon consists of a tower located at the center of a large courtyard, facing a set of surrounding buildings. The cells of the buildings, and the inmates within, are completely visible from the tower, but the inmates, who are sequestered from each other, cannot see if the guard is in the tower. So, the inmates must act as if surveillance is ever-present, in effect causing them to rule themselves because they take the surveillance for granted. This epitomizes a new disciplinary technology, where power does not operate like a force from the outside, but works through inner self-scrutiny, the subject disciplining itself (and thus ruling himself) according to what he takes to be a hidden guardian. (Holstein and Gubrium 2000: 78)

The panopticon, as the excerpt shows, symbolizes efficient control over the minds of others in the institutional organizations that Foucault studied. Following Holstein and Gubrium (2000), we wonder what degree of choice troubled individuals may have when they visit institutional sites whose discourse, according to Foucault, is governed and structured by constraining social conventions and written and unwritten rules. Foucault advised his followers not to accept "knowledge at face value but to analyze these so-called sciences as very specific 'truth games' related to specific techniques that human beings use to understand themselves" (Foucault 1988: 18).

However, as we have already emphasized, Foucault himself did not explore actual text and talk in interaction. Instead, he preferred to reflect upon discourse from a distant theoretical perspective. Following Foucault, proponents of critical discourse analysis (CDA)[21] explore talk in interaction in the quest for power-displaying discursive resources (Thornborrow 2002). These discourse analysts often use concepts such as "hegemony", "ideology", "class", "gender", "race", "discrimination" and "interests" (van Dijk 2001: 343).

For example, Ribiero (1996) studied a female patient's discharge interview from a psychiatric institution where she had been interned for 20 days. Assuming a CDA perspective, the author shows that the doctor's discursive contribution repeatedly confines the patient within the framework of the mentally ill instead of enhancing the fact that she is about to resume control over her life after her release from hospital. Thornborrow (2002) criticizes the prescriptive orientation of the CDA approach that assigns power and inequality to institutional discourse. Focusing on Fairclough's analysis of another doctor–patient interaction (Fairclough 1992: 138–139), Thornborrow makes the following comments:

> When we begin to look at the detail of talk, it becomes less clear that we can describe the operation of power in discourse in terms of one participant 'controlling' the turn taking organization. While it seems clear that this talk constitutes a particular form of institutional discursive practice, that speaker identities and participant status are asymmetrical, and that there is an institutional agenda at work here (the business of symptom description, diagnosis and subsequent proposed treatment), I would question Fairclough's interpretation of the doctor as doing things like 'controlling questions' and the patient doing things like 'accepting' turns (p.144). As we saw on two occasions in the talk, P [the patient] pursued her own turn without waiting for D's [the doctor's] offer, and, on one occasion, D abandoned a question entirely in response to the way P had designed her preceding turn. (Thornborrow 2002: 21)

In this excerpt, Thornborrow shows that Fairclough's analysis is based on an a priori CDA assumption that institutional context *always* comprises existing relations of power and status. Instead, she advocates a micro-analytic examination of interaction to see what actually takes place (Thornborrow 2002). We can conclude and say that Foucault's panoptical approach to institutional discourse – an approach that has inspired CDA – emphasizes that self-construction in institutional discursive practices is by and large shaped by nondiscursive historical forces. Foucault himself did not explore actual text and discourse.

The second approach to discourse that is described in this subsection is institutional conversation analysis (ICA) (Drew and Heritage 1992; Drew and Sorjonen 1997; Heritage 1997). Following the more traditional conversation analysis (Sacks 1992), whose roots are anchored in phenomenology and ethnomethodology,[22] ICA focuses on the local construction of institutional life as it is unfolded in the sequential real-time talk and interaction in institutional settings. Drew and Heritage define ICA in the following excerpt:[23]

> Institutional interactions may take place face-to-face or over the telephone. They may occur within a designated physical setting, for example a hospital, courtroom, or educational establishment, but they are by no means restricted to such settings ... Rather, interaction is institutional insofar as participants' institutional or professional identities are somehow made relevant to the work activities in which they are engaged. (Drew and Heritage 1992: 3–4)

Thus, ICA foregrounds the relevance of naturally occurring talk as a means to "get into the 'black box' of social institutions" (Drew and Heritage 1992: 5), in lieu of traditional sociological means such as questionnaires, structured interviews, ethnographic observation, and participants' commentaries and self reports. Drew and Heritage (ibid.) further describe the characteristics of institutional discourse. First, the turn-by-turn design of institutional talk is goal- and task-oriented (i.e., participants have goals and attempt to attain them through the accomplishment of institutional tasks). For example, in the corpora presented in our book, troubled selves call up the hotline service to solve their problem, and during the telephone conversation they accomplish various tasks such as the presentation and negotiation of their problems with para-professional volunteers.

Another feature assigned to institutional discourse is asymmetry (i.e., participants' discursive rights and obligations are not equal). For example, in our radio corpora, it is the host who initiates the interaction and has the right to terminate it, and not the lay callers or the psychologists who participate in the interaction. However, asymmetry does not necessarily mean that that radio hosts control the lay participants, as Thornborrow (2002) emphasizes in her criticism of CDA. For example, in Chapter 4, we show how two institutional representatives – a radio program host and a female psychologist – align themselves with a lay caller against another institutional representative.

In conclusion, we can say that ICA focuses on the local construction of institutional life as it is unfolded in the sequential real-time interaction in institutional settings. ICA foregrounds the importance of naturally occurring discourse in which self-construction is often accomplished via personal stories that lay selves and professionals co-construct. In Chapters 3–8, we will examine closely how self-revealing narrative formats[24] are first presented by lay participants in institutional problem discourse and how they are subsequently negotiated with professional and para-professional others.

So where exactly can we situate postmodern selves when they seek help in one of the sites described earlier? Are they imprisoned in pan-optical discursive and narrative practices according to Foucault? Or are they perhaps given a choice, space, and possibilities in institutional interactions according to institutional conversation analysis? As we mentioned previously, Holstein and Gubrium (2000) propose a happy end to the story of the self in the following words:

> If Foucault works in a historical register, and ethnomethodology in an interactional one, we tell the story of the self at the crossroads of narrative, social interaction, culture and institutional life. Working historically, Foucault had little access to the everyday operation of discourses, of discursive practice. We are more tuned to everyday interaction as it bears on self construction. At the same time taking direction from Foucault, we are more deeply concerned with the resources and conditions of self-construction that is typical of ethnomethodology. While certainly appreciating the *hows* of self construction, we are equally interested in the various *whats* – that extend to discourse and surrounding institutional environments of talk and social interaction. (Holstein and Gubrium 2000: 96–97)

What these authors are suggesting to theoreticians and empirical researchers interested in self-construction, then, is to be inspired by two complementary beacons. Mind the historical macro-forces that are at work, they suggest, and at the same time, pay attention to how the troubled selves attempt to express possibility and options in everyday social interaction that can be identified via micro-analysis.

Inspired by the constructivist paradigm (Lincoln and Guba 2000) and following current scholarship that advocates the use of micro- and macro-analytic approaches,[25] we explore self-construction in interactional telephone, cyber and face-to-face problem discourse. Figuratively speaking, we adopt the "panopticon" metaphor, the symbol of Foucault's prescriptive approach that emphasizes that powerful forces shape institutional discourse. At the same time, we accept "the local weaving of meaning by verbal looms located in workshop rooms."[26] The latter constitute our symbol of the environments of possibility and change that one can be engaged in when viewed from the non-confining perspective of institutional conversation analysis. In Chapter 2, we will present our interfacing four-world model of discourse analysis that is based on theoretical and methodological arguments that justify the marriage of micro- and macro-analyses.

Having set the boundaries of our book between the panopticon and the workshop room, we can now turn to examine our corpora in the quest for an answer to a central intriguing question: How is meaning constructed by professional and lay participants visiting the telephone and cyberspace sites explored in this book? This general question can be further subdivided into two specific questions: (1) To which discursive resources do participants in telephone and cyberspace problem discourse resort in order to accomplish their complicated tasks of problem presentation? (2) To what extent are these resources related to the interactional and meaningful construction of problems and solutions?

To answer these questions we advance two interrelated theoretical claims derived from the empirical evidence presented in this book. These claims have practical implications that are elaborated on in Chapter 9. The first provides an answer to our first specific question. It stresses that participants in problem discourse often present their troubles through detailed narrative discourse as well as succinct story-internal tropes. These are discursive resources that constitute interrelated versions of the troubled self. This claim establishes a meaningful connection between detailed narrative self-construction and succinct organizing figurative language (Kupferberg and Green 1998) that is often produced within the story to express the inexpressible (Gibbs 1994).

The second claim provides an answer to our second specific question. It stresses that the expressive, summative, interactional, and often multi-actional figurative language identified, described, and interpreted in our book constitutes a central discursive bridge that facilitates self-presentation and enhances the co-construction of solutions. These figurative and narrative resources of self-construction are employed in public radio interactions as well as in the more private hotline service that is not influenced by the overhearing audience. Therefore, at times they are used and at others abused, depending on a plethora of contextual resources that will be unfolded in the following chapters.

To recapitulate: In Chapter 1 we position ourselves as researchers in relation to relevant scholarship that inspired our study of interactional problem discourse. To this end, we define the historical origins of the technologies of self-construction. Then, we describe the characteristics of two approaches to institutional discourse that mark the theoretical boundaries of our book: Foucault's macro-approach and micro-analytic institutional conversation analysis (ICA). Figuratively speaking, the boundaries of our book are marked, then, by two architectonic tropes. The "panopticon" epitomizes Foucault's prescriptive approach. "The local weaving of meaning by verbal looms located in workshop rooms" constitutes our figurative representation of the environments of possibility and change viewed from the non-confining perspective of ICA.

At first glance, these sources of inspiration seem incompatible. In Chapter 2, we provide a detailed explanation how these approaches can be married in our four-world model. To this end, we present a detailed theoretical introduction that provides the background to our methodological framework. In Chapter 2, we also present our corpora, and then we describe how we produce our interpretive interface that relates the micro-analyses of the corpora to the broader contextual resources that are at our disposal as researchers. Bearing in mind the theoretical and methodological frameworks established in Part 1, Chapters 1 and 2, we continue in Chapters 3–8 to examine how the troubled selves we host in this book present their problems and attempt to negotiate possible solutions with professional and para-professional others.

Our interpretive analyses of these lay and professional voices show that the metaphorical boundaries presented in Chapter 1 should be redefined. Chapter 9 – the concluding chapter of the book – emphasizes how (i.e., by which discursive resources) and when (i.e., in what circumstances) the boundaries between the "panoptical institution" and "the workshop rooms" are abolished and then redefined by professional and lay participants.

Chapter 2
Theoretical and methodological frameworks

In Chapter 1, we set the boundaries of our book between the "panoptical institution" and "discourse-analytic workshop rooms". In Chapter 2, we present a detailed theoretical framework that justifies this alliance and provides the background to our methodological framework. Our theoretical approach embraces current definitions of discourse analysis that show how micro- and macro-levels should be interfaced. In addition, we espouse an integrated functional approach to problem discourse. This approach combines institutional conversation analysis (ICA), context-based discourse analysis, and narrative inquiry. Then, on the basis of this theoretical foundation, we present our interfacing four-world model of discourse analysis.

1. Theoretical framework

1.1. Functional approaches to discourse

To study how meaning is constructed in problem discourse, we espouse a theoretical framework anchored in ICA that was presented in Chapter 1, context-based discourse analysis (Duranti 1997; Hymes 1974; Linell 1998) and a narrative approach to self-construction (Bruner 1997).[27] These functional approaches share the view that language is a tool of human communication that is always related to and embedded in a specific context.

Following ICA, the first approach listed earlier, we micro-analyze naturally occurring telephone and cyber problem discourse. At this local level, we explore how sufferers' problems are presented and negotiated with professionals by means of discursive resources in the sequential production of discourse. However, we differ from some conversation analysts, headed by Schegloff (1997), who privilege only those aspects of context that participants "show that they have attended to, or are being influenced by" (Tracy 1998: 8). Instead, we align ourselves with the more context-oriented ethnographers of communication who emphasize the significance of pre-existing contextual resources that are reflexively related to discourse in a broader contextual space. Examples (2–4) illustrate how our integrated functional approach is applied in a micro-analysis. Example (2) is an excerpt taken from the opening of an institutional telephone conversation[28] between a radio host (H) and a troubled caller (C):[29]

Example (2) Turn-taking

1   H: The two of us together and each of us alone. Let's go on.
2   C: Hello.
3   H: Hello. Go ahead.

Example (2) illustrates how "the discursive mechanics of the social construction of reality" (Heller 2001: 250) can be micro-analyzed. In this example, the host and the caller interactionally accomplish several tasks that are identified via a close turn-by-turn examination. Methodologies like content analysis or the grounded theory often obscure the major features of the interaction because they do not study the sequentially organized turns, but rather require that categories be set in advance, as in the case of content analysis, or be developed during the analysis, as in the case of grounded theory (Titscher et al. 2000).

The host's first turn (line 1) performs two institutional tasks. It reminds those members of the overhearing audience at home who have just turned on the radio what they are listening to. In addition, the host orients himself to the actual participants of the ongoing radio program (i.e., psychologists and callers) and signals that the program is in progress. In response to the host's directive, a caller who has been accepted into the real-time interaction greets the host (line 2). The host responds and signals to the caller that she can go on (line 3). It is evident from this interaction that the turn-taking right is asymmetrical, and it is the host who assigns turns.[30]

Following context-based discourse analysis, the second approach listed at the beginning of this subsection, we rely on contextual resources as we engage in the analysis of problem discourse. For example, the analysis of Example (2) is based on our acquaintance with the radio program. We know, for example, that this radio program deals with psychological issues and attempts to solve callers' problems. We also know that the radio team consists of an experienced host and two psychologists and that anonymous callers are screened by the program operators prior to gaining access to the program. The asymmetrical character of Example (2) is not maintained in Example (3) from our hotline corpus. The participants are a lonely 80-year-old widower (C) and a hotline volunteer (V):

Example (3) The boundaries between institutional and non-institutional discourse

1 C: To judge by your speech, you are not a senior citizen.
2 V: What do you mean by a senior citizen?
3 C: An adult past 50. You're not. You're younger.
4 V: True.
5 C: Perhaps you are only 40.
6 V: Less than 40.
7 C: Less than 40?
8 V: Right.
9 C: I can tell by your speech.

Example (3) shows how at a certain point an institutional interaction becomes a friendly chat based on personal interest when the older male caller addresses the younger female volunteer – the institutional representative – with personal questions that are quite irrelevant to the task she is expected to accomplish (i.e., assist the caller in finding a solution to his problem). In brief, Example (3) illustrates how a close examination of talk reveals that institutional talk is not always asymmetrical, a finding that obliges the researcher to avoid sweeping generalizations and concentrate on the local features of each interaction in its relevant context.

We also adopt a narrative approach to self-construction that views narrative discourse as a gestalt configuration of life (Brockmeier 2001)[31] that is made up of linguistic building-blocks such as syntactic structures, lexical choice, tense shift, pronouns, constructed dialogue, and tropes. These functional resources are used by narrators in their attempt to construct and co-construct globally coherent verbal dimensions of the self. We explore these discursive resources by looking at them rather than through them (Capps and Ochs 1995) in the quest for inter- and intrapersonal dimensions of the narrated past world as well as possible future worlds.[32] Following the conversation analytic perspective, we will now show how ICA can be combined with the narrative analysis of a story.[33] Example (4) from our radio corpus shows that the host signals to the caller that she can present her problem and that she chooses to unfold a personal story:

Example (4) Unfolding a personal story

```
1  H: "The two of us together and each of us alone." ((addressing the next
2     caller)). Good evening. Go ahead, please.
3  C: This feeling has accompanied me in many situations, but I would like
4     to talk about a specific case. About three years ago, my brother was
5     killed in an accident ((pause)). Now, he was missing for three weeks
6     and ((pause)). They discovered the body, and ((pause)) there was
7     some sort of investigation ((pause)). But that's not the important part.
8     He was my younger brother, and ((pause)) it happened when I was 30
9     years old and he was 28, and when we were children we were
10    friends. That is we were very close to each other. That is, I was, I was
11    really like a mother to him.
```

In Example (4), the host allows the caller to take a longer narrative turn (lines 1–2) comprising a personal story (lines 3–11) that shows what the source of her problem is. Following Labov's structural components of a past tense personal story,[34] we divided the story into several elements, including evaluation, or self-building resources. For example, orientation, or the background of the story, is provided in lines 3–4. The problem-causing complicating action is unfolded in lines 4–7. Then, in lines 7–11, the narrator produces repetition – a self-revealing evaluative resource – to emphasize how close she was to her brother. Repetition is only one of the evaluative devices that reveals the caller's self. In Chapters 3–8 of our book, our micro-analyses show how callers use a variety of evaluative devices that construct dimensions of their troubled narrative selves in the interaction, and how the institutional representatives relate to these self-presentations. In these chapters, we specifically emphasize the contribution of figurative evaluative devices to problem talk.

We will now present three tenets underlying the functional approaches that we have outlined. These tenets can be profitably described within the boundaries of the mind-world-language triangle described in Chapter 1, section 2. The first tenet relates to the centrality of language. Accordingly, we hold that meaning-making processes are accomplished via "linguistic looms" located in the "workshop rooms" of problem discourse sites. The "workshop" metaphor foregrounds the constitutive function of language beyond its ability to reflect or mirror (Stewart 1996). However, this workshop is also constrained, as we argued in Chapter 1, by panoptical institutional forces that limit the range of possibilities provided by the workshop.

The second tenet relates to the world. Following Drew and Heritage (1992), Linell (1998) and van Dijk (1997), we replace the term *world* – one of the three terms that constitute the semantic triangle described in Chapter 1 – with the term *context*. Context is not an objective construct out there in the real world, as we have already shown. Participants constantly construct and co-construct the cultural, social, psychological, and historical contextual resources that are relevant to them during the interaction in the "workshop room" of problem discourse sites.

The second tenet, then, holds that language is reflexively related to context, and the two mutually constitute each other (Linell 1998).[35] The following excerpt shows how Linell (1998: 264) defines reflexivity in the spirit of Bakhtin (1981):

> Any stretch of discourse, created in actors' interaction with other actors, is embedded in a matrix of contexts. However, it is not simply embedded or situated in contexts, but has a *reflexive* [emphasis in the original] relationship to the contexts. Discourses and contexts mutually constitute and select each other, and hence they form a basic, indivisible whole.

This definition of reflexivity emphasizes the bidirectional relationship between discourse and context. Participants in discourse, and the researchers who study them, constantly relate to relevant contextual resources in their interactional construction of meaning. Focusing on problem discourse, the genre[36] explored in this book, we assume that participants' discursive contributions are shaped by context. Moreover, in the process of verbalizing their problems, participants often develop awareness and insights that may further influence the context in which they live.[37] Therefore, reflexivity means that participants are reacting to contextual constraints that they themselves are actually making, so that action and reaction become part of the same discursive process (Richard Watts, personal communication).

The third tenet relates to the mind. Does language mirror intrapersonal processes, or is it an interpersonal workshop where they are constructed? Social constructionism (Gergen 1994) emphasizes that meaning is primarily constructed in interactional and communal context. Discursive psychology, a radical version of social constructionism

(Anderson 1997; Edwards 1997; Shotter 1999), argues that discourse offers an exclusive perspective on mental life, and problem discourse is a landscape where knowledge and self are locally co-constructed and transformed. Linell's (1998) less radical version, entitled dialogism, allows for monological *as well as* dialogical activities that provide room for self-agency and choice. Other scholars such as Brockmeier (2001), Craib (1998), Frie (2003), Gubrium and Holstein (2001), Holstein and Gubrium (2000), McAdams (1993, 1996), and Wertsch (1998) also align themselves with the second perspective. Hutton (1988) exemplifies inter- and intrapersonal approaches to the mind by relating to Freud's and Foucault's diametrically opposed technologies of the self in the following excerpt:

> According to Freud our destinies are shaped by the drama of conflicts within our minds. Foucault approaches the problem of the psyche from the opposite tack. It is not the internal working of the mind that initially interested him but the emerging array of asylums that have fostered scrutiny of the mind over the past three centuries. (Hutton 1988: 125)

The excerpt emphasizes that Freud's psychoanalytic theory investigates the internal architecture of the individual psyche, whereas Foucault, as we have already shown in Chapter 1, is interested in the external architecture of collective mentalities that are shaped by social and cultural forces in various institutions (Hutton 1988).

We align ourselves with scholars who emphasize the contribution of both interpersonal and intrapersonal processes to the creation of mental life. We do not accept the assumption that the mind is primarily an interpersonal rhetorical product. We argue, in this vein, that the self consists of biopsychosocial dimensions. Our book specifically focuses on how socio-cultural and psychological components of the self are co-constructed and transformed when troubled selves are engaged in a dialogue with professionals in one or several of the sites we visit in the book. Thus, the "curing talk"[38] co-produced in such sites constitutes "the locus of ongoing, constantly changing mental life" (Chafe 1994: 36) that is unfolded and transformed in the *here and now*. The ongoing problem discourse constitutes a temporary world where the complexities of the *there and then* troubled past and the possibilities of a better future can be fully explored.[39]

Unearthing the unconscious implies that there are intrapsychic contents and processes that can be revealed by means of various methods.

In fact, Freud's psychoanalytic theory and praxis focused on such notions through his "structural model" that describes inner structures (i.e., the *id*, *ego*, and *superego*) and contents (i.e., fantasies, drives, memories, and complexes). Some of these are even assumed to be phylogenetic (i.e., relating to the evolution of the species; Freud 1917). Freud also emphasized that cross-cultural intrapsychic innate contents such as symbols have archaic roots, a claim that was reinforced in Jung's theory about archetypes and the collective unconscious (Jung 1959).

Many of the post-Freudian psychological theories kept the basic intrapsychic assumption even though their orientations were diverse.[40] Following Freud, neo-analytical theories assumed that conscious processes are produced by the ego, although they accepted the explanation that intrapsychic contents exist (Bergman 2000). Contemporary analytical theories further assume the therapeutic co-construction of meaning that engages both the therapist's and patient's unconscious processes (Beebe and Lachmann 2002).

Intrapsychic contents influence our mental life and can be manifested in our conscious and/or unconscious verbal and non-verbal behaviors. Sometimes they may constitute the basis of conflicts underlying normal and abnormal behavior. A conflict is defined as "a mental struggle that arises from the simultaneous operation of opposing impulses and drives. External (environmental) or internal demands are termed intrapsychic when the conflict is between the forces within the personality; extrapsychic when it is between the self and the environment" (Werner et al. 1984: 22).

1.2. Global coherence

Coherence has been at the forefront of scholarly attention in text and discourse analysis for the past two decades, but it is still a controversial construct.[41] A current definition of coherence emphasizes that it is a dynamic context-dependent discourse process. Bublitz (1999: 2–3) defines the process in the following excerpt:

> Coherence is not a state but a process, helped along by a host of interacting factors situated on all levels of communication (from prosodic variation to textual organization, from topic progression to knowledge alignment). As a process, coherence is not taken for granted but, depending on situation, genre or text type, rather viewed as being more or less tentative and temporary, continually in need of being checked against new information which may

make adaption and updating necessary ... It is also a cooperative achievement because it depends on both the speaker's (or writer's) and the hearer's (or reader's) willingness to negotiate coherence. (Bublitz 1999: 2–3)

Bublitz's definition foregrounds interpersonal dimensions of coherence in naturally occurring speech and writing. Other scholars emphasize both inter- and intrapersonal aspects of meaning construction in discourse. On the intrapersonal level, the process is accomplished when participants make hypotheses about the knowledge, beliefs, values, and feelings of other participants (Gernsbacher and Givon 1995). Cooperation among participants is achieved on the interpersonal level and can bring about successful construction of coherence or failure in communication (Linell and Korolija 1997). The study of successful or unsuccessful construction of global coherence can be conducted via micro-discourse analysis – a close examination of natural discourse in which participants' verbal behavior is encoded in their turn-taking design, turn completion and lexical and syntactic repetition (Coates 1995; Kupferberg and Green 2003).

Local coherence is often manifested in various interrelated discourse resources such as sequentially ordered discourse turns or repetition, for example, when one of the participants repeats what another participant said. Global coherence is defined as the gist of the text, or its central theme (Linde 1993; Linell and Korolija 1997; McAdams 1993; van Dijk 1997). Global and local coherence are related when a sequence of turns or the repetition of lexical items enables participants to focus on the central theme (Linell and Korolija 1997).

Recent empirical evidence from life-story interviewing shows that personal stories unfolded by the same narrators at one time point or across time points cohere globally (Bar-Kol and Kupferberg 2001; Kupferberg and Gilat 2001; Kupferberg and Green 2001). Other studies show how global coherence is achieved in interactional institutional discourse (Kupferberg and Gilat 2002; Kupferberg and Green 2003). In Chapters 3–8, we present, interpret, and explain a large number of examples showing how participants in interactional problem discourse continually attempt to achieve global coherence by using figurative bridges to attain this end.

1.3. Narrative evaluation

In this subsection, we focus on self-construction in narrative discourse, and in subsection 1.5, on self-construction in figurative language. Across the chapters of the book we explore how narrative and figurative patterns are related to each other and to the construction of global coherence in telephone and cyber problem communication. Troubled selves unfolding their problems often produce different genres of narrative discourse such as specific and generic (or habitual) stories as well as figurative language such as metaphors, similes, and the like. Accordingly, narrative discourse and figurative language are often associated with self-construction in problem discourse.

For example, Example (4) presented in subsection 1.1 shows how a troubled caller unfolds her problem via a personal story. At the end of the story (lines 10–11), she produces an emotion-displaying simile "That is, I was, I was really like a mother to him", which summarizes the caller's feelings toward her deceased brother. Our analyses in Chapters 3–8 show how self-construction is accomplished via narrative discourse and tropes and how the two patterns are related to each other. These resources have been defined as constituents of our changing remembered self.[42] Research has mainly focused on each of the two, but to our knowledge not on the connection between them (McMullen 1996). Nor has it shown how tropes are related to central themes of narrative discourse (Reinhart 1995) and what their evaluative function is.

The narrative turn in the human sciences[43] foregrounded the idea that "the story form, both oral or written, constitutes a fundamental linguistic, psychological, social, cultural, and philosophical framework for our attempts to come to terms with the nature and conditions of our existence" (Brockmeier and Harré 2001: 40). Narrative discourse comprises various genres (Ochs 1997), e.g., specific, generic, future, and hypothetical stories (Kupferberg and Ben-Peretz 2004; Ochs 1994).

Specific and generic personal stories are unfolded in spontaneous everyday as well as institutional discourse when humans attempt to render their existence sensible and coherent (Bruner (1997). Radio, hotline, cyber, and clinical problem discourse is particularly rich in personal stories.[44] A specific personal story was illustrated earlier in Example (4) where the narrator unfolds her problem and her perspective on the problem-inducing "events which took place at specific unique moments in a unique past time world" (Polanyi 1989: 17).

Generic personal stories constitute a skeletal narrative genre (Ochs 1997) that is derived from specific stories by a process of abstraction (Brewer 1988). This process takes place when narrators repeatedly verbalize the meaning of related experiences. For example, a generic story is verbalized in Example (4), line 3, constructing the meaning of a recurring experience ("This feeling has accompanied me in many situations").

Labov (Labov 1972; Labov and Fanshel 1977; Labov and Waletzky 1967)[45] defines six elements of personal narrative structure: *abstract*, which summarizes the gist of the story, *orientation*, which provides the background, *complicating action*, or the sequence of events, which creates a problem or an unexpected situation, *evaluation*, which provides the narrator's attitude, *resolution*, which shows what happened finally, and *coda*, which shifts the narrator's perspective into the present.[46]

Narrative evaluation "is the means used by the narrator to indicate the point of the narrative, its raison d'être: why it was told" (Labov 1972: 366). Following Labov, scholarly attention has focused on evaluative linguistic devices that narrators use interactionally when they co-construct the local meanings of their experience. These resources are subjectivity markers (Georgakopoulou 1997) – discursive self-builders that display affective, cognitive, socio-cultural, and behavioral dimensions of the self.

Evaluative devices have been explored in literary texts, elicited interview data, and everyday conversation (see Cortazzi 2000 for a critical overview). However, few studies have focused on evaluation in naturally occurring institutional discourse where troubled and sometimes suicidal participants have a real need to verbalize their problems and seek help.[47]

In view of the highly contextualized nature of evaluative resources, Georgakopoulou (1997) does not advocate the study of preconceived lists of evaluative devices defined a priori of discourse analysis, but prefers to link them to the specific context in which they are produced. In this book, we espouse Georgakopoulou's recommendation.[48] Thus, for example, the grammar of agoraphobics (Capps and Ochs 1995) consists of certain evaluative devices such as lexical choice of mental verbs, place adverbs, syntactic transitivity that marks low levels of agency, and *irrealis structures* (Fleischman 1990).[49] These display the agoraphobic's helplessness. In the discourse of the addicted, to use another example, lexical and syntactic repetition identified in personal stories are evaluative devices interpreted as discursive features reflecting the obsessive-compulsive dimension of this disorder (Green and Kupferberg 2000). This book further explores the evaluative role of linguistic resources, especially figurative ones, in interactional problem discourse.

1.4. Worlds of discourse

Current definitions of discourse analysis emphasize that it can be conducted at micro- and macro-levels that should be interfaced. Drawing on the integrated functional approach to problem discourse presented in subsection 1.1, we explain in this subsection how we microanalyzed our corpora and then related these analyses to our theoretical and practical contextual resources at a macro-level.

Miller (1997) illustrates micro- and macro-analyses with examples from micro ethnomethodology and conversation analysis on the one hand, and Foucauldian analysis on the other. He recommends establishing an interface between the micro- and macro-levels by placing the local co-construction of reality and conditions of possibility of the former approaches within a global context of the latter.

Following Miller (ibid.), Holstein and Gubrium (2000: 98) define "analytical bracketing", their version of an interpretive analytic interface. These researchers suggest shifting between the micro-level of analysis and the broader level where pre-existing resources are used for interpretation. Although we agree with these authors that interpretive analysis should involve micro- and macro-levels, we find it difficult to accept that researchers can bracket or completely block the influence of pre-existing resources when they explore micro-levels of analysis.

Accordingly, we explore and interpret the sequential production of problems at a micro-analytic level in the quest for evaluative discursive resources – self-builders that participants produce and co-construct. Then, our interpretive interface relates this micro-analysis to the broader contextual resources that are at our disposal as researchers. We have chosen to define this heuristic process in terms of world-making.[50] To this end, we propose a four-world model that consists of the participants' worlds of the present, past, and future, and the researchers' world that embraces the participants' worlds and relates them to global contextual resources.

The participants' points of departure are in the here and now of their problem discourse in which both their troubled narrated past worlds and their future worlds of possibility are co-constructed. In her study of family dinner discourse, Elinor Ochs (1994) describes how the present, past, and future are interwoven in the narrative format: "Stories are not only reconstructions of past experience but *preconstructions* [emphasis in the original text] of future experiences as well. Stories may imply or make explicit what will, might, could, or should (not) happen next. They craft lives-in-progress, allowing interlocuters continually to (re)create their past, present, and future selves at once" (ibid.: 108).

To describe the construction of participants' worlds in problem discourse, as well as the researchers' interfacing interpretive world, we define discourse time as present, past, and future worlds of experience constructed by means of discursive resources such as evaluative devices, and a variety of time-building linguistic means such as tense, aspect, and lexical items.

Hence, in the spirit of Ricœur and Brockmeier,[51] we assume that when troubled narrators address professionals and para-professionals, their point of departure is the "here and now" present moment of the interaction from which they can explore the problem-causing past worlds as well as future worlds of possibility and change. We also assume that they can travel back and forth from one world to the other.

In this way, discourse time frees them from the oppressive, ever-changing, ephemeral and linear "nows" of chronological time, which is often measured by clocks, and enables them to construct their tormented narrative past as well as more adaptive future worlds in the present. Particularly suitable for these trans-world excursions are evaluative devices such as constructed dialogue and tense shift that serve to bring the past into the present. Constructed dialogue heightens dramatization (Bar-Kol and Kupferberg 2001; Georgakopoulou 1997), recycles the past voices of significant others and the narrators' own voices, and even expresses double voices (Bakhtin 1981). Example (5) from our radio corpus illustrates how the narrator,[52] whose mother died unexpectedly in her arms, uses constructed dialogue to recycle the meaningful voice of her deceased mother:

Example (5) Constructed dialogue

1   You know, I remember that a month before she died we were driving in
2   my car and then we were stuck at a traffic light. She said to me: "Look,
3   you have to take into account how much time I'll live. You have to,
4   you'll have to cope with it. Don't be so dependent on me."

Tense shift (Pillemer, Desrochers, and Ebanks 1998; Schiffrin 1981) is another self-building resource that shows that troubled selves relive the past in the present. Georgakopoulou (1994) stresses that the intensity of the shift from past to present is more powerful when constructed dialogue and tense shift are combined in the same utterance. Example (6) from our radio corpus[53] illustrates how the narrator – a mother of seven children – uses tense shift when she describes how her lover, the children's father, left her. The relevant verbs in lines 1 and 2 are italicised:

Example (6) Tense shift

1   ((sighs)) It's hard to define it. It was simply something that, you *remain*
2   hanging in the air. You, you *crash* suddenly. *I'm trying* to come down
3   from the dream to reality. That man ruined my life. He simply ruined my
4   life. He simply dragged me down with seven babies.

Bamberg's analysis of narrative positioning (Bamberg 1997b, 1999, 2001) constitutes another effective procedure that narrative researchers can profitably employ to establish an interface between micro- and macro-levels. Positioning is a discursive activity that was originally defined as how narrators locate themselves in conversation in relation to one another.[54] This activity constitutes "a dynamic alternative to the more static concept of role" (Langenhove and Harré 1999: 14).

Bamberg's definition of positioning parsimoniously captures the traditional concept of evaluation (see subsection 1.3) and the interactional dimensions of narrative discourse. Bamberg (1997b) describes the researcher's construction of participants' positioning by means of evaluative devices at three interrelated levels whose dimensions can be captured in terms of three heuristic questions. At level one, the researcher examines how participants position themselves in relation to significant others in the narrated past events.

At level two, the researcher explores how participants position themselves discursively vis-à-vis other participants in the present ongoing interaction. At level three, the researcher summarizes the first and second levels and in addition, using macro-level resources, he shows how participants position themselves in relation to themselves (i.e., how they want others to view them). In other words, at level three the researcher finally constructs the participants' selves that were partially displayed at levels one and two.

Our recent study of hotline discourse suggests that the order of the analytic levels depends on the goal of the study (e.g., self-construction in Bamberg's studies and solving hotline callers' problems in our study. See Kupferberg, Green, and Gilat 2002). In our attempt to explore hotline discourse, we realized that we had to modify the order of the levels suggested by Bamberg (1997b) because our study focused on the description and interpretation of hotline problem discussion rather than on mere self-construction. Self-construction, the ultimate objective of life-story interviewing (i.e., Bamberg's level 3), constituted one resource among many others that we used in our analysis.

In this book, we have chosen the term *world*, rather than *level* because it can contain the multidimensionality and complexities of problem discourse. World-making is a heuristic procedure that first calls for the breakdown of the complex discourse gestalt into self-revealing linguistic resources that display inter- and intrapersonal dimensions in the participants' worlds of the present, past, and future. Then, the linguistic resources identified in these worlds are examined closely, reassembled, and synthesized in the researchers' interpretive interfacing world. In the world of the present, narrators position themselves in relation to themselves and professional others in the ongoing problem discourse. Therefore, it is in this world that they negotiate the contents of the troubled past and relate to possible future worlds.

In the researchers' world, we summarize the micro-analysis of the participants' present, past, and future worlds and show how it can be interfaced with theoretical and contextual resources at our disposal. The transition from micro- to macro-worlds is a circular process in an action-oriented book such as ours, where the findings foregrounded in the interpretive analyses are subsequently applied in actual problem-discourse (Linell 1998; Sarangi and Roberts 1999b).

1.5. Discourse-oriented perspective on figurative language

Another evaluative discursive resource that has been associated with self-construction but has not been sufficiently explored in naturally occurring discourse is figurative language (e.g., metaphor, simile and analogy) (McMullen 1996; Reinhart 1995). In this subsection, we define our functional discourse-oriented perspective on figurative language in naturally occurring problem discourse and distinguish it from approaches to figurative language that have attempted to explain trope interpretation and production by means of decontextualized models.[55]

Leezenberg (2001) proposes classifying semantic, pragmatic, and conceptualist approaches to figurative language interpretation according to two criteria: the level of linguistic theory where figurative interpretation is accounted for, and the kind of knowledge involved in the interpretation of tropes. In the following excerpt, Leezenberg elaborates on his classification:

> Semantic theories focus on conventionalized knowledge of some sort (not necessarily aspects of meaning in the more restricted sense, but also 'stereotypes', 'connotations' and the like); pragmatic approaches emphasize the role of non-linguistic or world knowledge; while conceptualistic approaches regard mental representation and the ability to think in analogies as the key to our metaphorical competence. (Leezenberg 2002: 11)

One of the most influential twentieth-century theories of metaphor is Lakoff and Johnson's (Johnson 1987; Lakoff 1987; Lakoff and Johnson 1980)[56] conceptualistic approach, often dubbed "cognitive semantics". This approach attempts to account for the ubiquity of metaphorical expressions in everyday spoken and written language. These are surface linguistic expressions of underlying cognitive constructions that enable humans to conceptualize abstract and inexpressible areas of experience in terms of familiar embodied (i.e., determined by our body and mind) target ones, as well as familiar areas that we wish to highlight (John Kennedy, personal communication).

For example, emphasizing cognitive aspects and downplaying their communicative use, adherents of cognitive semantics would argue that the following figurative expressions from our corpus of radio problem discourse, "This feeling has accompanied me in many situations" (see Example (11), line 3, in Chapter 3), and "I am in the middle of this crisis" (see Example (15), lines 20–21, in Chapter 3), are dominated by two conceptual metaphors, *EMOTION IS MOTION*[57] and *LIFE IS A JOURNEY*, respectively. Leezenberg explains that this approach is based on "a familiar phenomenological argument that meaning and truth are not just relations between symbol systems and the world, but are mediated by human intentionality of subjectivity" (Leezenberg 2001: 137).

Giora (2003) proposes another theory-driven conceptualistic model that leans on cognitive and intuitive factors and emphasizes the role of salient meanings in figurative and non-figurative language comprehension and production. The following excerpt summarizes *the graded salience hypothesis* underlying her model:

> More salient meanings – coded meanings foremost on our mind due to conventionality, frequency, familiarity or prototypicality – are accessed faster and reach sufficient levels of activation before less salient ones. According to the graded salience hypothesis, then, coded meanings would be accessed upon encounter, regardless of contextual information or authorial intent. Coded meanings of low salience, however, may not reach sufficient levels of activation to be visible in a context biased toward the more salient meaning of the word. (Giora 2003: 10)

This model claims that our linguistic behavior is shaped by salient meanings of words and fixed expressions. Salience, according to Giora, is determined by the following factors, which shape the functioning of the mental lexicon and override the effects of context in language production and comprehension: frequency of occurrence, familiarity, conventionality and prototypicality (Giora 2003: Chapter 2). The theory of graded salience is primarily based on laboratory experiments in which paid participants were requested to perform controlled tasks on the basis of which the functioning of the mental lexicon was described.

Both cognitive semantics and the salience theory present their a priori theoretical claims that can be further validated qualitatively by a close examination of discourse. Our approach to tropes is different. We assume that there is more to human communication in troubled circumstances than the identification of linguistic manifestations of underlying conceptual tropes and salient meanings. Accordingly, we explore naturally occurring problem discourse produced by sufferers who have urgent needs to speak or write about their problems and are often in acute distress. This micro conversation-analytic examination of the interaction is carried out to see how participants make use of figurative and non-figurative evaluative and positioning self-builders when they accomplish the institutional tasks of problem presentation and construction of solutions.

Moving from decontextualized studies of figurative language to studies that focused on therapeutic settings (Erickson 1983; Ferrara 1994; Ingram 1994; McMullen 1996), we see that figurative forms expressed by clients often match major themes of therapy (McMullen 1996). McMullen and Conway (1994, 1996) further show that the most common classes of intrapersonal tropes produced in psychotherapy are those of self and of emotion. Following Siegleman's idea (1990) of key metaphors as markers of change that can chart the progress of therapy, McMullen (1996) emphasizes that future research should focus on clients' key metaphors or salient theme-related instances, which often capture the clients' concept of self and their state of mind. These studies foreground the centrality of key tropes in psychotherapy, but do not explain how these metaphors are related to major themes of therapy.

Current studies by the present authors explore the evaluative functions of tropes in naturally occurring face-to-face, telephone, and cyber problem discourse (Green and Kupferberg 2000; Kupferberg 2004, in press; Kupferberg and Ben-Peretz 2004; Kupferberg and Green 1998, 2003; Kupferberg, Green, and Gilat 2002) in educational and non-educational settings. These studies show how narrators often use self-disclosing figurative language.

For example, in a face-to-face interaction (Kupferberg and Gilat 2002), a teacher trainee unfolds a personal story that constructs the meaning of his mother's hospitalization. The narrator also produces a story-internal trope (i.e., "a bang") that enables him to conceptualize his feelings: "The minute I entered the hospital, I receive such a bang, because I don't like hospitals." In other words, the narrator presents two versions of his self: a detailed narrative version as well as a succinct figurative one (Kupferberg and Gilat 2002).

Empirical evidence concerning the summative function of tropes within the narrative format is also provided in life-story studies (Bar-Kol and Kupferberg 2001; Kupferberg and Gilat 2001; Kupferberg and Green 2001). Focusing on epiphanies, or turning-point moments that are verbalized in narrative discourse (Denzin 1999), these studies provide further discursive evidence that there is a connection between tropes and the personal story in which they are unfolded. Accordingly, interviewees often produce narrative *and* figurative versions of their self. Using such central tropes, they display inter- and intrapersonal dimensions of the self that cohere globally across the different stories. In other words, certain tropes summarize the main themes in different personal stories unfolded by the same narrator, and constitute markers of global coherence.

This book further explores how central tropes used in naturally occurring problem discourse enhance the process of global coherence in *interactive* problem discourse. In Chapters 3–8, we explore the figurative language that narrators produce when attempting to unfold the meaning of their troubled experience in problem discourse. Our book, then, does not propose an explanatory model, but rather sets out on an exploratory journey to see what actually happens in interactional discursive processes.

As we have already emphasized, former studies show that figurative forms are ubiquitous in spoken and written discourse. When we attempt to conceptualize poorly defined or inexpressible, complex or emotionally charged domains of experience (Gibbs 1994; Kövecses 1990, 1998), we often resort to more familiar vehicle domains (Gibbs 1994; Lakoff and Johnson 1980). Troubled narrators use tropes (Ferrara 1994; Green and Kupferberg 2000; Kupferberg and Green 1998, 2003; Kupferberg, Green, and Gilat 2002; McMullen 1996) to express central themes of personal experience, or topic concepts, in terms of more familiar vehicle domains. Accordingly, the corpora of this book, which were often produced in acute emotional states of mind, enable us to examine closely how sufferers make use of tropes in their attempt to make sense of their lives and find possible solutions to their pressing problems.

Below, we define the types of tropes to which troubled selves resort in the examples presented in the book. A metaphor asserts that the more complex topic shares one or more features with the more familiar vehicle (e.g., "Life is a journey"). A simile is a hedged or weaker version of a metaphoric expression (Glucksberg and Keysar 1993). The weakening effect is achieved by means of words such as *like* or *as* (e.g., "Life is like a journey").

Kennedy and Chiappe (1999) and Chiappe and Kennedy (2001) do not accept the explanation that metaphors are stronger than similes. They argue that "the metaphor form is preferred over the simile form when the similarity between the topic … and the vehicle … is quite high. Indeed, similarity was found to be more important than familiarity, another potential factor that might affect preference for one form or another" (ibid.: 249).

An analogy verbalizes a more explicit statement of the similarities between the topic and the vehicle (Pribram 1990). For example, at the peak of a national crisis that took place in Israel in 1998, one adolescent wrote: "The present situation in the country is like the tension before one gets the results of an important test that will affect one's life" (Kupferberg, Gilat and Green 2000). Formulaic phrases such as proverbs, slogans and sayings are summative expressions of wisdom that are "generally learned and used as wholes" (Honeck 1997: 79) (e.g., "to be or not to be").

Hyperbole, like verbal irony and understatement, distorts the truth. Hyperboles "assert more than is objectively warranted" (Gibbs 1994: 391) (e.g., *The lion and the snake*, the hotline caller presented in Chapter 5, says that in addition to the problems he has presented, "there are a million other problems"). An oxymoron is a trope that combines "contradictory or incongruous words" (Merriam-Webster dictionary 1997) (e.g., "cruel kindness"). Finally, synecdoche is a trope in which a part is put for the whole (e.g., the gay woman presented in Chapter 7, produces two synecdoches that evoke persecuted stereotypical male evil-doers: *That person didn't have horns and she didn't have a beard*).

2. Methodological framework

2.1. Corpora

Our corpora consist of 92 radio calls, 33 hotline calls, and 48 cyber interactions. These corpora constitute actual interactions that "would have taken place anyway, whether or not we were present. In this regard, the speech analyzed can be regarded as authentic naturally occurring language speech" (Ferrara 1994: 19) rather than elicited speech obtained by different techniques, or discrete items garnered from different sources. Another salient feature of the corpora is that most of the interactions involve an unseen party: the overhearing radio audience (Bell 1992; Hutchby 1995)[58] and the virtual community whose presence has to be taken into consideration (Thornborrow 1997, 2002).

Callers participating in the radio corpora are first interviewed by station operators who attempt to screen the calls. Therefore, when callers are finally on the air, they have to verbalize their story again. The operators write a short abstract describing the contents of the caller's story to facilitate the subsequent intervention of the radio team. For example, callers participating in "The two of us together and each of us alone" are first interviewed by the program operators. The structured interview consists of the following items: the caller's name or pseudonym, family status, age, occupation, education, prior participation in the program, the caller's agreement to participate in the program, writing skeletal versions of the callers' stories, and general comments on the caller's fitness to participate in the program. Example (7) presents the skeletal story produced by the operator who interviewed the caller we entitled *In a big bang* (see Chapter 4, section 1):

Example (7) "She experienced a big bang"

1 She had an exceptional, perhaps even abnormal relationship with her
2 mother who died in July, seven years ago, and since then she has
3 experienced separation anxiety. For example, she's afraid to allow her
4 family to take any step for fear that they will abandon her. She doesn't
5 allow them to drive a car, go away, call on her for fear that they will
6 have to drive back home. Her mother died in her arms from a sudden
7 heart attack in the middle of a festive event. She experienced "a big
8 bang" [the quotation marks are used by the operator] so that she wakes
9 her husband in the middle of the night to make sure that he's alive. She
10 doesn't know what to do. She is helpless. She's not afraid for herself.
11 She says she's not bored. She's very busy, but this anxiety haunts her all
12 the time. It is very difficult for people who live with her. She wants to
13 change.

Example (7) shows that when the first verbalization of the story takes place, there are two participants: callers and radio operators, gatekeepers whose function it is to select media-worthy callers and block the access of others. The operators' comments summarize the callers' potential. Below we list some of their comments:
(1) "Excellent, she's OK."
(2) "A simple girl, talks all right."
(3) "Sounds great."
(4) "Sounds OK, but the telephone line should be checked."
(5) "Sounds more than OK, but extremely depressed. Sighs."

(6) "Sounds like a teacher."
(7) "Perfectly all right. Anonymity is very important for her."
(8) "Sounds nice and clear."
Callers participating in the radio program have to experience this filtering process whereas all callers addressing the hotline via telephone or cyberspace are accepted.

In this book, we focus on two radio programs. The first, "The two of us together and each of us alone", provides callers with a site where they can seek the professional help of psychologists. The second, "Night birds talk", merely invites callers to unfold exceptional stories, but no professional help is offered. The callers can, however, address the overhearing audience and seek help.

Research has shown that participants in radio programs are constantly aware of the unseen overhearing audience and that this awareness creates tension between the lay callers' goals and those of the radio team (Thornborrow 2002). Consequently, program hosts generally control topic selection and the question–answer turn-taking system (Heritage and Greatbatch 1992), and assume exclusive rights to ask questions (Green and Kupferberg 2000; Kupferberg and Green 1998, 2003; Montgomery 1991). In addition, they often provide their evaluation of the meaning of lay narrators' stories (Thornborrow 1997).

This asymmetry is sometimes relaxed when the narrative voice of ordinary people overpowers the institutional radio voices (ibid.). For example, motivated by an urgent need to address the overhearing audience for help, on the one hand, and assisted by the lenient attitude of the host who was ready to give in as long as an exceptional story was produced, on the other, several narrators presented in Chapter 8 were able to express the meaning of addiction and codependency in spite of the host's tendency to direct the interaction to other domains.

2.1.1. " The two of us together and each of us alone" corpus
Chapters 3 and 4 are based on 53 radio calls recorded in 1997 and taken from the popular Israeli program, "The two of us together and each of us alone," which has been hosted by Mr. Yovav Katz since 1979. The program is broadcast between 11 p.m. and 2 a.m. by the commercial Second Channel of the Israel Broadcasting Authority. In this popular weekly program, anonymous callers discuss their

problems with the radio team, which consists of a host and two experienced clinical psychologists. Topic-focused programs are opened by the psychologists, who introduce the topic. In general programs, however, there is no introduction. In a conversation conducted on Tuesday, August 21, 1997, the host admitted that he preferred the topic-focused programs where callers relate to the same issues.

The broadcast interactions might be profitably divided into three phases with somewhat different functions: the reception phase, when the host attempts to elicit relevant information from the caller, the problem-discussion phase, when the caller and the psychologist negotiate possible solutions, and the brief dismissal phase.[59] We identified a variety of constraints that might undermine successful communication in this program: "The psychologists' preference for certain callers, technical communication failures and other scheduled breaks including the news and information broadcasts, callers' and team's awareness of the overhearing audience, team's attempt to place callers in a predefined cognitive set, callers' language disturbances, nervousness, and limited proficiency in Hebrew" (Kupferberg and Green 1998: 119).

Chapter 4 is based on the analysis of 13 calls produced in two programs conducted in 1997. These calls differ from the calls in Chapter 3. Having analyzed the first 40 calls, we discovered that certain tropes constitute central organizing elements that summarize the essence of the problem and sometimes enhance interpersonal communication. Yovav Katz, the host, agreed to collaborate with us on two programs broadcast in July and August 1997, respectively.

At the beginning of each, the host asked potential callers to open their call with a title or a name they had chosen for their problem. In the July program, several operators requested and were granted the consent of three callers to be further interviewed by the authors after the program. We focus on these interviews in Chapter 4.

2.1.2. "Night birds talk" corpus
Chapters 7 and 8 are based on 39 broadcast telephone interactions recorded in 1998 between lay callers and the host of "Night birds talk". This radio program was broadcast once a week between midnight and 2 a.m. from 1975 to 2001 by the non-commercial Israel Defense Forces (IDF) radio station, *Galei Zahal*. The host, Gideon Reicher,

stressed that the goal of the program was to provide the audience with "breathtaking personal stories" (Gideon Reicher, personal communication). Hence, the host framed the program by inviting potential callers to narrate exceptional stories after announcing the topics to be presented in the program. The interactions included in the book were produced in four programs entitled "Attraction and Repulsion", "Failures and Triumphs", "Drives and Instincts", and "Quarreling and Making Up".

2.1.3. Hotline corpus

In Chapter 5, we present excerpts from three hotline interactions selected out of a corpus of 33 calls between para-professional volunteers at the Israeli telephone emergency service (ERAN) and troubled callers. ERAN is an acronym comprising the first letters of the Hebrew words *ezra rishona nafshit* 'mental first aid'. The description of ERAN is based on Gilat and Latzer (in press), Gilat, Lobel, and Gil (1998) and Latzer and Gilat (2000).

ERAN, like similar services in other Western countries, offers round-the-clock help to troubled callers. The latter may remain anonymous and terminate the interaction whenever they want to. The volunteers' pre-service training lasts one year. Subsequently, the new in-service volunteers are supervised by senior volunteers on a regular basis. In-service volunteers have three roles: listening in, effecting emotional, cognitive, and behavioral changes, and, when the need arises, advising the callers to turn to other sources of help.

New callers and frequent callers constitute different populations in terms of gender, age, content, and pattern of the interaction, reliance on additional support services, and the type of help requested. New callers often present problems related to family and interpersonal relationships. Frequent callers who do not succeed in solving their problems via other agencies tend to present problems of an intrapersonal nature such as loneliness, self-esteem, depression, anxiety and mental illness.

Calls are usually conducted in three phases. First, callers are encouraged to present themselves and the problem. Then, callers and volunteers discuss the problem and suggest candidate solutions. Sometimes, callers talk about their problem while the volunteers listen in. In the third phase, prior to terminating the call, the volunteers and/or callers relate to the effect of the call on the caller.

2.1.4. Cyberspace corpus

In Chapter 6, we present two cyber[60] multilogues[61] selected out of a corpus of 48 interactions between troubled netizens (Crystal 2001) and digital answerers, including para-professional volunteers. In such an asynchronous multi-participant forum,[62] "the interactions are stored in some format, and made available to users upon demand, so that they can catch up with the discussion, or add to it, at any time" (ibid.: 11).

Crystal (2001) emphasizes that asynchronous forums comprise written messages that often display properties of speech. For example, the messages expect or demand an immediate response as in spoken language, and display much of the urgency and energetic force that is characteristic of face-to-face conversation. However, they lack immediate feedback, and their rhythm is slower than that of phone calls and face-to-face interactions. When a problem is presented, it is entitled by the troubled writer. The other messages are indexed linearly in relation to the first message. This organization constitutes the map of the messages.

Current scholarship emphasizes that cyber problem discourse has two faces (Barak 2000). On the one hand, it encourages greater exploration and expression of the self. On the other, "the tales of relationships formed under these circumstances also contain darker themes ... Online communities can be sites of betrayal, violence and – ultimately – disintegration" (Reid 1998: 40).

2.2. Data collection and analysis

The hotline telephone data was collected by ERAN's professional coordinator. The latter listened in by earphones and produced verbatim stenographic representations as well as a description of relevant aspects of the speech production. This was a necessary step because the recording of calls is strictly forbidden. The examples presented in Chapter 6 were published in an instructional brochure co-authored by Gilat and Kupferberg and distributed to ERAN volunteers at the 2002 ERAN annual meeting. Other corpora were recorded and transcribed. We view transcribing as an interpretive process that is connected to the aims of the study (ten Have 1999). Because the study focuses on figurative and non-figurative resources, the transcripts display all the verbal devices, but do not include paralinguistic devices such as kinesic cues and prosodic elements.

To analyze the data, we adopted a qualitative method that is located in the middle of the interpretive continuum between the phenomenological and hermeneutical poles,[63] and inspired by Bamberg's three-level analysis of positioning (Bamberg 1997b, 2001). The method was first used in life-story interviewing (Kupferberg and Green 2001), and then it was adapted to problem discourse (Kupferberg, Green and Gilat 2002).

Following our four-world model, we analyzed the participants' discursive gestalt in order to identify figurative and non-figurative self-building evaluative devices that position the participants in three worlds. In the world of the present, we wanted to see how troubled narrators situate themselves in relation to themselves and professional others during the ongoing problem discourse. In the world of the past, which is unfolded in the present, we wished to explore how participants relate to inter- and intrapersonal dimensions of their troubled self in the narrated past. As for the future, we were curious to find out how participants relate to possible or future worlds. Then, we summarized the analysis in our world, the researchers' world that constitutes an interface between the micro- and macro-levels.

We analyzed the data independently using micro and macro resources. Then, we synthesized our findings. The goal of the sequential micro-discourse analysis was to explore discursive resources including figurative language in order to see how troubled callers and digital writers, as well as professionals and para-professionals, co-constructed problems and solutions via evaluative devices. The micro-analysis was guided by "the next turn validation" (Peräkylä 1997). This methodological procedure aims at the discovery of preceding or following cotext (Korolija 1998) that provides confirming evidence that what one participant said had also been noticed and used by other participants.[64]

Our goal in the psychological analysis was to assess the callers' problems and identify the intra- and interpersonal dimensions of their selves in terms of psychological theories and clinical experience. Then, guided by "multiple investigators' triangulation" (Douglas 1976), we synthesized the two perspectives in an integrative interpretive interface. Together, the next turn validation and multiple investigators' triangulation enabled us to reach an accord at a given time that we hoped other scholarly eyes would find trustworthy (Lincoln and Guba 1998; Mishler 2000).

Our units of analysis are hierarchically ordered. Following Hymes (1972), we define our spoken and digital global units as speech events in which sufferers unfold their problems and discuss them with other participants. Telephone calls are further divided into turns and utterances, respectively. A turn is defined as the time when one party speaks until a change takes place and another party takes over (ten Have 1999). Utterances express full (e.g., I get up in the morning) and incomplete (e.g., I looked) ideas.

Digital speech events are divided into sequences of messages, messages, sentences, and clauses, respectively. Each unit begins with a problem-message written by a troubled digital sufferer and followed by anonymous answerers' messages as well as the messages that the troubled self writes in response to the answerers' messages. Following Crystal (2001), we propose viewing digital messages as digital turns taken by participants in the asynchronic multi-actional speech event.

In both telephone and digital turns, we also identified specific and generic stories and organizing figurative resources. Generic stories and organizing tropes were verbalized within the extended narrative formats. These narrative and figurative units are central to the analyses in this book that show how they are interrelated. Specific stories were produced by the troubled narrators in extended turns or problem messages. In Chapters 7 and 8, the host, as our analyses show, is involved in the construction of the callers' personal stories and this is displayed in the turn-taking design.

The original unabridged Hebrew corpora were analyzed, and then representative excerpts displaying organizing tropes were translated by a professional translator, a native speaker of English. Subsequently, two bilinguals read the Hebrew and English versions of the excerpts and evaluated the adequacy of the translated versions. The readers suggested several minor changes that we accepted.

The following symbols are used in the examples. Verbal description is indicated by double parentheses (e.g., ((laughs))). Authors' comments are indicated by square brackets (e.g., [the second child]). Organizing tropes and figurative structures produced in response to them are indicated by italics (e.g., *Am I their floor rag?*). Incomplete utterances are indicated by a comma (e.g., It was simply something that, you remain hanging in the air.). Constructed dialogue is marked by quotation marks (e.g., She said: "Good morning").The roles of hotline participants are marked by the following letters: C (caller), H (host), P (psychologist), and V (hotline volunteer). When two psychologists participate in the program, it is indicated by numbers (e.g., P1 and P2).

In the running text, organizing tropes and figurative structures produced in response to them are indicated by italics (e.g., *Am I their floor rag?*). Figurative language that is not interpreted as organizing is indicated by quotation marks (e.g., "I was the best source of light in the market"). Conceptual metaphors are indicated by small capital italics (e.g., *EMOTION IS MOTION* and *LIFE IS A JOURNEY*). Finally, to distinguish between the different troubled callers and digital writers who are described in this book, we decided to define them by using one of their organizing tropes as their representative names (e.g., *Amputating the cancerous leg* presented in Chapter 3, Examples (8–10)). In the cases of callers that did not produce organizing figurative language, we use a representative utterance (e.g., "One can talk about all kinds of subjects" in Chapter 3, Example (18)) or a representative digital sentence (e.g., "I was the best source of light on the market" in Chapter 6, Example (54)). The "List of the troubled selves" is presented on page ix.

Finally, Raviv and Abuhav (2003) list several recommendations that are pertinent to the ethical codex of radio and cyber psychology. These authors stress that research based on media and internet data should eliminate details that may be detrimental in any way to callers or cyber writers. This recommendation has been implemented throughout this book.

3. Overview of the book

Part 1 consists of two chapters that present our theoretical and methodological frameworks. In Chapter 1, we position ourselves as researchers in relation to current scholarship that inspired our study of interactional problem discourse. First, we define the historical boundaries of the technologies of self-construction. Then, we focus on the characteristics of postmodern discourse via two points of view on institutional discourse: Foucault's panoptical approach and the more open-ended institutional conversation analysis.

These approaches located our book between two architectonic tropes. The first trope is the "panopticon" – the epitome of Foucault's prescriptive macro-approach. The second is "the local weaving of meaning by verbal looms located in workshop rooms" – our figurative representation of institutional conversation analysis. These sources of inspiration seem incompatible at first glance. Accordingly, in Chapter 2, we present a theoretical introduction (section 1) that justifies the union between the two approaches and provides the background to our methodological framework (section 2).

At the end of the theoretical introduction, we propose our four-world model of discourse analysis (subsection 1.4). The model shows how micro- and macro-approaches can be interfaced in the researchers' world that embraces the participants' worlds of the present ongoing interaction, troubled past, and possible future and relates them to global contextual resources. In section 2, we present the methodological considerations that guide the application of the model in the study of the participants' discursive gestalt.

Our analytic investigation of figurative bridges in telephone and cyber problem discourse is presented in Parts 2 and 3, Chapters 3–8. These chapters contain excerpts from our naturally occurring corpora. These excerpts are accompanied by our interpretive comments that highlight the discursive, social and psychological dimensions of the corpora within the interpretive four-world model we have proposed in Chapter 2.

Chapter 3 focuses on organizing figurative language phenomena whose summative and interactional functions enhance interpersonal radio problem discourse. This chapter also emphasizes the multilogical function of figurative conspiracies – a data-driven construct we coined to describe the joint work of various discursive resources that sufferers produced in their attempt to express their troubled experience.

In Chapter 4, we describe how we tested the presentational and interactional functions of these tropes by collaborating with a radio host who, at our request, asked callers to entitle their problems in order to assist the team. The chapter shows how two externally-directed callers negotiated their problems figuratively with the radio team.

Chapters 5 and 6 explore dramas unfolded in hotline and cyberspace. These chapters also show that in states of emergency, the need to resort to unambiguous non-figurative language arises.

In Part 3, we focus on the discursive construction of control in the exceptional stories of callers participating in "Night birds talk". This program aims at providing a site for the voicing of exceptional stories but does not offer mental help like the site we visit in Chapters 3 and 4. In Chapter 7, two callers use figurative resources when they negotiate issues of control with the radio host. In Chapter 8, we further show how addicted and codependent callers use organizing figurative language to construct their self-portraits, altered states of consciousness, and conceptualization of time and of the withdrawal process.

Part 4 consists of Chapter 9 and an Epilogue. In Chapter 9, we summarize the theoretical and practical dimensions of the organizing figurative language that was identified, described, and interpreted in Chapters 3–8. We also show how our findings can be used to redefine the boundaries we set in the introduction. Finally, we relate to the practical implications of our findings in therapeutic and educational settings.

The Epilogue emphasizes that our interpretive analyses constitute one stance out of many possible others that can be used to explore problem discourse. Therefore, we conclude the book by inviting additional scholarly eyes to examine our corpora and our interpretive interface from other theoretical and methodological perspectives in order to shed more light on problem discourse.

Part 2
Figurative bridges in radio, hotline and cyber discourse

Chapter 3
Organizing tropes

In Chapter 3, we analyze excerpts from calls broadcast in the radio program "The two of us together and each of us alone",[65] in order to answer the questions raised in section 2 of Chapter 1. (1) How is meaning constructed by professional and lay participants visiting the telephone and cyberspace sites explored in this book? (2) To which discursive resources do participants in telephone and cyberspace problem discourse resort in order to accomplish their complicated tasks of problem presentation? (3) To what extent are these resources related to the interactional and meaningful construction of problems and solutions?

Bearing in mind the Foucauldian panopticon and the conversation analytic looms in the workshop rooms – the tropes that set the boundaries for the study of our corpora – Chapter 3 aims at providing answers to these questions. In section 1 we present our analyses of several effective and ineffective interactions, respectively, and explain the reasons why some calls were effective and others were not. The effective interactions are presented in subsection 1.1, and subsection 1.2 contains the ones we interpreted as ineffective.

One of the excerpts in subsection 1.2 is from our hotline corpus. At first glance, this appeared to be an exception, but actually it constitutes a "treasure" that illuminates the other examples presented in the chapter (Peräkylä 1997: 212). Our interpretive interface of the data analyzed in this chapter is summarized in section 2 in terms of the four-world model we presented in subsection 1.4 of Chapter 2.

1. The troubled caller makes a phone call

1.1. Effective interactions

The first caller, an eloquent 49-year-old woman, participates in a general program that does not open with a scholarly introduction like the topic-focused ones (see Examples (20) and (21) in Chapter 4). This

48 *Organizing tropes*

caller taught us an unforgettable lesson about problem discourse. When she was finally on the air, she insisted on using figurative language to facilitate her communication with the radio team. Yovav Katz, the experienced program host, finally complied with her request. Examples (8) and (9) below are illustrative excerpts from this call:

Example (8) "I left the cage, my wings are broken"

```
 1  C: I'm a poetic person because I'm not so comfortable in prose. Can I
 2     tell you something more rhymed so that you will understand my
 3     situation?
 4  H: Do you really want to open with rhymes?
 5  C: Yes. Instead of an identity card.
 6  H: I'm afraid of it.
 7  C: It won't hurt anyone.
 8  H: No, no, no. That's not what I'm afraid of. I'm afraid that there'll be a
 9     real barrier between us.
10  C: It will make the opening easier for me.
11  H: OK. It's all right. It's fine.
12  C: ((confused laughter)) I left the cage, my wings are broken, but when
13     I learn to fly, I will muster inner forces. I asked God to preserve my
14     energy. I escaped the bars, my soul endangered. On each of my
15     feathers there is a lot of makeup.
16  H: Yes, it's beautiful.
```

Example (8) was produced in the reception phase of the call. First, the caller and the host negotiate metalinguistically the aptness of figurative language for self-presentation in problem discourse (lines 1–11). Positioning an assertive self in relation to the host in the world of the here and now, the caller demands to express her problem by means of tropes, which constitute, in her opinion, "an identity card" (line 5). The host doubts their usefulness. In his opinion, talking metaphorically is talking with "a real barrier" (lines 8–9), but later he complies with the insistent request, and accepts figurative language (line 11).

To shift the focus from the ongoing interaction to the narrated past world, the caller produces a poem that depicts a painful process of terminating a marriage. There are two salient self-building discursive resources in the poem: utterances high on the narrative agency scale[66] and an analogy. These resources are embedded in a carefully planned (Ochs 1979) poetic text that positions the caller in two worlds: in relation to her husband in the past, and in relation to the radio team in the present.

The caller displays an active initiating agent in the narrated past. This is accomplished by repetition of the first person pronoun[67] "I", the grammatical subject of three transitive verbs: "left", "asked" and "escaped" (lines 12–14). Repeating these utterances,[68] the caller establishes an assertive determined self, a characteristic that is also identified in our analysis of her speech in other parts of the ongoing interaction. It is interesting to note that the caller erases her husband from the narrated world, possibly because her marriage was traumatic and painful.

The second self-building resource is an emotion-disclosing analogy. The analogy describes how the caller ended the relationship, or rather how she wants to present it to the radio team and the overhearing audience. The caller compares herself to a bird whose wings are broken and who "left the cage" (line 12). Subsequently, she produces a more optimistic future story (Kupferberg and Ben-Peretz 2004; Ochs 1994), in which she will learn how to fly (lines 12–13). In Example (9), the caller redefines her marriage using another painful trope:

Example (9) "Amputating the cancerous leg"

```
1   C: Now I will go on talking literally. I am getting a divorce on Sunday
2       after 28 years of marriage.
3   H: So what can I say?
4   C: I wanted it and I got it. Now, what do I do with it? Twenty years are
5       quite a long period of time. I got used to it. Yes. It becomes second
6       nature. I call it [getting a divorce] amputating the cancerous leg so
7       that I will be able to stand again on one stable leg. This is a
8       paraphrase, and it is not real. I will stand on one leg, and the other
9       one does not function anymore. It is not there. But I will be more
10      stable when I stand on one healthy leg than on two.
```

In Example (9), the caller uses another trope to describe her marriage and the process of getting a divorce. Now, she describes it figuratively in terms of "a cancerous leg" that will be "amputated" when she gets the divorce. Elsewhere in the interaction, in a section that is not presented in this chapter, the caller also entitles herself "a broken marionette". These tropes constitute succinct and painful self-portraits that the caller produces during the interaction.

The caller's marriage experience, which is encapsulated in tropes (e.g., "My wings are broken", "Amputating the cancerous leg", and "The broken marionette"), may have provided the psychologist with important information about her. In addition, he probably noticed her repetitive and resolute demand to present her problem figuratively in the reception phase (Example (8), lines 5, 7 and 10). In our opinion, the syntax of agency and tropes, the evaluative resources used by the caller, display emotional, cognitive and behavioral dimensions of her troubled self in the narrated past world as well as in the ongoing telephone interaction. Example (10) illustrates how the psychologist relates to the caller's discursive construction of her problem:

Example (10) "The amputated leg" and "the phantom pain"

1 P: There's a phenomenon that I don't think you're taking into consid-
2   eration, but I will elaborate on your metaphor about the amputated
3   leg with which you are, I hope, familiar. It's called a phantom pain
4   [An imaginary pain experienced by amputees when no limb is pre-
      sent].
5 C: Yes.
6 P: You sometimes feel a kind of a ghost pain after the amputation.
7   ((pause))
8 C: Yes, it seems to hurt.
9 P: Yes, one feels the pain as if it were there.
10 C: And the longer the illness goes on, the stronger the pain.
11 P: That may be your experience. What I want to stress is that I'm glad
12   to hear that you're healthy and sane despite all those violent images,
13   and you do have two legs and yourself, and it sounds as if there is a
14   lot in this.

In his response to the caller, the psychologist acknowledges that he has noticed[69] the painful figurative versions of her troubled but resolute self in the narrated world. Concentrating on "the amputated leg" (line 2) – the psychologist's version of *Amputating the cancerous leg*, the emotion-disclosing trope produced by the caller (see Example (9), line 6) – the psychologist stresses that the caller is sane and healthy, and reframes (Rosen 1982) her metaphor with a new and more optimistic metaphor that defines her marriage as a "phantom pain" (line 3). Thus, *Amputating the cancerous leg* becomes both a presentational and dialogical figurative vehicle that enhances the interaction. In this book, tropes that accomplish such complex tasks are dubbed organizing tropes, and they are indicated by italics. In addition, when we refer to the troubled selves we hosted in the book, we use the organizing tropes that they produce as representative names.

What does the caller mean when she entitles her self *Amputating the cancerous leg*? It is possible that she the caller wishes to emphasize that now that she no longer has a husband, she has a physical disability that might make future achievement difficult. However, the time limit, one of the factors shaping radio problem discourse,[70] must have forced the psychologist to abandon *Amputating the cancerous leg*'s past, which was summatively organized in painful tropes. Consequently, instead of unearthing the intrapsychic contents of these figurative forms and elaborating on them, the psychologist efficiently shifts the focus of the interaction to a better future in which, he thinks, the narrator's pain will instantly cease.

The example shows that the trope constitutes a story-internal organizing component of global coherence within the caller's detailed version of the story, which, as the caller avows, facilitates her problem presentation. In addition, it is noticed by the psychologist, who makes professional therapeutic use of one of the several organizing self-building resources produced by the caller by sending a modified trope that downtones the dimensions of her problem. Located in our fourth interpretive and interfacing world, we regard the caller's trope as a communicative bridge over which the psychologist sends his healing, future-oriented message. The fact that the psychologist notices the trope constitutes "the next turn validation". This methodological procedure aims at the discovery of preceding or following cotext that provides confirming evidence that what one participant says has also been noticed and used by other participants.

In conclusion, the troubled caller presented in Examples (8–10) goes on the air determined to present her agentive self via a poetic text that she has planned at home. At the beginning of the interaction, her strength is further revealed when she persuades the host, the voice of the institution, to listen to her tropes. Having convinced him that poetic language is apt for the presentation of her problem, the caller produces two highly planned versions of her problem: a poetic text, and several organizing emotion-disclosing tropes that constitute the gist of her tormented past.

The psychologist notices these detailed and succinct versions of the problem, as well as the resolute self presented in the worlds of the past and the present. Bearing in mind the limited time allotted to him, he chooses to reframe the caller's figurative contribution with a healing metaphor. The example shows that the trope constitutes a story-internal organizing component of global coherence that enhances the time-bounded radio interaction. It is not at all clear to what extent this interaction provides the caller with a solution such as a positive perspective on her problem or coping strategies that she can use in the future.

The next caller is a more prosaic 35-year-old female divorcée whose brother died in an accident. This call is part of "Wrong Decisions", a topic-focused program opened by the host who presents the topic, introduces the professional team and provides information to facilitate telephone communication. Then, there is a 16-minute introduction in which the psychologists present the topic, exhibiting their expertise by means of professional knowledge.

The following conceptual metaphors – or in terms of Lakoff and Johnson (1980) the manifestations of deeper conceptual tropes underlying and determining our thinking – occur in the psychologists' introduction in various versions: *IDEAS AND EMOTIONS ARE OBJECTS IN THE BODY, IDEAS AND EMOTIONS ARE MOVING OBJECTS* and *LIFE IS A JOURNEY*. The second trope – *IDEAS AND EMOTIONS ARE MOVING OBJECTS* – is produced three times in the topic-focused program: first in the team's introduction, and then in two calls. In Example (11), the caller produces a detailed personal story to present her problem to the host and to the media community:

Example (11) *I was really like a mother to him*

```
1   H: "The two of us together and each of us alone." ((addressing the next
2       caller)). Good evening. Go ahead, please.
3   C: This feeling has accompanied me in many situations, but I would like
4       to talk about a specific case. About three years ago, my brother was
5       killed in an accident ((pause)). Now, he was missing for three weeks
6       and ((pause)). They discovered the body, and ((pause)) there was
7       some sort of investigation ((pause)). But that's not the important part.
8       He was my younger brother, and ((pause)) it happened when I was 30
9       years old and he was 28, and when we were children we were
10      friends. That is we were very close to each other. That is, *I was, I was*
```

11	*really like a mother to him.* That is, I always saw to it that he did his
12	homework and stuff. After I got married, our relationship was not
13	very good, mainly because ((pause)) my ex-husband did not really
14	get along with him. The last time I saw him was when ((pause)) we
15	quarreled and ((pause)) I was very angry because he was so irres-
16	ponsible and we quarreled about all kinds of things. What I remem-
17	ber are the last words I said to him. He was very angry and hurt,
18	and it has nothing to do with the accident, but it was our last talk.

Having produced an orientation utterance[71] dominated by a conceptual trope that was produced by the psychologists ("This feeling has accompanied me in many situations", line 3), the second caller delves into her past without delay. She does not attempt to tighten her ties with the radio team as the first caller did. Paralinguistic features such as pauses, sound stretches and low volume identified in her contribution show that it must have been difficult for this caller to express herself.

She unfolds two personal stories: the accident story (lines 4–11) and the quarrel story (lines 12–18). It is noteworthy that she verbalizes the more traumatic accident story first, although this ordering does not match the chronological order of the events. As she unfolds the accident story, it turns out that it constitutes the orientation or the contextualizing background of the second story, since it is rich in evaluative devices that illuminate the relationship between the caller and her deceased brother.

The accident story opens with the problem-causing complicating action (lines 4–6). Then, the narrator produces several emotionally charged utterances that position her vis-à-vis her brother (lines 8–12) in the narrated past world. The caller uses two discursive resources to build this relationship. She uses repetition, a characteristic emphatic linguistic resource in therapeutic discourse, to mark the age difference (lines 8–9) and her feelings (lines 9–11). The emphasis on the age difference is surprising because the caller was only two years older than her brother, and this age difference does not necessarily explain the caller's intense emotions and responsibility toward her brother.

The organizing simile in lines 10–11 (*I was really like a mother to him*) summarizes, in our opinion, the detailed story that exposes the caller's emotional state. The trope constitutes a succinct story-internal version of the detailed narrative format. The emotional intensity packaged in the trope is intensified by the stance adverbial "really" that the caller uses to emphasize the special bond with her sibling.[72] The trope positions the caller simultaneously in two worlds: in relation to her brother in the narrated past world, and in relation to the radio team whose help she is seeking in the present. Following Chiappe and Kennedy (2001), we argue that the caller produced an emotion-displaying simile rather than a metaphor because she was aware of the fact that she was not the biological mother.

The quarrel story (lines 12–18) is about an incident that must have hurt the deceased brother. Although she does not say it explicitly, it is possible that the sister thinks that the words she uttered in their last quarrel (lines 16–18) were somehow related to her brother's death. This may have resulted in the strong guilt feelings that have plagued her ever since. It is also possible to assume that the sister did not do effective awareness-raising "grief work" (Freud 1917) (i.e., elaboration on the meaning of her brother's death). As a result, she must have continually expended her energy in unfruitful attempts to understand her loss, a process that affected her well-being. Our interpretation is supported by the paralinguistic evidence mentioned earlier that shows that it was very difficult for the caller to express herself. It is evident that the feelings expressed in the call and other *unconscious contents* could not be elaborated on in a 16-minute radio speech event.

In the quiet intimacy of the psychologist's clinic, the process of grief work could have comprised several stages (Green 1985). The first stage would have focused on cognitive elaboration of information related to the brother's death and search for new explanatory information, including the probability of suicide. The second stage would have attempted to make the caller aware of conscious and unconscious emotional contents related to her relationship with her late brother (e.g., guilty feelings, and anger towards the deceased) – succinctly encapsulated in the organizing trope *I was really like a mother to him*. Then, in the next stage, the therapeutic process could have tried to bring about relief from the emotional and libidinal investment in the dead brother in order to direct those energies towards actual and healthier goals and relationships.

In brief, our analysis shows that the caller unfolds her problem by means of two specific stories and several evaluative resources, including a story-internal organizing trope that summarizes the essence of the problem. Interpreted within the two personal stories, *I was really like a mother to him* – the figurative version of the caller's self – summarizes inter- and intrapersonal dimensions and constitutes a succinct version of the caller's feelings, thoughts and behavior in relation to her brother in the narrated past world. The narrative and figurative patterns may have attracted the attention of the psychologist[73] participating in the program, provided him with shared knowledge concerning the caller's problem and facilitated the choice of intervention, despite the limitations characteristic of this speech situation. Example (12) is an excerpt from the discussion phase, showing how one of the psychologists participating in the program makes functional use of the organizing story-internal metaphor to help the troubled caller:

Example (12) *You were to some extent like a mother to him*

1   It often happens that when we look back, we have a choice. Do we
2   choose to look back at the last words we said, or is our choice to look
3   at the other things you describe? That's a very courageous relation
4   ship which you describe by saying that *you were to some extent like a*
5   *mother to him*, and brought him up, and you were very good and
6   understanding to him. In other words, what do we really choose to
7   remember? You can also look at all the other good things you shared
8   with your brother and say what a wonderful relationship it was, and
9   you are left with the choice. What do you want to remember? Be
10 cause your memory is yours. The memory of your brother remains in
11 you. It is your companion. And you can choose which part of your
12 life with your brother will be your companion for the rest of your
13 life.

During the brief intervention illustrated in Example (12), the psychologist advises the caller to replace the negative experience that has been her companion (lines 7–13) with more positive memories about the times she spent with her brother. Echoing a conceptual trope that he produced earlier in the introduction to the program (i.e., IDEAS AND EMOTIONS ARE MOVING OBJECTS), the psychologist uses a strategy that is probably grounded in cognitive therapy (Beck 1976) to advance this intervention. Accordingly, he repeatedly stresses that the caller can rely on her common sense, sift through the memories she has, and choose to remember only the positive ones (lines 6–13).

Moreover, the psychologist summarizes the core of his answer to the caller by means of a revised version of her simile (lines 4–5): *You were to some extent like a mother to him.*[74] The reformulated trope is also accompanied by a stance adverbial "to some extent", a diminisher or downtoner (Biber et al. 1999) whose function is to moderate the intensity of guilt and responsibility displayed by the caller's organizing trope, and which she must have experienced in relation to her brother. The fact that the psychologist uses the caller's own figurative form indicates, in our opinion, that he must have noticed this organizing component in the caller's narrative contribution unfolded in the telephone interaction. In this way, the psychologist's turn validates the significance of the caller's trope for both participants in this interaction.

In conclusion, Examples (8–12) show that organizing figurative components of the past world produced by callers within the detailed narrative versions of their problems in the present are noticed by the psychologists and constitute functional discursive resources. The two callers presented in subsection 1.1 produce the tropes in the reception phase of the call as they unfold their lot to the program host. These enhance the interactional negotiation of effective solutions that can be implemented in the future.

1.2. Ineffective interactions

Successful presentation of the sufferer's problem in the reception phase is not always conducive to the interaction. Examples (13) and (14) show that although the caller, a 37-year-old male, produces relevant self-building tropes, the team's attitude toward him undermines the success of the interaction. In Example (13), the caller presents his problem to the host:

Example (13) *Life is like a jail*

1   H: Hello.
2   C: Good evening.
3   H: Good evening. Go ahead.
4   C: I was born in a world that was imposed on me. There are two con-
5   trasts in it: the spiritual and the earthly. I am a spiritual man by
6   nature. Since I was a child, I have been a book-loving person. There
7   are three thousand books in my library. The problem is that most
8   people are exactly the opposite of me. They are totally earthly.
9   Therefore *life is like a jail*. I am a prisoner, and they are my jailers.
10   They guard me, all those earthly people. I decided to get married.

11	Because I got married and I have children and because I also have to
12	make a living and survive, I work in an office as a clerk, a junior
13	clerk. My work is boring, robot-like, monotonous. I earn a low
14	salary, and I don't have time to read all those books I have – the
15	three thousand books I have. I have no time to read them because I
16	have to work from morning to night, and I have very little time to
17	read or write. I have written a book, but I want to write a few more,
18	H: What will be in your books? What will you write?
19	C: Theoretical books, philosophical books, historical books that span the
20	disciplines. That's my dream. That's my fantasy. I dream about a
21	spiritual world, a huge temple in which everyone is wearing white
22	clothes and discussing philosophy.

This caller chooses to present his problem via a brief resumé rich in evaluative resources. These show that he perceives his narrated life in terms of two diametrically opposed domains: the "spiritual" and the "earthly". These domains are presented at the beginning of the call (line 5) and are subsequently elaborated upon throughout Example (13). Although the caller mentions his marriage (lines 10–11), he chooses not to go into detail during the short telephone interaction.

To construct his dual existence vis-à-vis significant others in the past world, the caller uses four discursive resources: lexical repetition, modality of obligation, negative utterances and organizing tropes. Numerous lexical items pertaining to one of the two diametrically opposed domains are embedded in the example. Modality of obligation (line 11) and negative utterances (lines 14–15), the second and third discursive resources, further indicate the caller's helplessness (Green and Kupferberg 2000) vis-à-vis significant others, and thus intensify the power of the "earthly".

The caller uses a simile and a metaphor to summarize the two domains: *life is like a jail* (line 9) and "I dream about a spiritual world, a huge temple" (line 20–21). Both figurative structures designed and constructed by the caller enclose him within their imaginary boundaries, even though he is not aware of it and thinks that he can escape from the earthly *jail* and find shelter in the imaginary "huge temple" (line 21).

The imaginary diametrically opposed architectonic structures display an inflexible perspective on life in terms of absolutes with no intermediate states. They probably indicate rigid thinking (Rokeach, McGovney, and Denney 1960) or emotional immaturity. Example (14) illustrates how the psychologist relates to this summative contribution:

Example (14) *You said that you're imprisoned in some sort of a small jail*

```
1   P:  As you were talking, I had a lot of questions in my mind, and I was
2       calculating three thousand books. It's interesting to calculate how
3       many pages there are in your library. And what's the average number
4       of pages in each book? And how many lines are there on each page?
5       The fact that you have three thousand books, and that you declare
6       that you are a spiritual man, and you said that you're imprisoned in
7       some sort of a small jail, you are also transmitting a feeling of
8       superiority over us. We are earthly people. We are less important
9       than you. But I'm asking myself if this feeling that you live in a jail,
10      don't you think you would feel the same if you did something else,
11      and if you were able to read a lot and write a lot?
```

Example (14) shows that the psychologist does notice the powerful self-disclosing organizing *jail* simile (lines 6–7), but decides to make fun of the caller. The psychologist asks several questions relating to the number of books, pages and lines in the caller's library in order to highlight the caller's obsessive behavior (lines 2–4). He seems to be reproaching the caller for his comments regarding his large library (lines 5–9).

As in Examples (10) and (12), the psychologist relates to the trope produced by the caller. Using a chain of two premodifiers ("some sort of", "small"), he minimizes the awesome dimensions of the caller's confining structure (lines 6–7, *You said that you're imprisoned in some sort of a small jail*), but does not relate to the intrapersonal significance of the confining figurative resources the caller produces. Subsequently, the host intervenes and forces the caller to terminate the conversation because, as the host explains, the caller is identified as a frequent caller who repeatedly unfolds the same problem. In brief, the example shows that the third caller uses figurative resources to display the essential components of his problem. However, in the asymmetrical institutional context of a radio program whose hidden goal is mainly entertainment, these succinct versions of the caller's troubled self cannot be fully explored.

The example illustrates the tension that is often created between the voices of lay callers and institutional representatives in media discourse. Oriented to the overhearing radio community, the host, who controls the turn-taking system, decides that this frequent caller's voice is not interesting enough. The caller is unable to overpower the institutional voice in the dialogical but asymmetrical interaction.

Examples (15) and (16) are taken from a topic-focused call that is also interpreted as ineffective. The caller is a 52-year-old divorcée with four children. She does not present her problem clearly in the reception stage, but insists that the team ask her questions:

Example (15) "It will be easier for me if you ask me"

```
1   H:  Hello.
2   C:  Yes.
3   H:  Good evening.
4   C:  Yes.
5   H:  Yes. Go ahead.
6   C:  It'll be easier for me if you ask me ((confused laughter)). I can say
7       that after I listened to your experts' introduction, I am calmer. That
8       is, I got answers that are related to my dilemma.
9   H:  Tell me more about it.
10  C:  ((sighs)) I'm very nervous. I've never been on the air. It'll be easier
11      for me if you ask the questions.
12  H:  How old are you?
13  C:  I sound young, although I am past 50. I'm 52.
14  H:  So you've made wrong decisions?
15  C:  Now that I understood very well what wrong decisions mean in
16      Hebrew, because it's not my native language. But today I think it
17      [her marriage] was a waste of my time. Today I'm at a different place
18      ((laughter)).
19  H:  Yes. Tell us the story from the beginning.
20  C:  Aha. From the beginning? It's very difficult because I'm in the mid-
21      dle of a crisis.
22  H:  Yes.
23  C:  That's why I said that if you ask me the questions, I'm willing to talk
24      in order to solve some of my riddles.
```

Example (15) illustrates the reception phase of the call. The caller does not present her problem. Instead, she prefers to talk about the experts' introduction and requests that the team ask her questions. In lines 6–8 and 15–16, the caller relates to the effect of this introduction on her understanding of her own problem. Her figurative language echoes the experts' tropes. The caller defines the present stage in her life (lines 20–21, "I'm in the middle of a crisis") using a variation of the psychologists' conceptual metaphor (*LIFE IS A JOURNEY*). Later on, in phase 2 of the interaction, which is not presented in this chapter, she makes further use of figurative language to describe the experts' introduction when she explains that the team's introduction is "a star falling from heaven".

Since the caller does not make a clear contribution in phase 1, as we see in Example (15), it seems that the psychologist misinterprets what she says. The host intervenes by providing an alternative interpretation via a metaphor. This is illustrated in Example (16):

Example (16) "This was the only merchandise in the market"

1   P: I understand from what you say that your relationship with this man
2   who was your husband for so many years was somehow very
3   important because he was a Sabra [a prickly pear, denoting native-
4   born Israelis] and you felt like,
5   C: No, don't interpret it.
6   P: I am not interpreting.
7   C: He was unimportant.
8   P: What?! Unimportant?
9   C: ((Laughing bitterly)) That's right.
10 P: OK. You say that what existed then, doesn't exist anymore.
11 C: No, no, no ((pause)) no.
12 H: Was there no choice? Was he the only merchandise in the market?
13 C: Yes, yes, yes! How did you know?
14 H: That's what you said.
15 C: Right. That's how it was. There was no choice.

If we consider the caller's incoherent problem presentation illustrated in Example (15), it is not surprising that the psychologist and the caller misunderstand each other, as shown in lines 1–11. The psychologist attempts to explain why the caller agreed to get married (lines 1–4), and then in line 10 he purports to explain how the caller feels at present. Both attempts are unsuccessful, as is evident from the caller's protests in lines 5 and 11. The host intervenes in line 12, producing a trope that is in keeping with what the caller wants to say, as the caller's turns in lines 13 and 15 show. In this way, the host's metaphor enhances the construction of local coherence. Having engaged in various discursive tasks other than problem presentation, the caller realizes in phase 2 of the interaction that it is too late. She repeatedly expresses her disappointment via comments, some of which are figurative. Her comments are illustrated in Example (17):

Example (17) "This puzzle – I have to find the missing part"

1　C:　My riddles were only partially solved. You didn't understand me. I
2　　　still have many questions. Today I feel that ((pause)) this puzzle, this
3　　　puzzle, I have to find the missing part. You don't know me. I'd like
4　　　to be in touch. Can we talk afterwards?

The caller defines her state of mind in terms of "riddles" and "a puzzle". These figurative definitions of her acute need to make sense of her life contradict what she says in Example (15) (lines 7–8), and elsewhere in the interaction (i.e., the psychologist's introduction was like "a star falling from heaven").

In conclusion, various factors identified in this call seem to have undermined its success. The caller does not present her problem coherently at the beginning of the call; she is nervous and her proficiency in Hebrew is limited. In addition, although the caller defines her problem as a crisis in Example (15) (lines 20–21), the psychologists, who are aware of the fact that the telephone interaction is about to end, do not probe her problems any further.

"One can talk about all kinds of subjects", the next caller, specifies that he is married to a woman who is much younger than he is. The caller probably suffers from a language disability or an emotional problem and therefore does not succeed in presenting his problem coherently in the reception phase. In Example (18), he talks about different topics in parallel and the host does not understand what he wants to say:

Example (18) "One can talk about all kinds of subjects"

1　H:　Hello.
2　C:　Hello.
3　H:　Good evening.
4　C:　Good evening. Good evening.
5　H:　Go ahead please.
6　C:　Well, I'll skip the compliments to your program,
7　H:　Why? Don't! ((laughs)) I'm joking. It's OK. It's OK.
8　C:　You deserve it. I'm calling because I think that this problem concerns
9　　　quite a few couples, that one can talk about all kinds of topics, about
10　　children, their upbringing, running a household, financial affairs,
11　　going out, even about friends' problems. But there are certain taboo
12　　domains, and actually they are the most intimate domains.

62 *Organizing tropes*

13 H: Yes,
14 C: What does love measure when it begins with romantic words and
15   includes enjoyable earthly matters concerning sex, the physical.
16   There's such a barrier between the two domains,
17 H: Yes,
18 C: When one of them is free, he's at the table in front of the children.
19   Also at night. But what does love measure when it includes physical
20   touch as well as, how can I put it, the depth of each other's hearts.
21   These things are often totally separate, from the general point of view
22   and from the individual's point of view. OK?
23 H: Yes, I was about to hurry you up, but it's good that you're hurrying
24   yourself up.

It is difficult to understand what the caller wants to say. Careful reading of Example (18) shows that "One can talk about all kinds of subjects" probably wants to clarify what love is and how the emotional and physical components of love can be integrated. However, the caller is unable to express his ideas. The host and psychologists listen in patiently, probably realizing that this caller has escaped the scrutinizing panoptical eye of the gatekeeping operators. Then, the caller, like *Life is like a jail*, is politely dismissed from the rating-oriented radio program. It is evident that "One can talk about all kinds of subjects" should have chosen another site to present his problems.

At first glance, the next call appears to be an exception when it is compared with previous calls discussed in this chapter. Our interpretive comments will show how this exception actually constitutes a treasure that illuminates the meaningful connection established in Chapter 3 between narrative and figurative self-construction. This caller is a woman who probably experienced an interpersonal trauma, but refuses to provide the hotline volunteer with specific narrative clues. As a result, the interaction focuses on abstract themes such as infidelity, self-confidence, assertiveness, and extreme changes in a person's life. These themes are not anchored in a specific context. Example (19) illustrates the abstract nature of this interaction:

Example (19) "Like you're the world's only sucker"

1 C: ((pause)) ((coughs)) I wish you were a magician. I wish you could
2   make time fly backwards.
3 V: Do you want me to move time backward? I hear that something is
4   bothering you, right?

5   C: Yes. Can you do it?
6   V: Well, you know it's a wish, and I'm a human being exactly like you,
7   but let's talk a little. Maybe other things will happen when we talk.
8   C: Why is life unfair? I have to ask you a question. Does it sound
9   reasonable that people, the most responsible ones, the ones whose
10   heads are on their shoulders, the ones who understand, the ones who
11   pay attention to every single detail, at some point become extremely
12   irresponsible?
13 V: Please tell me what this has to do with you.
14 C: I prefer not to go into detail, but I would like to know that I am not
15   the only crazy person in the world, like you're the world's only
16   sucker. Do you understand what I mean?

The volunteer urges the caller to unfold specific stories (lines 3–4, 6–7, 13) in order to obtain information about the caller's problem-causing experiences. The caller refuses to unfold her story in public, and resorts to various evaluative resources that distance her verbal contribution in the present from the narrated past world. Lines 1–2 are a sequence of two wish utterances and a trope (i.e., "a magician") that conspire to distance the caller from the ongoing interaction. The trope assigns supernatural powers to the volunteer, and may imply that the caller's problem is complex. However, a wish utterance orients the discourse toward the domain of irrealis (Fleischman 1990), and in this way weakens the illocutionary effect obtained by syntactic repetition and a metaphorical comparison with a magician. This figurative conspiracy constitutes an interactional bridge to which the participants resort in the first four turns of Example (19) (lines 1–7).

In lines 8–12, the caller uses other distancing devices that further separate her discursive contribution from the narrated past. She uses a complex utterance consisting of a rhetorical yes–no question in which the noun "people" is defined by four restrictive relative clauses. In the absence of a contextualizing story, the relative clauses fail to refer to anything. The caller also uses a figurative conspiracy consisting of a simile and the indefinite second person pronoun. Thus, the simile (lines 15–16), which could have been a powerful organizing trope of the caller's emotions had she unfolded a narrative format, conspires with the indefinite second person "you", and constitutes another distancing device. In sum, this caller produces tropes that may have provided the gist of her experience, but because she refuses to unfold her story, both the volunteer in the here and now and the researchers constructing the fourth interpretive world that is tuned to the participants', are left with unanswered questions.

2. Summary

Our interpretive interface of the data analyzed in this chapter is summarized in this section in terms of the four-world model that we presented in Chapter 2, subsection 1.4 and whose boundaries are set by the Foucauldian panopticon that overlooks the conversational workshop rooms. Bearing this framework in mind, we describe and compare how the six troubled callers presented in Chapter 3 fared in the telephone sites they visited.

We discover that callers are meticulously scrutinized twice – first by the radio station operators who interview them to see if their stories are interesting (see Example (7) and the comments following it in Chapter 2). Then, once they are accepted into the public arena of radio problem discourse, the panoptical eyes of the host and the psychologists further probe their narrative and figurative productions and verbal skills. Those callers deemed media-worthy are allowed to proceed.

The six interactions presented in Chapter 3 are summarized below. The first two, *Amputating the cancerous leg* and *I was really like a mother to him*, are approved by the media gatekeepers and therefore they are allowed to present their troubled narrative and figurative contributions. *Amputating the cancerous leg*'s voice is loud and clear from the moment she is on the air. Because the program is general and no introduction is provided, she assertively demands to present her own introduction via a planned poetic text that she must have composed before the program. The caller undermines the authority of the host who is doubtful of the discursive adventures that the lay caller unexpectedly proposes to undertake in his program.

When the host finally complies with her request, the determined and agentive caller unfolds a painful story that is summatively organized by means of self-revealing tropes – the succinct versions of her resolute but suffering self in the world of the past. Examples (8–10) show that the caller's narrative and figurative contribution presented at the beginning of the interaction enhance the time-bounded radio interaction. One of the tropes she produces constitutes a story-internal organizing component of global coherence that is recycled by the psychologist in his answer.

Although the second caller, *I was really like a mother to him*, participates in a topic-focused program, she is not influenced by the psychologists' scholarly introduction and their conceptual tropes. Driven by strong needs to express the intrapersonal meaning of her troubled past world, she disregards salient tropes that the psychologists produce in their authoritative introduction. Instead, she produces her intrapersonal narrative contribution in the first phase of the interaction and, as in the case of *Amputating the cancerous leg* before her, her story contains an organizing trope that constitutes a functional and dialogical resource that the psychologist uses.

Always under the panoptical eye, these media-worthy callers, then, produce organizing tropes in the reception phase of the call as they are unfolding their lot to the program host, the psychologists and the overhearing audience at home. These figurative forms constitute summative versions of the callers' narrated worlds. The fact that the psychologists notice these tropes provides validating evidence (Peräkylä 1997), confirming that what the callers say is also relocated by the psychologists from peripheral consciousness (Chafe 1994) into the ongoing interaction. In this way, these forms enhance the interactional negotiation of effective solutions that can be implemented in the future. In other words, these examples show that organizing tropes may have acted as discursive instruments that prevail over the limitations characteristic of this speech situation.

Life is like a jail, the third caller presented in Chapter 3, uses figurative and narrative resources to display the essential components of his problem at the beginning of the call. However, the succinct versions of the lay participant are not fully explored by the institutional representatives of the media. Oriented to the overhearing radio community, they collaborate to terminate the interaction with this frequent and tedious caller whose repeated stories are not likely to improve the rating of the program.

Various factors identified in the fourth interaction seem to have undermined the success of "This puzzle – I have to find the missing part". She does not present her problem coherently at the beginning of the call and instead compliments the radio psychologists on their introductory explanation. She is also nervous and her proficiency in Hebrew is limited. As a result, precious time is wasted before the caller can finally explain why she has called in. Thus, although the caller describes her problem in terms of "a crisis", the psychologists, who are aware of the fact that the telephone interaction is about to end, do not probe her problems any further. Under such circumstances, the co-construction of a solution is practically impossible.

"One can talk about all kinds of subjects" is not able to present his problem clearly. The host and the psychologists do not understand what the caller wishes to express, and therefore the caller, who has evidently chosen the wrong site to unfold his problems, is politely dismissed from the rating-oriented radio program.

Another caller who does not get along well is "Like you're the world's only sucker". We present this hotline interaction in Chapter 3 because it sheds light on the functions of organizing tropes, a central construct described in this book. Although this caller produces figurative language that may have provided the gist of her experience, she refuses to unfold her detailed story. Therefore, both the volunteer in *the here and now* of the ongoing interaction and the researchers reflectively constructing the fourth interpretive world that is tuned to the participants', are left with unanswered questions.

Chapter 3 shows that in the public arena of a rating-oriented radio program, some lay callers are more successful than others. Those who produce intriguing narrative and figurative versions of their problems in the first phase of the interaction have a better chance to fare well in the time-bounded public site: negotiating the meaning of their past world and sometimes constructing possible future alternatives.

Other suffering souls like *Life is like a jail* and "One can talk about all kinds of subjects" have evidently entered the wrong site. In the public arena of radio discourse, whose main goal is the entertainment of the overhearing audience rather than healing, their tedious and incoherent self-constructions are not accepted by the media representatives, who hasten to banish them in an eager quest for more rating-worthy callers. These ineffective interactions show that radio problem discourse is multilogical, not dialogical, a multiparticipant situation in which the unseen participant plays a significant role.

Finally, "This puzzle – I have to find the missing part" and "Like you're the world's only sucker" do not manage to solve their problems for other reasons that illuminate and reinforce the successes of *Amputating the cancerous leg* and *I was really like a mother to him*. "This puzzle – I have to find the missing part" wastes precious time on complimenting the media representatives and therefore fails to present her problem in the reception phase.

"Like you're the world's only sucker" is a deviant case which calls for special attention and explanation. Produced in the more private and rating-free domain of the hotline service, it is ineffective because the caller produces tropes with no contextualizing personal stories. In other words, she does not provide the volunteer with information about problem-causing past events. Therefore, it is impossible for the volunteer and the researchers to construct relevant dimensions of the caller's self. This interpretation is validated by the volunteer's repeated requests for the caller to provide a contextualizing narrative format.

The chapter shows, then, that the expressive figurative resources of troubled callers deemed media-worthy constitute pithy subjectivity markers – the gist of the more detailed version of the callers' narrated world. These tropes sometimes enhance the co-construction of global coherence in the world of the present, within which the tormented problematic past worlds and possible or imaginary future worlds are constructed.

Tropes are particularly conducive to the success of the call when they are produced at the outset of the short interaction. In this way, callers who present inter- and intrapersonal dimensions of their troubled selves through personal stories and organizing tropes in the reception phase of the interaction make a salient contribution to the subsequent psychological intervention in the problem-discussion phase with the professional others. If our interpretations are correct, these participants are able to overcome a plethora of factors that undermine communication in circumstances that do not seem conducive to problem discussion.

We define organizing tropes in relation to the personal story in which they occur as story-internal figurative forms that summarize other evaluative resources and constitute succinct versions of emotional, cognitive, socio-cultural, and behavioral dimensions of the caller's troubled self. In other words, these tropes enable callers to construct relevant inter- and intrapersonal dimensions of the past in the present, and sometimes even relate to the future.

To our mind, this third chapter offers illuminating examples revealing two significant aspects of problem discourse: the relationship between narrative formats and evaluative positioning resources within the story, and the centrality of organizing tropes – summative and hierarchical versions of other repeated patterns in a personal story. These tropes fulfilled presentational and dialogical functions in the interactions explored in this chapter.

The empirical connection established between narrative and figurative self-construction in problem discourse provides answers to questions raised in studies that foreground the centrality of key metaphors in problem discourse, but do not explain how these metaphors are related to major themes of this genre (McMullen 1996; McMullen and Conway 1994). The discovery of the organizing function of self-building tropes is supported by empirical evidence in studies that focused on self-construction in life-story interviewing of teacher trainees, and school principals (Bar-Kol and Kupferberg 2001; Kupferberg and Gilat 2001; Kupferberg and Green 2001).

Chapter 3 also shows that only some callers are endowed with media-worthiness. This characteristic enables them to gain access to the time-bounded and overhearing audience-oriented program, present their troubled stories and negotiate them with the media representatives. Based on the interactions presented in Chapter 3, we define media-worthiness as a gift comprising assertiveness and readiness to argue with the media representatives in order to present one's own perspective as well as good story-telling skills including the ability to focus on the essence of the problem by means of figurative resources. The production of both narrative and figurative formats lubricates the professional participants' attempts to orient the time-bounded conversation towards a meaningful closure.

Finally, media-worthy callers present their versions of the problem for the media representatives and for the overhearing community that is eager to penetrate their reality and hear attention-holding stories. In fact, these callers are allowed to attain their personal goals because at the same time they serve the goals of the media. The pragmatic significance of media-worthiness is that callers who are not endowed with these gifts are denied access to the program.

Chapter 4
Open your call with a title

In Chapter 3, we discovered that the panoptical eye of the radio team relaxes its surveillance when media-worthy callers like *Amputating the cancerous leg* and *I was really like a mother to him* are spotted. These troubled selves are allowed to present their problems and weave their detailed narrative formats and succinct organizing tropes. In addition, it is evident that because these discursive contributions are constructed in the first phase of the relatively short interaction, the psychologists are sometimes able to use them for therapeutic ends.

Following our action-oriented goals presented in Chapter 1, we show in Chapter 4 how the insights gained in Chapter 3 are applied in the very same radio program. We decided to collaborate with the program host in order to see to what extent the presentation of a title in the reception phase of the call would be conducive to the construction of the caller's past and future worlds within the world of the present. At our request, the cooperative host urged potential callers to open their call with a title. In this chapter, we present excerpts from a topic-focused program and a general one, respectively. The programs were broadcast on Tuesday, July 24, 1997 and Tuesday, August 21, 1997.

1. Topic-focused program: "I advise you to hate your mother"

In this section, we present excerpts from a call made to a topic-focused program that dealt with "separation anxiety". There are four parties in the program: the host, two clinical psychologists, program operators, and five callers who are approved by the program operators and thus gain access to the program. In their introduction, the psychologists, a woman (P1) and a man (P2), discuss the meaning of "separation anxiety" at length in an attempt to establish an understandable conceptual frame of reference. Selected excerpts from their introduction are presented in this section.

The psychologists do not concur on the definition of the sources of "separation anxiety", the topic of the program. The woman emphasizes that it is a universal normative experience, whereas the man considers it a pathological condition that afflicts some human beings but not others. Example (20) illustrates how the female psychologist defines the meaning of "separation anxiety":

Example (20) "We wander around with a small hole in our stomach"

1   P1: Separation anxiety is something that we all experience. We're born
2   with it. The question is if it is normal. The very fact that we are
3   separated from our mother's womb, we are detached from her, five
4   minutes after we're born. Ever since then we wander around with a
5   small hole in our stomach that we call separation anxiety. Since
6   birth, any relationship is always accompanied by pain, or the fear
7   that we will be abandoned or left alone.

It seems that the female psychologist aligns herself with Bowlby's (1973) theory, when she explains that "separation anxiety" is created at birth, during the emergence of a new individual from the body of its mother. The psychologist emphasizes that this universal experience constitutes the source of "separation anxiety". Following our definition of organizing tropes in Chapter 3, we suggest that the psychologist produces a central figurative resource that encapsulates her perspective on the essence of this universal phenomenon: "Ever since then we wander around with a small hole in our stomach that we call separation anxiety" (lines 4–5). The trope provides a succinct definition of "separation anxiety", viewed as an intrapsychic experience that stems from an interpersonal experience (i.e., the separation from the mother's womb at birth).

In Example (21), the male psychologist presents his perspective on the phenomenon. He shifts the focus of the introduction from universal aspects to pathological and interpersonal ones, characteristic of those who suffer from "separation anxiety":

Example (21) "As if they are leeches"

1   P2: There are people who experience this anxiety very intensely. They
2   cling to other people as if they're leeches, and they're afraid to
3   leave them, like a child holding on to his mother's dress, afraid to
4   let go. Surely, this anxiety affects the quality of their life. And

5   then, there is the other side of this leech. These are people whose
6   separation anxiety is so intense that they are afraid to take any risk
7   and establish any relationship.

The male psychologist attempts to explain to the overhearing audience and potential callers what the pathological dimensions of "separation anxiety" can be by resorting to phenomena that some, but not all human beings experience. These are summatively defined in terms of two similes ("As if they're leeches" in line 2 and "like a child holding on to his mother's dress, afraid to let go" in lines 3–4). Both figurative forms shift the focus of attention from the intrapsychic domain constructed in Example (20) by "a small hole" to an interpersonal domain constructed via "as if they're leeches" and "like a child holding on to his mother's dress, afraid to let go". Produced one after the other, these tropes probably show that the psychologist attempts to establish a connection between the "child holding on to his mother's dress" and the offensive parasitic "leeches" clinging to others for their own benefit.

In response to the psychologists' introduction, five callers choose to unfold their problems in public. These callers entitle their problems in terms of the erudite institutional introduction that prefaces the program. Example (22) illustrates how one of the five, the fourth caller, responds to the host's directive and entitles her problem. She is a 50-year-old woman whose mother died suddenly of a heart attack in the middle of a festive event seven years before she herself calls the radio station. The caller's first verbalization of her troubled past was summarized in Chapter 2, Example (7), and was evaluated by the program operators as "excellent":

Example (22) "My title is like everybody else's"

1 H: The two of us together and each of us alone. Let's go on.
2 C: Hello.
3 H: Hello. Go ahead.
4 C: Well, my title is like everybody else's. It's separation anxiety. Only
5   in my case it's not about him or her, or about children, but rather
6   about death. Are you listening? ((sighs))
7 H: Yes. Of course.
8 C: ((sighs and laughs)) My heart is beating fast. Can you hear my
9   breathing?
10 H: We can hear you loud and clear.

Having listened to the former three callers and probably influenced by the psychologists' introduction, the fourth caller begins by adopting the topic of the program (line 4). In this way, she positions herself as a fit member of the temporary night community (Katriel 1998) that was first inaugurated by the psychologists' authoritative introduction, and then reverberates and is locally perpetuated throughout the calls.

The caller must have been very anxious, as she admits in line 8, and as the audible sighs she produces indicate. After she produces a title that satisfies the directives of the program host, this suffering soul, like *I was really like a mother to him*, and unlike "This puzzle – I have to find the missing part", hastens to unfold her individual discursive contribution via two personal stories. These narrative formats are not arranged chronologically, as we see in Example (23). The first story provides the context in which the caller's problems arose:

Example (23) "My mother died in a big bang"

1 Well, OK. ((sighs)) Seven years ago I spoke with a psychologist about
2 this subject, and he promised me that the matter usually lasts about half
3 a year, that is the time of rehabilitation after death ((pause)) ((sighs)),
4 and it has lasted seven years. It's a wild anxiety that I don't share with
5 anyone, but I radiate it all around me. Seven years ago *my mother died*
6 in my arms, all of a sudden, *in a big bang*, during a festive event without
7 any prior warning.

Narrating the first story (lines 1–4), *In a big bang* constructs the relevant context for her problem: an anxiety that makes her life unbearable. The story comprises orientation (line 1–2), and a problem-inducing complication action (lines 2–3), that focuses on a promise made by a psychologist, probably the caller's therapist, that her grief work (Freud 1917) will be over in half a year. The caller stresses that she has been suffering from anxiety for seven years.

The coda of the first story (lines 4–5) comprises a figurative definition of how the anxiety has influenced the caller's life at intrapersonal ("wild anxiety") and interpersonal ("but I radiate it all around me") levels. This definition recycles discursive resources produced earlier in the program by the psychologists and a former caller. It also expresses the caller's individual productions. Aligning herself with the psychologists, she calls her problem "an anxiety", adding an individual intensifying contribution via the adjective "wild" (line 4). The trope (line 5, "but I radiate it all around me") was worded almost identically by a caller who was on the air before her.

The first story constitutes the background of the second story that unfolds how the caller's mother died. The caller provides several details that constitute the context of the painful personal story. She also uses a trope to explain the intensity of the emotions created after the death of her mother (line 6, *in a big bang*). The trope is produced by the caller three times: twice during the interaction and once in the short preliminary interview conducted by the program operators (see Example (7) and comments in Chapter 2). In each of the production instances, the trope constitutes a summative and central evaluative self-displaying resource that performs at least two functions. It constructs the intensity of the loss the caller experienced when her mother died, and it provides the radio psychologists with a valuable self-builder that can be further explored.

This organizing trope shows that although the caller complies with the host's request to give a title and relates to the conceptual framework constructed by the psychologist, the individual trauma she experienced is finally expressed through an individual trope that constructs and displays *her* personal agony. However, as we see later on, the psychologists do not relate to this self-builder and choose to elaborate on the contents and tropes that they presented in their introductory comments in Examples (20) and (21).

Then, in a section of the interaction that is not presented in this chapter, the caller describes her life since the *big bang*. She says that she has been constantly afraid that people who are close to her will die. To illustrate what she means, the caller produces generic stories that focus on her daily routines. For example, she always checks to see if her husband and children are breathing while they are asleep. She also emphasizes that she did not do so before her mother's death. In response to these daily routines, the host chooses to focus on the caller's relationship with her mother rather than on her present life, as we see in Example (24):

Example (24) "She doesn't want to get close to me"

1 H: It means that you had a very special relationship with your mother,
2 C: Very special ((sighs)). For seven years I have been thinking about
3   her, 22 hours a day. Then, I sleep for two hours and dream about her
4   all the time, and the dreams are so real and so strange. I don't talk to

74 *Open your call with a title*

```
5       people about them. These are dreams that can't be described. The
6       main motive in each dream is my mother who was such an
7       affectionate person, and I was the most precious thing she had, and
8       she used to hug me and caress me and help me bring up my children.
9       She used to do so much for me. In all my dreams she always turns
10      away from me. She doesn't want to speak with me. She doesn't want
11      to get close to me. She avoids me. She only cares for my brother. She
12      runs away from me. She doesn't let me come near her. She has
13      nothing to do with me. This is repeated in every dream, each night in
14      a hundred dreams. And the person who is close to me, that's my
15      brother. I could talk with him, but my brother's son was recently
16      killed in a car accident, and I can't go to him and tell him my story
17      when he has such a painful story of his own.
```

In Example (24), *In a big bang* chooses to continue talking about things that are constantly on her mind instead of relating directly to the host's comment in line 1. The caller describes the anxiety that she has experienced since her mother's death through generic stories that describe her waking hours as well as her dreams. During the day, she keeps thinking about her mother (lines 2–3). The mother is also a central figure in her dreams at night (lines 3–4, 5–6 and 9–14). The caller details the dead mother's behavior in the dreams and compares it with that of the living mother. The affectionate and caring parent who inhabited the world of the living avoids her daughter in dreams.

Avoidance is constructed via a chain of negative utterances (lines 10–13): "She doesn't want to speak with me", "She doesn't want to get close to me", "She doesn't let me come near her", and "She has nothing to do with me". It is also manifested in verbs that denote distance: "She always turns from me", "She avoids me", "She only cares for my brother", and "She runs away from me".

Careful reading of the caller's narrative productions indicates that the sudden death of the caller's mother must have caused a trauma from which *In a big bang* has not been able to recover. Example (24) comprises discursive evidence that the caller probably suffers from a Post-Traumatic Stress Disorder (PTSD) (American Psychiatric Association, DSM IV, 309.81), as the following symptoms indicate. The caller reports having intrusive distressing recollections (lines 2–3), recurrent distressing dreams about the event (lines 3–4) and premonitions that it is about to recur. In addition, the caller emphasizes that she suffers from insomnia (line 3) and hypervigilance (ibid.).

At this discursive junction, the host invites the female psychologist to join the discussion. The psychologist's comments are summarized below. She chooses to position herself in relation to the caller in the present temporary world as an understanding, friendly, and empathetic professional who has been listening carefully and wishes to share her thoughts with the caller. The psychologist defines the caller's experience as a trauma, and, adopting a psychological approach to trauma interventions that emphasizes the healing effect of speech (Foa, Keane, and Friedman 2000), explains to the caller that the therapeutic intervention in which she engaged following her mother's death must have been unsuccessful.

Accordingly, the psychologist uses two figurative forms to describe the dire consequences of that ineffective intervention. She tells the caller that "the explosive charges of the trauma have not been dismantled" and describes the caller's clinical post-traumatic status in terms of "an open bleeding wound". Subsequently, the psychologist adds that the caller did not take into account the possibility that her mother would pass away. In response to the last interpretive comment, the caller unfolds a story presented in Example (25):

Example (25) "Don't be so dependent on me"

1 C: You know, I remember that a month before she died we were driving
2   in my car and then we were stuck at a traffic light, and she said to
3   me: "Look, you have to take into account how much time I'll live.
4   You have to, you'll have to cope with it. Don't be so dependent on
5   me."
6 P1: Yes.
7 C: And I said to her: "I don't want to think about it because the day
8   you go, I'll go with you."

In Example (25), the narrator unfolds a personal story that shows that she agrees with the psychologist. The story relates to a conversation that took place before the mother's death. *In a big bang* uses constructed dialogue, an evaluative device indicating that the caller was probably reliving the meaningful conversation that took place in the world of the past. At the same time, the decision of the caller to display the conversation with her dead mother at this point in the interaction may be an indication that the ongoing interaction makes her mindful of the content of her mother's words and conscious of the fact that her mother was realistic and understood that the relationship might be harmful when the mother passed away. Thus, the mother's voice that is heard within the caller's narrative is also the voice of the daughter whose awareness may have been raised. Example (26) shows how the female psychologist comments on the personal story presented in Example (25):

Example (26) "Get out of the circle of dependence"

```
1    I think that what your mother told you intuitively and wisely was to get
2    out of the circle of dependence and intimate relationship you had, and
3    you chose to stay there like children who think that Mommy will be
4    there forever. You have chosen to remain inside the relationship.
```

Echoing a trope produced by the narrator at the beginning of the call, but not cited in the book ("How can I get out of this vicious circle?"), the psychologist summarizes figuratively the dead mother's advice. Then, she emphasizes that the daughter chose to stay inside the circle of dependence (lines 2–4). In addition, the psychologist stresses that the mother was realistic, understood that the symbiotic relationship might be harmful to the daughter when she (the mother) passed away, and may have tried to prepare her daughter for the inevitable end. Example (27) shows how the male psychologist relates to the problem:

Example (27) "I advise you to hate your mother"

```
1    P2:  I'd like to tell you some harsh things,
2    C:   Oh.
3    P2:  The other psychologist is signaling to me that I'm too harsh,
4    C:   I'm also afraid,
5    P2:  No, there's nothing to be afraid of. What I'm going to say to you is
6         meant to help you, and not make it harder for you. I think that what
7         my colleague [the female psychologist who related to the caller's
8         problem] tried to ask you is why you keep mourning your mother
9         rather than saying goodbye to her. This is related to the type of
10        relationship you had with your mother. And when a person is her
11        mother's best friend, it usually means trouble. A mother is a
12        mother, and a friend is a friend and these things should not be
13        mixed together. Now, I'm going to say something that may be hard
14        for you to accept. A child has to learn to love his parents and hate
15        them. And parents who don't make it possible for their children to
```

16		hate them, actually prevent them [the children] from loving them.
17		You and your mother had a relationship in which, for various rea-
18		sons that can't be revealed in a radio program, you weren't able to
19		or couldn't express the anger and hate you felt toward your mother.
20	C:	No. Really!
21	P2:	No?
22	C:	No! No! The people who knew her would tell you she was an
23		angel. One can't hate such a person.
24	P2:	Look. Let me tell you,
25	C:	There was nothing to be angry about.
26	P2:	I think that if you want to be cured, you must know that your
27		mother wasn't an angel. I am ready to vouch for that. I won't tell
28		you what I think.
29	C:	Maybe today she is an angel.
30	P2:	((laughing)) Yes, maybe today. Maybe she's an angel.
31	C:	Please, don't speak badly of her.
32	P2:	No. What I'd like to do is show you all those things, that your
33		brother was her favorite child, not you.
34	C:	No. Never. Only in my dreams. Never.
35	P2:	The dream says something about reality. And you don't have the
36		guts to face the feelings that could actually cure you. Death is a part
37		of our life. It's clear to us that we'll go away from here, and our
38		friends will go away from here, and finally our children will go
39		away from here. Now if you really want to be cured, I think you
40		have to face your mother in the flesh, not as an angel. And if you
41		believe in angels, then I think it'll haunt you for the rest of your
42		life. I advise you to hate your mother.

Example (27) shows how the male psychologist and the caller negotiate the mother's influence on her daughter, but fail to reach global coherence. We will begin with a brief summary of the content of the example and then present our analysis. The male psychologist strongly advises the caller to hate her mother, who, in his opinion, discriminated against her in favor of her brother. In this way, the male psychologist thinks, the caller can cure herself. The caller repeatedly protests and attempts to convince the authoritative psychologist that he is wrong. Both the female psychologist and the host voice their objections to the psychologist's aggressive strategy.

The psychologist's first turn alerts the caller to the harsh content of his advice (see line 1 and also later lines 13–14). The caller and the female psychologist react strongly to this surprising piece of advice (lines 2, 3, and 4). In light of their remonstrative responses, the psychologist mitigates his tone (line 5) and emphasizes that his ensuing message will help the caller (lines 5–6). He then resumes his combative approach, however, aligning himself with the comments made by the female psychologist (lines 6–9: "I think that what my colleague tried to ask you is why you keep mourning your mother rather than saying goodbye to her"). Subsequently, the psychologist advises the caller to hate her mother (lines 14–15). This directive is produced after the psychologist prepares the caller for the fact that what he is about to say is hard to accept (lines 13–14).

His simplistic advice is probably derived from his interpretation of Mahler's Separation-Individuation concepts (Mahler 1963), and it can be linked to the beginning of the chapter when he talks about leeches. Shifting the focus to the pathological domain, the psychologist probably assumes that people who suffer from separation anxiety are adults who cling to their mothers like leeches, and therefore the solution that he proposes is an instant and absurd command: Hate your mother!

This piece of advice is accompanied with an implicit warning that intensifies the effect of the shocking recommendation (lines 17–18). The warning is implicit in the psychologist's hypothetical story, emphasizing that had they talked in the privacy of the clinic, he could have been more explicit. The caller's terse but protesting "No. Really!" meets with the psychologist's surprised but assertive rhetorical "No?", which actually constitutes a powerful panoptical assertion (lines 21).[75]

In her attempt to vindicate her dead mother's honor, the caller resorts to a trope: "an angel" (lines 22–23). In lines 26–31, the male psychologist and the caller use the "angel" trope interactionally as a discursive bridge that enables them to negotiate the dead mother's character. They fail, however, as we have shown, to reach global coherence (i.e., reach an agreement concerning the main topic: who the mother was) (see Chapter 2, subsection 1.2) since each of them interprets the trope "angel" differently. The caller defines her mother as a person who had several virtues that made her worthy of the title "angel" (lines 23, 25 and 29). She emphasizes that other people would also be of the same opinion (lines 22–23).

The argument gains momentum when the male psychologist resorts to new discursive weapons. He produces an authoritative "Let me tell you" (line 24), to which the caller relates with another verbal protest (line 25). Then, using a conditional, lexical choice, and modality of obligation (lines 26–28), he warns the caller that if she wants to be cured, she must accept that her mother was not an angel. It is noteworthy that at that point, the psychologist defines the caller's problem as an illness, in keeping with his introductory comments in Example (21), and he hastens to use an amplifying linguistic resource such as "vouch" to support his instant diagnosis (line 27).

In other words, the psychologist unequivocally says that the caller's problem is caused by her dependent relationship with her mother and not by the traumatic experience of her mother dying in her arms. In her despair, the caller gives in, and suggests that "maybe today she is an angel" (line 29). The psychologist complies with the caller's insistent demand to entitle the mother "an angel" as long as it only means that the mother is not alive now (line 30).

Then, the psychologist relates to the caller's dreams described in Example (24). He interprets the dreams as an indication that the mother discriminated against her daughter in favor of her son, reminds the caller that she has to be cured, and repeats his therapeutic advice: "I advise you to hate your mother" (line 42).

We think that even if the psychologist's approach is anchored in relevant theories about loss and separation, he should have let the caller gain awareness and discover the real meaning of her relationship with her mother on her own. The psychologist probably knows that in the public arena of a radio program, there is no time for intrapsychic processes of exploration. The aggressive alternative he chooses is evidently not accepted by the caller, the female psychologist, and the host.

Our interpretation is validated by the caller's turns that constitute "the next turn validation" (Peräkylä 1997). In addition, in a telephone interview we conducted the following day (see Example (29) below) the caller provides discursive evidence that supports our interpretation. In Example (28), a real drama takes place on the air when the host and the female psychologist attempt to rescue *In a big bang* from the combative psychologist:

Example (28) "I don't know if you're using the right word"

1 H: ((addressing the male psychologist)) I don't know if you're using
2   right word. I don't know if, ((incomprehensible. All the participants

3   the talk at once))
4 C: ((referring to the word "hate")) It's a shocking word.
5 H: But one can certainly talk about anger,
6 C: Anger. Yes. I'm angry because of what D. [the male psychologist]
7   said. It has nothing to do with my mother ((incomprehensible. All
8   the participants talk at once))
9 P2: It's true. I wanted to tell you at the beginning that it would have
10   been an easier solution.
11 C: ((laughs))
12 H: But if you changed the word "hate" into the word "anger",
13 P2: ((addressing the host)) Why are you doing this?
14 C: ((relating to the host)) Yovav is really merciful. He's saying the
15   right things. Yes, I'm willing to think about the idea of anger.
16   Perhaps I'm angry that she abandoned me.

In Example (28), the host and the female psychologist attempt to mitigate the harsh impact of the male psychologist's comments in Example (27), and thus provide evidence that validates our interpretation of Example (27). The host proposes to change the psychologist's wording (lines 1–2) and later advises the caller to be angry at her mother instead of hating her (line 5). The host's first turn is accompanied by a jumble of unintelligible speech (lines 2–3) when all the participants talk at the same time.

Encouraged by the unexpected support granted by the institutional representative, the caller says that she is shocked by the use of the word "hate" (line 4). When the host puts forward his alternative (line 5), the caller avows that she is angry at the psychologist, not her mother (lines 6–7). Her comment is followed once again by a jumble of unintelligible speech (lines 7–8). When the host repeats his idea of replacing the word "hate" with "anger" (line 12), the male psychologist protests, using a rhetorical question (line 13). The caller concludes by redefining the host's idea of "anger" in terms of her perspective on the death of her mother: "Perhaps I'm angry that she abandoned me" (line 16).

To recapitulate: In response to *In a big bang*, the female psychologist chooses to position herself in relation to the caller in the present temporary world as an understanding, friendly, and empathetic professional who has been listening carefully and who wishes to share her thoughts with the caller. It seems that she relates to an approach to trauma that emphasizes the healing effect of speech. Accordingly, she explains that "the explosive charges of the trauma have not been dismantled", thus implying that future psychotherapy may help the caller. It is evident that she does not attempt to administer instant intervention on the air, since she is probably aware of the limitations of the telephone interaction on the one hand and the severity of the caller's problem on the other. Therefore, she chooses not to open up the discursive productions of the caller: her trauma-perpetuating generic stories and her intense emotion-displaying organizing trope.

Assuming an authoritative attitude of an almighty knower, the male psychologist offers his instant diagnosis of the caller's problem that rings familiar Freudian bells. When he urges the caller aggressively to accept his authoritative formula, he encounters the opposition of all the other participants, including the female psychologist and the host, who support the caller in this unique interaction. A real media drama takes place on the air when the host and the female psychologist join forces with the caller, whose suffering is probably augmented rather than alleviated following her unsuccessful discussion with the male psychologist.

At our request, the host asked the callers who participated in this topic-focused program if they would agree to be interviewed by telephone after the program. Three out of the five participants agreed. In a telephone interview conducted the following day, we asked the participants three questions: (1) Why did you make the telephone call? (2) How did the host relate to your problem? (3) How did the psychologists relate to your problem? We produced verbatim representations of what the callers said. Example (29) presents an excerpt from *In a bang*'s reflective answers to our questions:

Example (29) "I didn't accept what the other psychologist said"

1   I made the call because I had disturbing dreams. Therapy didn't help
2   me. I like the program. I like the host and his voice. If I had to rate
3   him on a scale from one to ten, I'd say he's ten. I didn't accept what
4   the other psychologist [the male psychologist] said. The people who
5   listened to him reacted like me. The idea of hating my mother! The
6   good thing was that Yovav [the host] straightened things out.

The caller validates our interpretation regarding the male psychologist's intervention. She also emphasizes that the host was on her side. We believe that she may need further psychotherapy to solve the post-traumatic syndrome she suffers from. In this respect, the short radio program could not help her.

2. General program: "I don't know how to get close to my middle son"

Example (30) below shows how the host opened a general program on Tuesday, August 21, 1997:

Example (30) "Open your call with a title"

1	This is Yovav Katz, your program host. "The two of us together and
2	each of us alone." Tonight the line is open to topics of your choice.
3	Our phone numbers are 6910260, 6910208, or 6910269. From time
4	to time, we broadcast an open program and you can talk about the
5	topic of your choice. In most cases, we choose topics for discussion
6	and focus on them. So this is your chance. Make good use of it and
7	call us. Tonight Dr. T [a female psychologist] is with us. We have a
8	special request for you. Since this is an open line program, and each
9	of you will most certainly choose a different topic, we ask you to
10	begin your call with a title or a name that you have chosen for your
11	topic. Open your story with a title, and then we'll continue our
12	conversation.

In Example (30), the host entices potential troubled selves to make a phone call. The host provides important information, and, which concerns us most, asks callers to open the call with a title. Five callers respond to his opening. Three adults and a ten-year-old boy produce figurative titles, while the fifth caller – a 29-year-old new immigrant whose proficiency in Hebrew is limited – is "non-figurative". This caller responds to the host's directive to entitle her problem, saying "It's about the relationship of a daughter and a successful mother." Example (31) shows how the ten-year-old boy and the host co-construct the opening of the call. The participation of a child in an adult program broadcast between 11 p.m. and 2 a.m. (see Chapter 2, subsection 2.1.1) is quite unusual. This is probably the reason why the young caller was easily granted access to the rating-oriented radio program:

General program: "I don't know how to get close to my middle son" 83

Example (31) "It all comes from the dreams"

1 H: Hello?
2 C: Yes.
3 H: I am ten years old.
4 H: Mmmm.
5 C: Yes, and I have a brother who is five and a half, and he's scared at
6   night. He's afraid. He gets up at night and he always says: "I'm
7   scared."
8 H: And you?
9 C: I think that it all comes from the dreams.

Despite his young age, the eloquent boy presents his figurative title coherently, displaying responsibility toward his younger brother: "I think that it all comes from the dreams." Another figurative caller was a young woman who has been separated from her husband for a long time because of her academic studies. In response to the host's request to entitle her problem, she says: "It's difficult to define it, but maybe I would call it 'body and soul united'." Then, a male caller defines his problem figuratively in the following words: "I am the little prince in a world of social whores". Finally, excerpts from the call made by the fourth figurative caller – a 28-year-old married woman and mother of three – are presented below in Examples (32–36). Example (32) is an excerpt from the reception phase of this call:

Example (32) *I don't know how to get close to my middle son*

1 H: Tonight I have asked callers to start by giving us a title for the topic
2   they are going to talk about. What's your title?
3 C: It's difficult for me to sum it up by giving a title. But I could say that
4   it's a problem of communication. *I don't know how to get close to my*
5   *son, my middle son.*
6 H: OK, so let's examine the problem you have.
7 C: Please help me. I'm very nervous.
8 H: ((reassuringly)) Yes. OK. From your title, I can understand that it's
9   difficult for you to get close to your middle child, and I also
10   understand that if he's your middle child, then you have three
11   children.
12 C: Correct.
13 H: How old are you?
14 C: Twenty-eight.
15 H: How long have you been married?

16 C: Six years.
17 H: So what's your problem?

In Example (32) the host reminds the caller to entitle her problem, orienting himself simultaneously to the overhearing audience, the significant other in radio communication (lines 1–2). Approved by the watchful eyes of the program operators, this troubled caller makes a phone call and presents her problem in a temporary interpersonal telephone relationship. The caller says that it is difficult for her to entitle her problem (line 3), and thereupon summarizes figuratively the core of her past world within the boundaries of the present ongoing interaction (lines 4–5).

The title emphasizes that the caller does not know how to communicate with her middle child. Using the collective directive "let's" (Biber et al. 1999) (line 6), the host authoritatively but pleasantly acknowledges that he is constantly aware of the presence of the radio team as well as the overhearing audience. When the caller admits that she is very nervous (line 7), the experienced host repeats the caller's figurative definition reassuringly (lines 8–9). Then, he elicits more information in a question–answer sequence (lines 8–17). In Example (33), the caller unfolds her problem:

Example (33) *There is a buffer inside of me that I can't define*

```
1    Right after my wedding I conceived, and my first son was born
2    joyfully. After my first son was born, I conceived again, and my
3    second son was born ten months and two weeks after my first son. I
4    must have been very exhausted mentally and physically. And I had a
5    problem. How could I accept this child? I must emphasize that he
6    was born at home, and in addition to the pain, I also had a feeling of
7    rejection. What is he doing to me? Why is he kicking me? Perhaps I
8    really wasn't ready for another pregnancy, for child-rearing. As I was
9    bringing up the two of them, I discriminated against him, consciously
10   or unconsciously I see it now. He is already four and a half, and I can
11   tell by his behavior that he demands more attention from his
12   surroundings and from me. But it's difficult for me to get close to
13   him. It's difficult. *There is a buffer inside of me that I can't define.*
```

In Example (33), the articulate caller further delves into her past world, which has already been summatively entitled via a trope in Example (32). She unfolds a personal story that consists of a problem-inducing complicating action and evaluative devices depicting her differential positionings in relation to her sons. The complicating action comprises two important events: the birth of her first son (lines 1–2) and the birth of her second son (lines 2–3), which took place ten and a half months after the first.[76] The caller positions herself in relation to her first and second sons. As far as the first son is concerned, the caller uses the explicit emotion-building adverb "joyfully" to describe the significance of the birth of her first son (line 2). It is much more complicated for her to explain her feelings toward the second son (lines 2–13), although she manifests a high level of self-awareness and diagnoses her mental and physical condition when she conceived the second son (lines 3–4). Then, she uses lexical choice, rhetorical questions and a doubt-building stance adverbial – evaluative resources that conspire to position the caller in relation to her second son.

To reinforce what she has already said in lines 3–4, the caller uses lexical items such as "pain" and "rejection" (lines 6–7) – explicit evaluative devices that further define her physical condition and emotional state of mind. Rhetorical questions (line 5 and line 7) constitute an evaluative resource that expresses her protest against the unexpected pregnancy. This powerful resource also situates her protesting but determined self in relation to the radio team whose help she is seeking. Finally, she uses the doubt-building stance adverbial "perhaps" (line 7), which must have unearthed an implicit underlying antagonism.

Elaborating on her attitude toward her second son, the caller finally admits in lines 9–10 that she "discriminated against him, consciously or unconsciously". The problem-inducing personal story and the evaluative resources unfolded in Example (33) are summatively organized by means of a trope, *There is a buffer inside of me that I can't define* (line 13). This trope further explains the caller's figurative title produced at the beginning of the call (Example (32), lines 4–5 : *I don't know how to get close to my son, my middle son*).

We see, then, that tropes summarize the gist of the narrated world and display it in the temporary present world that has been constructed in order to find a solution to the caller's problem. The first (i.e., *I don't know how to to get close to my son, my middle son*) relates to her conduct. The second (i.e., *There is a buffer inside of me that I can't define*) provides an explanation.

In our opinion, the young woman's tropes show that she rejected her second unexpected pregnancy as well as the idea of having another child so soon after the first child. The trope summarizing Example (33) refers to an inaccessible intrapsychic buffer that was created before the second child was born and may have undermined her ability to get close to her second child. In Example (34), the host elicits additional information about the caller's third son prior to requesting that the psychologist provide the caller with mental help:

Example (34) *He is my toy*

1 H: And how old is your third child?
2 C: A year and a half.
3 H: A boy or a girl?
4 C: A boy. I have three sons.
5 H: Three sons, but the third one is different.
6 C: The third son is totally different.
7 H: Could you tell us how?
8 C: He is really our toy, our sweetie pie. We are always hovering around
9   him. He is an extremely charming boy. He is attractive. He is
10   developing very well. I am very attached to him. *He is my toy.*

In Example (34), the caller positions herself figuratively vis-à-vis her third child. It is interesting to compare how she chooses to position herself in relation to each of her three sons, respectively: "My first child was born joyfully", *There is a buffer inside of me that I can't define*, and *He is my toy*. The caller's figurative and non-figurative utterances show that the first and the third sons are accepted and loved, but the middle son is rejected. The host probably feels at that point that he has elicited sufficient information about the caller's relationships with her sons, and accordingly asks the psychologist to negotiate a solution with the caller. In Example (35) the psychologist attempts to explain to the caller what her problem is and what she should do:

Example (35) "Now before the second child is born, he is already an obstacle"

1 When the first child arrives, you are very happy, and then when he
2 [the second child] is born, you don't have time to be with him. And
3 you feel upset about it, because you are already pregnant with the
4 third child. All the joy of the first year with your first child – the type
5 of joy that no mother will miss – you are unable to experience. It is
6 as if you are rebelling on behalf of your first child, and on your own

7	behalf. And then the second child arrives. Now before the second
8	child is born, he is already an obstacle, and you feel guilty. How can
9	it be that a child you are supposed to love – and you already know
10	what maternal love is – how come you can't give it to him? Now this
11	feeling of guilt is terrible, because the minute we feel we have
12	wronged someone, we become even more angry at the person who
13	caused this feeling. Do you understand what I'm saying?

In Example (35), the psychologist provides her interpretation of the caller's problem. She reformulates the caller's story and explains that the mother has guilt feelings because she does not fulfill her maternal duties toward her first child (lines 1–7). Careful reading of Example (33) shows that she does not understand what the caller says. The caller uses various evaluative devices, succinctly summarized by a trope (*There is a buffer inside of me that I cannot define*, Example (33), line 13), to position her protesting self vis-à-vis the second child, not the first. Moreover, the incomprehensible intrapsychic buffer to which she relates does not mean she has guilt feelings, but probably that she experiences a feeling of rejection toward her second son.

The psychologist disregards the verbal expression of the mother's feelings and interprets them as guilt feelings. Having provided her interpretation, and aware of the time limit, the psychologist hastens to recommend a coping strategy that the mother can use in a possible future world in order to solve her problem. There is no time to help the caller construct the meanings of the narrated past world succinctly presented via organizing tropes. Example (36) shows how the coping strategy is practically dictated to the caller:

Example (36) "There is a child inside of you and you have to come to terms with him"

1	P:	Look, how can you develop a relationship with your middle son?
2		You yourself used the word *middle* when you gave Yovav a title.
3		You said it's a problem of communication with the *middle child*,
4		which means that the words *middle child* are part of your vocabulary.
5		It's a word with a negative tag. You could develop a unique
6		relationship with this child. Which means you have to spend more
7		time with him. Are you going to reacquaint yourself with this child?
8		Is it possible for you to find half an hour to spend with him on a daily
9		basis?
10	C:	Theoretically yes, but in reality it never happens. *I feel there is some*

11   *sort of a buffer*. For example, I go to bed late, and he sleeps in the
12   afternoon, so it is difficult for him to fall asleep late at night. He's
13   awake, but I'm always busy with other things.
14 P: And if you were to do the right things, what would you do?
15 C: Perhaps I'd put everything else aside and I'd spend more time with
16   him. Ask him what he'd like to do, tell him a story, play with him.
17 P: Let me tell you what's happening between you and this child you
18   don't know so well. In reality, there is a child inside of you and you
19   have to come to terms with him, the child who interfered when you
20   wanted to enjoy your relationship with your first son. The other child
21   is on the outside. You don't know him so well. Do you understand
22   what I'm saying?
23 C: Yes.
24 P: And I advise you to get acquainted with him, because you may like
25   him very much, and he will look different from the child inside you
26   with whom you have to come to terms.

In Example (36), the psychologist recycles several tropes used by the caller earlier in the conversation, and proposes her interpretation. First, she relates to the trope *middle* used by the caller when she opens her problem presentation (Example (32), line 5). The psychologist describes the words "middle child" as having "a negative tag" (Example (36), line 5). It is not at all clear if this is what the caller had in mind.

Then, she proposes a behavioral change that, in her opinion, will solve the young mother's problem. She advises the caller to spend more time with her middle son. This strategy will, to her mind, change the caller's emotional stance toward her child (lines 5–9). The psychologist asks the caller if this change is feasible. The young woman's answer sounds hesitant (line 10) and shows that she has not accepted the psychologist's directive.

Subsequently, in lines 10–11 as if protesting against the psychologist's interpretation, the caller repeats the trope she produced earlier in the call: *I feel there is some sort of a buffer* (Example (33), line 13). The caller further explains how this buffer is manifested in everyday life at home when she does other things instead of caring for her second son (Example (36), lines 11–13).

The psychologist ignores the caller's verbal protest. She prefers to continue the conversation in the discursive direction she has chosen (line 14). Thus, instead of focusing on the meaning of the emotional *buffer*, the trope that encapsulates the caller's narrated world and that has been mentioned twice, she continues exploring the future enthusiastically but rather superficially, asking the mother if she knows what she would do if she were to spend time with her son.

It seems that the mother knows very well what to do (lines 15–16) and that she made the phone call in order to discuss more complicated matters. However, in this asymmetrical radio interaction where both participants know that the call has to culminate in some sort of happy ending, the caller is forced to follow the psychologist's recipe and adapt herself to the latter's directives.

In lines 17–22, the psychologist proposes a summative definition of the mother's problem that dovetails with her interpretation (see Example (35)). She begins her lecture with an authoritative "Let me tell you" directive (line 17), and explains that the internal buffer to which the caller related is actually her first son who was neglected when the second child was born. She adds that the mother does not know her second child very well (line 21) and should become acquainted with him.

The psychologist then proceeds to ask the caller if she has understood what the former has said (lines 21–22). She does not ask the caller if she accepts her interpretation. In this asymmetrical interaction, the caller has no choice but to comply with the psychologist. The institutional voice summarizes the caller's problem in a simplistic way that is not in keeping with the complexity unfolded by the caller.

Following Anderson (1997), we suggest that the psychologist is a modern therapist who is "certain about what he or she knows" (ibid.: 4). The postmodern therapist, on the other hand, is "a non-knower who is uncertain and regards knowledge as evolving" (ibid.). This example also supports Foucault's claim that therapeutic discourse is powerful and dominating. It is reasonable to assume that in the conventional clinical setting, there would have been more time to *open up* the tropes and analyze the intrapsychic and interpersonal meaning of the narrated past constructed by the caller instead of hastening to build a possible future.

In conclusion, analysis of *I don't know how to get close to my middle son* shows that the caller does open her call with an emotion-disclosing figurative title that constructs the gist of her past and that could have been conducive to an effective problem discussion. The psychologist notices the figurative title but does not explore it deeply. It is evident that radio problem discourse is a site where there is no time to construct the meaning of the conscious and unconscious contents of the caller's problem-inducing past. It is also possible that the psychologist is not able to identify the complex emotions constructed via the caller's organizing title. She opts instead for an easier direction that she emphasizes in her response.

3. Summary

In Chapter 3 we discovered that troubled callers who gain access to the radio program and who weave their detailed narrative formats and succinct organizing tropes in the first phase of the interaction, are sometimes provided with solutions to their problems. Accordingly, in Chapter 4 we show how the insights we gained in Chapter 3 are applied in the very same radio program by the program host who urged possible callers to open their call with a title. We assumed that callers who make focused contributions in the first phase of the interaction, facilitate the negotiation of solutions.

Both *In a big bang* and *I don't know how to get close to my middle son*, the callers presented in Chapter 4, show us that when asked to give a title to their complex problems they choose figurative titles that enable them to summarize the essence of their past worlds and present it to the radio team whose help they seek. However, the examples presented in Chapter 4 show that in the time-bounded and overhearing-audience-oriented program, even when callers make relevant presentations of their complex troubled past by means of detailed personal stories and succinct tropes, the psychologists cannot or do not want to explore the complexities of the narrators' past experience. Instead they opt for instant future-directed solutions.

In a big bang participates in a topic-focused program and presents her idiosyncratic narrative and figurative contributions in spite of the introductory *lectures* of the psychologists. The female psychologist who is probably aware of the limitations of the telephone interaction on the one hand and the severity of the caller's problem on the other does not attempt to administer an instant therapeutic intervention. Instead, she advises the caller to seek additional mental help. The male psychologist, on the other hand, assumes an authoritative attitude of an almighty knower and instructs the caller to hate her deceased mother. His instant diagnosis creates an unprecedented media drama in which other institutional representatives align themselves against him in favor of the caller.

Our interpretation of this unique drama is validated in two ways. First, participants' next turns provide us with additional discursive evidence that back up our interpretation. Second, in a telephone interview conducted with the caller the following day, the caller also supported our interpretation when she verbalized her reflective perspective on the radio drama that took place the day before.

I don't know how to get close to my middle son, the second caller presented in Chapter 4, opens her call with an emotion-disclosing figurative title that constructs the gist of her past. The figurative title is noticed by the psychologist but it does not enhance problem communication because there is no time to construct the meaning of the conscious and unconscious contents of the caller's problem-causing past. The psychologist opts instead for an easier direction, advising the caller to spend more time with her middle son, although it is obvious from the interaction that the caller's problem is related to a disturbing intrapersonal buffer.

In view of the studies that show that both lay and professional participants are aware of the advantages and disadvantages of the services provided by such programs (Raviv and Abuhav 2003), one can accept the fact that the psychologists who negotiate the problems of *In a big bang* and *I don't know how to get close to my middle son* cannot explore the complexities of their past worlds in a short telephone interaction. However, it is quite upsetting to see that the psychologists do not admit that fact, and instead attempt to provide instant, and in the case of *In a big bang*, even deleterious advice.

Chapter 5
Figurative conspiracies

In this chapter, we continue our exploration of problem discourse by shifting our focus from rating-oriented radio problem discourse that was presented in Chapters 3 and 4 to hotline telephone discourse. In this site, trained volunteers listen in in an attempt to effect some change or advise the callers to turn to other sources of help. Excerpts from three calls are presented in subsections 1.1, 1.2 and 1.3. In section 2, we summarize the main points of this chapter.

1. Hotline sufferers

1.1. "Am I their floor rag?"[77]

In this subsection, we focus on the summative and interactional functions of organizing figurative language in a hotline drama.[78] Examples (37–40) comprise illustrative excerpts from an interaction between a female volunteer and a 25-year-old woman. This 35-minute call is summarized below.[79] The call can be divided into three stages. In stage one, the extremely agitated but eloquent new caller lists her problems and positions herself in relation to significant others in her narrated world as well as to the volunteer whose help she is seeking within the boundaries of the temporary world of the interaction.

The caller describes herself as very short and unemployed, and emphasizes that she is obliged to live with her parents, who allegedly abuse her mentally and physically. The caller has appealed to several community services, but they were unable to help. The female volunteer asks what the caller's address is, and when the caller provides the information, the screaming voices of the parents are suddenly heard.

In stage two, the volunteer demands to talk with the mother. Following the volunteer's directive, the mother portrays a lazy, disobedient daughter who does not want to go out to work and who steals money from her parents. The mother does not understand what the volunteer is saying, even though the latter speaks slowly and repeats herself several times. In the third stage, the daughter attempts to convince the volunteer that her version of the story is true.

This call is unique because family dynamics and conflicts (Watts 1991) are presented in real time, when the caller and her mother communicate with the volunteer and make several unsuccessful attempts to communicate with each other. In other words, the problematic past world is not narrated, but is actually constructed on the air in real time. The caller's uncontrollable crying and the mother's screaming and cursing constitute a background soundtrack against which the caller's and her mother's contrasting narrative versions are produced. In this unexpected context, the volunteer is obliged to assume a judgmental role in order to determine who is telling the truth. Examples (37–40) show how the caller positions herself within the worlds of the past and the present. In Example (37), which is produced at the beginning of the interaction, the caller lists her problems:

Example (37) "I cannot live in this house anymore"

1   ((sounds extremely agitated)) I'm 25. I live with my parents. They beat
2   me up all the time. They beat me up and they abuse me. I cannot live in
3   this house anymore, and the problem is that I'm not working now. I'm
4   also what people call an extremely short person, and it's very difficult
5   for me to find a job, so I live on national insurance, and I have no place
6   to go.

Example (37) shows how the caller positions herself first and foremost in relation to the volunteer whose help she seeks, and for whom she describes the family dynamics at home. In other words, the example displays interpersonal relations in the present and inter- and intrapersonal relations in the past.

Interpersonal and intrapersonal dimensions are constructed by means of diverse linguistic devices. Physical abuse is constructed in generic stories (lines 1–2) by means of three consecutive transitive utterances that are high on the agency scale and in which the causal agent "they" – a "powerful metaphor for other" (Malone 1997: 73) – and verbs denoting violence (i.e., "beat up" and "abuse") are embedded. The generic stories position the helpless caller in relation to her abusive parents and reflect her anger at the causal agents (Bamberg 1997c, 1997d). Negative forms (lines 2–3 and 5–6) complete the list of the caller's problems and further display her state of helplessness.[80]

In response to this moving presentation, the volunteer asks the caller what her telephone number is because she probably intends to provide the caller with help when the telephone call is terminated. The caller produces two specific stories presented in Example (38) below, which contextualize and verify the contents of the generic presentation in Example (37):

Example (38) "My father beat me up with a rolling pin"

1   The story is as follows. We had an argument. They took things from me.
2   So I got angry, and I took her [the mother's] watch. Then I said to her:
3   "Give me back my things," because every time they like something of
4   mine, they take it from me. They take my things, the things I buy with
5   my own money, the national insurance money. So I said to her: "Give
6   me back the things that belong to me and I'll give you your things."
7   They cannot talk like civilized people, discuss matters in a nice way.
8   They start beating me, pushing me, beating me up. My father even beat
9   me up with a rolling pin.

The two specific stories (lines 1–8 and 8–9) are interrelated. They verbalize the meaning of a stormy family incident that must have taken place a few minutes before the call and probably induced the caller's angry emotional state (Power and Dalgleish 1997) at the beginning of the call. As in Example (37), it is the present relationship with the volunteer that matters and for which the caller verbalizes the meaning of her distress.

The first specific story consists of abstract (line 1), complicating action (lines 1–2 and 5–6), and evaluation constructed via generic stories stories (lines 3–4 and 7–8), showing how the daughter perceives the parents' behavior. Lexical and syntactic repetition of the verbs "give" and "take" in transitive utterances (lines 1, 2, 3 and 4) construct the complicated and childish family dynamics. Although the caller is the suffering recipient of injustice inflicted by the parents – the controlling agents in the triggering event of the first story (line 1, "They took things from me") – the caller reverses the balance of agency when she attempts to retaliate (line 2).

Retaliation is not her only coping strategy. The caller also tries to reason with her parents, and she uses constructed dialogue "to replay" (Georgakopoulou 1994) the original context in which the incident took place (lines 3 and 5–6). Finally, she uses third person singular and plural pronouns when referring to her parents (lines 1, 2, 3, 4, 5, 7, and 8).

In the second moving story that consists of one utterance (line 8–9), the caller resorts once again to lexical choice and repetition of transitive utterances to construct her helplessness in relation to her abusive father. For the first and only time during the call, the caller uses the noun "father". Elsewhere, when she refers to family members, she only uses third person singular or plural pronouns.

Example (39) is produced in stage three, after the caller's mother has presented a contradictory version of the dynamics at home. When the mother says that the parents do not discriminate against their daughter in favor of their son, the daughter's screaming and crying is heard, and she demands to talk with the volunteer forthwith:

Example (39) "But how much can a person swallow?"

1 ((sounds extremely agitated)) When I served in the army, I used to come
2 home every night. I never went out. I didn't have any friends. I didn't
3 ask her for anything. I would even buy my own clothes with the
4 miserable salary that they pay soldiers. I swear to you in the name of
5 everything that is dear to me that I have never asked them for anything.
6 But their son, they buy him everything. They buy him a stereo system
7 that cost four thousand shekels [about 1,000 American dollars at the
8 time]. They don't care. Now that he [her brother] has enlisted, he has a
9 lot of friends and every Friday night, every Saturday, every day: "Mom,
10 give me money. Give me money. Mom, give me money." I swallowed
11 it. But how much can a person swallow?

In Example (39), interpersonal relationships between the caller and her family members in the narrated world are constructed once again in order to convince the volunteer, who has been exposed to the mother's version in stage two, that the caller is telling the truth. To do so, the eloquent caller unfolds specific and generic stories, and makes use of amplifying linguistic devices (Eggins and Slade 1997) such as swearing, rhetorical questions, repetition, and a figurative conspiracy.

The parents' discriminatory attitude toward their offspring is verbalized through generic stories and one specific story. The generic stories depict the daughter's (lines 1–4) and the favorite son's (lines 8–10) respective military services. These stories are discursively distinguished by means of "but" (line 6), a coordinator of contrast (Quirk et al. 1985). Repetitive use of third person singular and plural pronouns constructs the caller's perception of alienation at home, where the caller's brother is further singled out by means of the possessive pronoun "their" (line 6). The caller even swears (lines 4–5) to assure the volunteer that she is telling the truth.

The purchase of the stereo system (lines 6–8), a specific story that is only partially unfolded, provides an illustrative context for the less detailed generic stories. Linguistic devices such syntactic repetition and tense shift show that this triggering external event (Power and Dalgleish 1997) must have upset the caller very much. The generic stories (lines 8–10) comprise repetition and constructed dialogue that conspire to reflect the caller's fury in the face of the inequity at home.

Finally, a rhetorical *wh*-question, which is syntactically an interrogative but semantically a forceful negative statement, conspires with a trope (lines 10–11) in an assertion that means that the caller cannot put up with the situation at home any longer. While the trope indicates that the caller accepts her lot in silence, the rhetorical question in which the trope is embedded constitutes a powerful protest against the situation. This figurative encapsulation of the narrated world is directed at the volunteer whose help the caller is seeking.

Example (40) is taken from stage three. The daughter attempts to present a convincing summary of her first version, which was presented in stage one, in order to get help from the volunteer:

Example (40) *Am I their floor rag?*

```
1   C: You see. This is the situation. So with all due respect, how much
2      can a person put up with? What is it? Am I their floor rag? What is
3      this?
4   V: I believe you. First, because I didn't hear your mother deny it, and
5      also because you're very convincing. You're very convincing.
6   C: How much can a person put up with? What is this? Are they mak-
7      ing a floor rag out of me? How much can I suffer?
8   V: There's no doubt in my mind that a change has to be made, an
9      intervention.
10  C: I suffer a lot. I swallow a lot. How much can I swallow? Are they
11     making a floor rag out of me? How much can I swallow? ((the
12     mother is heard screaming)) Do other people deserve to be treated
13     like the kings of the world? Am I their floor rag?
14  V: Before we talk about your studies and a job, there is no doubt in my
15     mind that a clean-up job is needed here. If you are threatened and if
16     you are beaten up, then it's very difficult to talk about progress. I'll
```

98 *Figurative conspiracies*

17   find out what the best thing is to do. You've given me your phone
18   number and I certainly think that this can't go on.

In Example (40), the volunteer finally aligns herself[81] with the caller against the mother (lines 4–5, 8–9 and 14–18). Encouraged by this change, the caller, who must have been aware of the volunteer's judgmental role during the call, hastens to provide a figurative summary of her detailed narrative contribution presented in stage one. This figurative summary is verbalized by means of four figurative conspiracies (lines 2, 6–7, 10–11, and 12–13).

These conspiracies consist of tropes and rhetorical questions that are produced repeatedly, and as a result are emphasized. We will focus on each evaluative device and then show how they work in tandem to construct the caller's interpersonal dimensions and enhance the interactive dialogue with the volunteer. The tropes (i.e., the *floor rag* metaphor and *like the kings of the world* simile) position the caller in space (i.e., her short stature) and within the emotionally charged past experiences in relation to significant others, *the kings of the world*.

It is also possible that the tropes present the caller's perspective on gender issues (Richard Watts, personal communication). Calling herself a *floor rag* the caller may have implied that she is burdened with stereotypically female chores. These are juxtaposed vis-à-vis the male *kings of the world* who in the context of her troubled world[82] comprise her father and brother and also her mother who must have aligned herself with the male figures against her daughter. In this way, she may have alluded to the parents' discriminatory attitude and to the fact that despite the fact that both she and her brother served in the army (see Example (39)), the parents preferred her brother to her.

The tropes are embedded in rhetorical questions[83] that constitute, as we have already shown, powerful assertions that the caller cannot put up with the situation at home any longer. In other words, these evaluative devices construct cognitive dimensions of a self that does not accept her lot and wishes to change. Finally, repetition of these figurative constructions indicates that what the caller was saying was extremely important for her.

It is also important to see at which discursive junctions these conspiracies are located. The caller produces them after the mother's version has been verbalized, in order to convince the volunteer that her (the caller's) version of the narrated past world is true. We chose *Am I their floor rag?*, the conspiracy in lines 2, 6–7, 10–11 and 13, as the organizing trope that summarizes the inter- and intrapersonal dimensions of the caller's tormented life (i.e., her stature, her strong determination to change her life and her parents' attitude toward her).

Am I their floor rag? also has a dialogical function that enhances interpersonal communication with the volunteer in the ongoing interaction. The self-revealing figurative conspiracies in Example (40) must have attracted the volunteer's attention, and she responds figuratively in line 15 by saying that *a clean-up job is needed here*. The volunteer's response does not relate to the emotional and cognitive dimensions of the caller's self that *Am I their floor rag?* may have displayed to her. She probably prefers to orient the talk toward a practical domain of doing because she understands that there is no time to elaborate on the meaning of these conspiracies: help must be sent to the abused caller at once.

In conclusion, the tormented hotline caller produces figurative conspiracies, or groups of evaluative devices including a trope that conspire to express several dimensions of her tormented self at meaningful discursive junctions of the hotline drama. The volunteer notices these conspiracies and makes use of them. Accordingly, we can say that they have a dialogical function that enhances interpersonal communication.

1.2. "The lion and the snake"

This call can be divided into two stages. The interaction is summarized below. In stage one, an eloquent frequent caller, a young adult homosexual who declares that he previously used other support services, briefly presents his problems. The list comprises loneliness, rejection by male friends, fear that he may have contracted HIV, failure in his university studies, clinically diagnosed depression, and his father's terminal disease.

In stage two, the female volunteer listens to the caller's problems. In the end, the caller tells the volunteer that he feels much better. The caller produces various tropes that position him in relation to significant others in the narrated world and further his communication with the volunteer. In Example (41), the hotline caller presents his problems:

Example (41) "But in addition there are a million other problems"

1   Shalom. I have many problems, but I only want to talk about one of
2   them. I want you to know that what I'm telling you is only a drop in the
3   ocean. I called because now this is on my mind. It bothers me, but in
4   addition there are a million other problems.

In Example (41), the caller positions himself vis-à-vis the volunteer in the ongoing interaction by means of interpersonal utterances (Halliday 1985):[84] "I want you to know" (line 2) and "what I'm telling you" (line 2). Emphasizing metaphorically that the problem he wishes to focus on is only a drop in the ocean (lines 2–3), and hyperbolically that there are a million other problems (lines 3–4), the caller presents his problems as an incommensurable domain that lacks a basis of comparison. In Example (42), he unfolds a specific story in which he contextualizes the rather abstract presentation of the problems in Example (41) by positioning himself in relation to one of his male friends:

Example (42) *As if I were trash*

1   ((sighs)) I had a very good friend, but he met some girl. Since then he
2   has treated me as if I were trash.

The specific story is one example out of several stories narrated by the caller to show that he is rejected by male friends. The organizing simile in *as if I were trash* positions him simultaneously in the tortured past world as well as the present ongoing interaction with the volunteer. The trope constitutes a succinct self-portrait that the hotline caller constructs in the online telephone interaction where he is negotiating the meaning of his problems, but as our analysis shows, the caller's idiosyncratic use of tropes may indicate that he doubts whether the portrait is successful.

Why did the caller produce a simile and not a metaphor? He may have done so because he did not regard the similarity between his humiliated self – the topic of the organizing simile *As if I were trash* – and the vehicle (i.e., trash) as high (Chiappe and Kennedy 2001). In this way, this trope, like the rhetorical questions used by the caller in Examples (39–40), has two functions: it foregrounds the caller's degradation and at the same time it is a protest against it.

In Example (43), produced at the end of stage 1, the caller and the volunteer negotiate figuratively what the focus of the interaction will be:

Example (43) *The lion and the snake*

1 C: I'm a person who's worried about what lies just ahead of me, not
2   what is lying ten kilometers down the road. If there's a lion in front
3   of me, and there's a snake at a distance of ten kilometers, I'm not
5   afraid of the snake ten kilometers away. I'm afraid of the lion lying
6   one meter away.
7 V: Let's see what the lion is and what the snake is.

The analogy presented in Example (43) can be interpreted at inter- and intrapersonal levels. By dividing his problems into urgent and less urgent ones, the caller signals to the volunteer in which direction the call should proceed. On the intrapersonal level, the analogy reflects a cognitive dimension of a self that is overpowered by problems, but is capable of appraising the situation.

Examined via a gender prism, the caller's tropes can be interpreted as relating to an additional unconscious level. The animals chosen by the caller to encapsulate his problems symbolize masculinity. The lion – the king of the animals – is conceived by the caller as powerful, dominant, swift and aggressive. The snake is a common phallic symbol. The caller is probably threatened by these two symbols that may be representative of the men who have abused and humiliated him, as he emphasizes in Example (42).

The female volunteer notices, or chooses to relate to the overt significance of the caller's figurative contribution, which explicitly indicates the discursive road that the caller has chosen. Using the same analogy, she communicates her acceptance (line 7). Subsequently, the volunteer listens to the caller talking about his urgent and less urgent problems, and at the end of the call, this frequent caller informs the volunteer that he feels much better.

In conclusion, the hotline caller presented in subsection 1.2 makes use of an organizing analogy that facilitates the accomplishment of two central tasks: problem presentation and negotiation of a solution. The fact that the organizing analogy is noticed and applied by the volunteer in this interaction as well as in the case of *Am I their floor rag?* constitutes a next-turn figurative response that validates our interpretation that the analogy, *The lion and the snake*, functioned as a central interactional device.

1.3. "My life is a story in a book"

This 80-year-old frequent caller is a retired widower who overcomes his loneliness by calling up the hotline service. Although the caller is not a native speaker of Hebrew, he expresses himself clearly. The call can be divided into two stages that are summarized below. In stage one, he unfolds generic and specific stories that focus on dramatic events in his life. These events are closely related to important events in the history of the State of Israel.

The female volunteer encourages the narration of a life story because she understands that this is what the caller is seeking. In stage two, this institutional talk becomes a friendly chat based on reciprocity and exchange of information. During this stage, the participants switch roles, and it is the experienced caller who gives advice to the younger volunteer, annulling at this discursive junction the panoptical positioning of the volunteer. Moreover, at times it seems that the lonely old male attempts to court the younger volunteer and in this pseudo romantic interaction she rejects him in the position of a male friend, but accepts the wise old man.

After the caller has told the volunteer several stories about his life, the latter understands that the caller wants to continue talking. The volunteer expresses her consent by complimenting elderly people on the interesting stories they unfold. In the end, the caller expresses his gratitude. In Example (44), the caller describes his problem:

Example (44) "I am a lonely man and all I want to do is talk"

1   You are all alone at home, wondering around for 24 hours. You look for
2   someone [in Hebrew the indefinite feminine pronoun "mishehi" is used].
3   Before I had this telephone number, I used to look up a number in the
4   telephone directory, and I used to talk. I used to ask the other person's
5   permission. "Do you want to talk with me? I am a lonely man and all I
6   want to do is talk." There were people who did talk, and there were peo-
7   ple who didn't. About ten days ago, the telephone rings at 6:30 in the
8   evening. "Tell my daughter that I am on my way to pick her up." I said:
9   "Wait, don't go. I think you reached the wrong number." Then it turned
10 out that she works there with you. She was so happy that she found me.
11 She called me up twice. But now she hasn't called for four days.

The lonely widower unfolds his problem via self-building generic stories (lines 1–7), a specific story (lines 7–11), and evaluative devices such as lexical repetition and constructed dialogue. The generic and specific stories locate the caller's lonely self vis-à-vis anonymous voices with whom he attempts to socialize on the telephone. The generic stories emphasize the interminableness of the situation and the intensity of the caller's search for occasional companions who can mitigate his loneliness.

The detailed specific story focuses on a recent event that makes the caller's narrative contibution trustworthy. As for the evaluative devices, repetition of lexical items denoting loneliness (e.g. "alone", "look for someone" and "lonely", lines 1–2 and 5) shows that the caller is probably aware of his loneliness. In addition, constructed dialogue (lines 5–6, 8, and 9) may be an indication that as the caller recycles his voice and those of anonymous others, he relives those precious moments. In Example (45), the caller and the volunteer negotiate the choice of the next topic:

Example (45) *My life is a story in a book*

1 V: At the beginning of the call, you said something about how you
2   found out about ERAN. I didn't understand you. How exactly did
3   you start calling us? Did you look us up in the telephone book? [We
4   preferred the literal translation "book" to the more adequate
5   "directory" because it must have influenced the caller's next turn.]
6 C: I have stories. *My life is a story in a book.*
7 V: Your generation, each one of you really has very interesting stories.
8 C: One can write a detailed and beautiful book about my life.

Produced after the caller has told the volunteer several stories about his life, Example (45) illustrates the interactional work accomplished in this call. The volunteer recycles prior cotext (Korolija 1998) to provide the caller with a new topic (lines 1–3). The caller must have sensed her keen interest to cooperate with him, but does not answer the questions she asks (lines 2–3) directly. He prefers to recycle a different type of prior cotext in which he unfolds his heroic past deeds. He signals his preference figuratively (line 6), inviting the empathetic volunteer to leaf through the pages of *the story in a book*. The volunteer expresses her consent by complimenting the interesting stories that elderly people unfold (line 7).

Thus, Example (45), as we have shown, is related to the interactional negotiation of solutions. The lonely caller explicitly states that he wants to go on talking, and the volunteer complies with his request and helps him find new topics. At the end of the call, the caller validates this interpretation by expressing his gratitude figuratively: "I feel that I cannot say goodbye to an angel. Believe me you are more than an angel."

In sum, the caller accomplishes what he wants most: to talk with an empathetic person. He signals his preference figuratively by means of an organizing trope that provides the volunteer with information about the caller in the narrated past world (i.e., a respectable person worth listening to), and at the same time communicates his need to continue talking with the volunteer in the ongoing world of the present.

2. Summary

In Chapter 5, we shifted the focus from rating-oriented radio problem discourse to hotline interactions. The three hotline callers, *Am I their floor rag?*, *The lion and the snake* and *My life is a story in a book*, produce story-internal past-building organizing tropes that are noticed by the volunteers and facilitate the interaction.

Am I their floor rag? seeks immediate help, but her mother's contradictory narrative version undermines her credibility. In order to regain the volunteer's trust, she produces an organizing trope that provides the volunteer with a useful summary of the inter- and intrapersonal dimensions of her troubled self. This tormented hotline caller's figurative production comprises, inter alia, figurative conspiracies – or groups of evaluative devices that work in tandem to express one or several dimensions of the troubled self and in which one of the discursive resources is a trope. This information, produced at a crucial discursive junction in the interaction, assists the volunteer in assessing the caller's situation. Similarly, *The lion and the snake* and *The story in a book* are frequent callers who signal to the cooperative volunteers figuratively what and how they want to conduct the call, and these directives facilitate the accomplishment of problem presentation and the negotiation of a solution.

The fact that the callers' organizing tropes are noticed by the volunteer constitutes a next-turn figurative response that validates our interpretations. For example, it shows that the analogy, *The lion and the snake*, functioned as an effective interactional device. Similarly, *The *story in a book* signals to the volunteer that he wants to talk with an empathetic person and a good listener. The caller accomplishes this task by means of an organizing trope that provides the volunteer with information about him in the narrated past world and at the same time communicates his needs in the ongoing world of the present.

Chapter 5 also raises a gender issue. Do men and women use tropes differently? Our interpretive comments show that the organizing tropes produced by the hotline callers may have aired unconscious gender products that were displayed in the telephone conversation, but were not employed by the volunteer, who may have noticed them but opted not to relate to them.

Chapter 6
Cyber multilogues

In Chapter 6 we explore dramas that are unfolded in cyber problem discourse to find out what characterizes the digital transworld journeys of participants who visit an asynchronous hotline forum. In section 1, we present two virtual interactions. In subsection 1.1, we provide a detailed analysis of a virtual drama triggered by a suicidal problem-message sent by *Why not be ahead of my time?* – a troubled 15-year-old boy. We show how the young troubled self positions itself figuratively in relation to significant and virtual others. We also describe how, in the course of a multilogue anchored in figurative junctions, the boy gradually changes his perspective on life.

In subsection 1.2, we present "I was the best source of light on the market", another digital sufferer. This sufferer produces a message that is rich in figurative forms, but devoid of any contextualizing narrative format. Consequently, as in the case of "Like you're the world's only sucker", this interaction constitutes a deviant case that further illuminates the interactive function of tropes.

1. Cyberspace sufferers

1.1. "Why not be ahead of my time?"

Three answerers respond to the 15-year-old's suicidal problem-message: two female answerers (A and B) and a hotline volunteer. Seven messages are presented below and the content of five others is summarized. In Example (46), the boy addresses the virtual community:

Example (46) *Why not be ahead of my time?*

1   The only way to be released from the jaws of life.
2   I don't know how to cope with the problems I have, so the only thing I
3   can do is let off steam and just write it all in one place. I don't expect
4   anyone to pay any attention to this message, but I'm sending it because
5   this is the only place where I can talk about everything incognito.
6   I am 15 years old. I get along with my friends.

7   I have quite a lot of friends and I also have a girlfriend. But still I can't
8   find my place in this world. I don't understand why. I have good friends,
9   good grades. Basically, I have all that a person could wish for at my age,
10 but something is still missing and I can't put my finger on it, but what I
11 do know is that recently I've been thinking about suicide. I don't under-
12 stand it, but a few days ago I heard on the news that it's common in
13 Israel for teenagers to commit suicide. The minute I heard it, I
14 immediately accepted the idea. This is more or less what I've been
15 thinking about lately. A few days ago, I was walking when I saw a truck.
16 For some reason, I felt the need to jump into the road and just let it run
17 me down. Maybe the fact that there were other people with me
18 prevented me from doing it, but still since then I have been thinking
19 about ways to do it. I know I wrote that I have friends, and I guess
20 they'll miss me if I do it, but for how long? We're still young, and surely
21 I'm not that important to them at this stage of their life. And what about
22 my girlfriend? Will she miss me? I know that she loves me very much
23 and I love her too, but is it enough? One always hears that love isn't
24 always enough. So maybe there's nothing really keeping me here on
25 earth. After all, the world will keep going even when I'm not in it, so
26 why is it important if I die or live?In the end everybody dies, so does it
27 matter if I die a little earlier than when I'm supposed to? I know that
28 someone reading this may think: "What? Is he crazy? Why is he
29 thinking about such a thing at this young age? He has his whole life
30 ahead of him." I know that this is what it looks like, but believe me, it
31 isn't like that at all. I see life from a different perspective than most kids
32 my age. I think that life is only one phase and death is another. I don't
33 believe in life after death, but I believe that life has to end sometime. So
34 let's say that I don't feel comfortable now. *Why not be ahead of my time*
35 *and move on to the next phase?* After all, my friends will join me
36 sometime. So it doesn't really matter when I die. I don't expect any of
37 you to understand me, but I'm asking you to think about what I've
38 written and try to understand me and my point of view. I'm sure you'll
39 understand me and perhaps it will give you a slightly different
40 perspective on life and our roles in this place that we call planet earth.

The problem-message can be divided into two parts: a digital presentation of the adolescent's problem to the virtual community and his suicidal solution (lines 1–19), and elaboration on the possible effects of this act on real-life significant others as well as cyberspace others (lines 19–end). The adolescent opens his presentation with a figurative title, "The only way to be released from the jaws of life", to position himself in the world of the present vis-à-vis the virtual community whose help he seeks in the message. The trope also positions him in the world of the past in which he must have been very discontented.

This figurative formulation of suicidal intentions is somewhat abstract. It is a modified version of a common formulaic phrase in Hebrew, "to be released from the bonds of life" (Rachel Frankel, personal communication). In the boy's version, life is defined in terms of an unspecified monster from whose jaws he wants to be released. Throughout the message, the boy elaborates on the meaning of suicide, displaying to others and clarifying to himself several dimensions of his adolescent self.

Having established his first ties with potential netizens (Crystal 2001) in the first lines (lines 1–5), the adolescent tries to define his problem. First, the eloquent digital writer contextualizes his message by means of two parallel lists. These discursive resources enable him to package maximum information in minimum discursive means (lines 7–8 and 8–11). Each list is followed by a sudden discursive transition from the state of "having" and "getting along" to an anticlimax of "missing" and "not having". This transition is marked by means of "but" (lines 7 and 10), a coordinator of contrast (Quirk et al. 1985).

The last clause of the first list (lines 7–8) is a figurative conspiracy through which the boy attempts to define what is missing in his life. The conspiracy consists of an emphatic adverbial ("still"), a negative modal ("can't") and a trope ("find my place in this world"). The trope emphasizes what the boy needs. The use of the telic verb[85] "find" may be interpreted as an indication that the discontented teenager skips the stage of "looking for", as he is anxiously and restlessly expecting to find instant results. The negative modal orients his endeavor toward an unreal realm. The boy concludes the second list with an oxymoronic statement that expresses a depressive feeling of emptiness: "I have all that a person could wish for at my age, but something is still missing" (lines 9–10).

The lists provide a contextualizing preface to the ensuing personal stories (lines 12–18) that constitute trustworthy past experiences. The first personal story is used by the teenager to show that the media legitimize his intention to commit suicide (lines 12–15), and the second (lines 15–18) provides an example illustrating how he almost committed suicide. The lists and the stories are repeated twice (in lines 7–8, 8–

11, 12–15, and 15–18, respectively). In fact, repetition is a salient evaluative device in Example (46). It enables the adolescent to establish importance in his message.

Negative clauses are also repeated in the message. These clauses, produced as an anticlimax to the lists (lines 7–8, 8, 10, 11–12) and elsewhere in the message (lines 3–4, 20–21, 23–24, 30–31, 32–33 and 34), constitute a discursive manifestation of the missing element that the boy attempts to define throughout the message. The stance adverbials "maybe" and "perhaps" (lines 17, 24, and 39) further intensify the construction of a realm of uncertainty and irrealis in this message.

The boy repeatedly refers to his ties with his age group in the first part (lines 6–7) and in the entire message (lines 19–23), foregrounding the significance of these interpersonal ties to him. It is intriguing that he refrains from relating to his parents and siblings. They are not even mentioned as people who will miss him after his death (lines 20–23). The erasure of parental figures from the adolescent's narrated world places them in the domain of the unsayable (Budick and Iser 1991). This domain is illuminated and foregrounded because the boy frequently refers to his peers, who not only seem to overpopulate his world, but also constitute the domain of the sayable.

Why are the parents' voices unheard in a suicidal message of this troubled adolescent? Perhaps it shows that the boy has experienced acute conflicts with them. Such conflicts are unavoidable in adolescence (Green 2002) when the processes of separation from the parent–child context and the exploration of possible individuation take place (Mahler 1963). This may have created an unbearable emotional load that is reflected in the removal of the parents from the narrated past world.[86] This interpretation is supported by lines 36–37 where the writer emphasizes that he does not expect to be understood.

In line 18, the adolescent shifts the focus of his message to examine the interpersonal significance of his solution. The shift from present and past tenses to future tense (lines 20, 22, and 25) and the repetition of questions (lines 20, 21–22, 22–23, 25–26, and 26–27), establish a domain of irrealis in a post-mortem script where the boy attempts to examine how his possible death might influence significant peers and virtual readers of his message. In the second part of his message, he is therefore no longer inhabiting the world of the past, but it is in the present multilogue with virtual cyber answerers that he is elaborating on future implications that concern him.

The questions are intensified by the stance adverbials "maybe" and "perhaps" (lines 17, 24, and 39, respectively), which establish a tone of uncertainty and confusion in the future script regarding the feelings of others. The future is succinctly summarized by means of a trope (line 25, "the world will keep going even when I'm not in it"), displaying the writer's state of alienation that is characteristic of this age group (Conger 1997).

Positioning himself in relation to possible readers of his message in the virtual community, the boy uses constructed dialogue that consists of three questions (lines 28–30). These may be interpreted as a "double voice" (Bakhtin 1981) of inquisitive possible others as well as the adolescent's own nagging self. In lines 31–35, the boy attempts to define his perspective on "life" and "death". It is evident that this is not an easy task. The writer resorts to a cluster of tropes to define the significance of suicide. This cluster is illustrated in Example (47):

Example (47) A cluster of tropes

1   I see life from a different perspective than most kids my age. I think that
2   life is only one phase and death is another. I don't believe in life after
3   death, but I believe that life has to end sometime. So let's say that I
4   don't feel comfortable now. *Why not be ahead of my time and move on*
5   *to the next phase?*

It seems that the task of presenting his perspective is very difficult, perhaps impossible. Tropes enable the boy to reformulate his definition of highly complex concepts such as life and death. To do that, he depicts two linear phases, echoing a conceptual metaphor that compares life to a journey (lines 1–2). But the next clause contradicts the definition ("I don't believe in life after death", lines 3–4). Then the boy emphasizes this belief with the next figurative clause: "but I believe that life has to end sometime" (line 3). Another clause produced later re-establishes the possibility that there is life after death where his friends will join him (Example (46), lines 35–36). These contradictory statements show that the adolescent is in a state of turmoil and is not able at that point in his life to conceptualize the meaning of death rationally (Green 1985).

The writer summarizes the cluster of tropes, and, in our opinion, the entire message, via two figurative conspiracies: *Why not be ahead of my time and move on to the next phase?* (Example (47), lines 4–5).

These consist of tropes packaged in negative rhetorical *wh*-questions coordinated by "and". Syntactically, these negative rhetorical questions are interrogative. Semantically, they are positive powerful assertions that repeat, and thus emphasize, the painful and at the same time attractive idea of suicide. In the first conspiracy, the writer asserts figuratively that he *can be ahead of his time*, expressing both his superiority and aloneness with regard to the others. The second completes the idea by explaining that the boy will actually move on to the second phase (i.e., death).

These conspiracies enable the boy to formulate a more explicit solution to his problem. This formulation differs from the abstract solution expressed in the title in Example (46), line 1. The first formulation of the idea was accomplished by means of a formulaic phrase. Now, he uses an analogy that verbalizes a more explicit statement of the similarities between the topic the boy attempts to explain (i.e., the meaning of life and death) and the vehicle he uses (i.e., finite phases along a temporal axis) (see Chapter 2, subsection 1.5).

Positioning himself in two worlds – in relation to significant others in the narrated past world and in relation to the virtual community he addresses – the boy uses the conspiracy to express feelings of independence and control that provide him and other adolescents who are in crisis and distress with the justification to annihilate or exterminate themselves through suicide (Or-Bach 2000).

In conclusion, several discursive resources constitute the central building blocks of the multilogue. They display the inter- and intrapersonal dimensions of the writer: repetition of lists, personal stories, lexical items, coordination, negative and interrogative clauses, and stance adverbials as well as figurative language (i.e., tropes, organizing figurative conspiracies, and a cluster of tropes). Like other teenagers, the boy repeatedly emphasizes interpersonal relations with peers (Green 2004), including his girlfriend, but surprisingly refrains from mentioning family ties. The message is also rich in contradictions of being popular and at the same time feeling alienated, helpless, and omnipotent, of knowing and not knowing what life and death are. These display the confusion of an eloquent, discontented, restless, impatient, anxious, and at times helpless boy who earnestly wishes to define the meaning of life. The turmoil engendered by suicidal thoughts may have caused disturbances in the boy's thinking about the meaning of the past, the present, and the future, which also resulted in the erroneous conceptualization of death as a reversible process (Green 1985).

Our interpretive analysis suggests that the boy does not really want to commit suicide, but implores the virtual community to help him. His first attempt at entitling his problem (line 1) is somewhat abstract. However, in the course of the message, the abstract monster presented in the title is replaced by another, more detailed but contradictory perspective – the idea of a bidirectional movement from life to death. Addressing cyberspace and formulating in writing what is on his distressed mind may have made it possible for the adolescent to examine his suicidal intentions. Thus, the ongoing interpersonal process with the cyberspace community may have been accompanied by an intrapsychic conflictual process (Green 2003a).

Is the boy aware of the fact that the gnawing monster that makes him think about death sometimes also threatens other adolescents? Does he know that he will eventually move on to adulthood, another phase in life? We think not, but the answerer who hastens to write to him has probably thought about it. Example (48) is the first response to the message:

Example (48) Answerer A

1   You may have found the solution on your own.
2   I read what you wrote. The truth is that I saw someone much more
3   mature. You are 15 and you have a different perspective on life than
4   most kids your age. I think that you have many reasons to be happy. In
5   our world, life is not easy. People criticize us out of self-defense, and
6   you have so many people who love you. The very fact that you haven't
7   committed suicide so far is because you see how important you are in
8   other people's eyes, and how much they will miss you. Perhaps this is a
9   period that will pass, or perhaps you simply have to be with yourself and
10 see all the gifts that God gave you and understand that there is much
11 more to life than throwing it away at such a young age. I will be happy
12 to hear from you.

The writer begins the message with a title (line 1). Then, she[87] foregrounds the positive dimensions she identified in the boy's message, consistently backgrounding his suicidal intentions (lines 2–11). In the end, she emphasizes that she will be happy to hear from him (lines 11–12). The title of answerer A's message seems to cohere with the figurative conspiracy formulated by the boy (Example (46), lines 7–8,

"But still I can't find my place in this world"). However, the answerer's careful wording shifts the emphasis from the domain of helplessness emphasized in the boy's message to a more secure world ("You may have found the solution on your own"). In this sentence, she also packages her answer in indirect modality to avoid sounding like a reproachful other (line 1).

Answerer A also modifies her reinterpretation of the boy's narrated past experience by reorganizing the boy's lists. Her list, however, comprises maturity, a different perspective on life, various reasons to be happy, and love given by many people. In this way, answerer A carefully backgrounds the missing component that is so salient in the boy's message. This discursive reframing is later summarized by the answerer's cluster of tropes: "see all the gifts that God gave you and understand that there is much more to life than throwing it away at such a young age" (lines 10–12).

She also modifies the boy's organizing figurative language (Example (46), lines 34–35, *Why not be ahead of my time and move on to the next phase?*) by proposing a sober, less extreme temporal division. Thus, instead of relating to the boy's extreme "life" and "death" phases, her response implies that life itself has other phases, and the present perplexing phase will pass (lines 8–9). Using cognition verbs (Quirk et al. 1985) (i.e., "see", "understand"), she repeatedly and therefore emphatically encourages the adolescent to find the solution on his own. Still on this interpersonal level, and displaying sensitivity to the teenager's emotional needs, she provides him with advice that is carefully packaged in indirectness by means of the epistemic stance adverbial "perhaps" (Biber et al. 1999, lines 8 and 9). In conclusion, showing utmost sensitivity to the troubled writer, answerer A shifts the discussion to a domain of hope and coping. Example (49) presents what answerer B wrote:

Example (49) Answerer B

1 The meaning of life.
2 No, you're not insane. You're just a very sensitive boy, perhaps more
3 sensitive than most kids your age, a boy looking for meaning in his life,
4 a boy looking for something, testing the limits of things. Maybe your
5 life is too good and you are trying to exert yourself to the utmost to see
6 what will happen. Well, nothing will happen, you'll waste an opportu-
7 nity that was given to you – and it is life – the opportunity to do some-

8   thing positive in this life. Instead of jumping in front of a car, look for
9   ways to give something meaningful to life, like helping suffering hurt
10 children who have no social life, volunteering in hospitals, delivering
11 food to the elderly, and there are many other institutions that are in
12 desperate need of good and sensitive people. True – we will all die. The
13 question is what we do with ourselves until then. Do we give up hope
14 and pity ourselves that we are not remembered? Feel superior that we
15 have chosen the moment of death? Or perhaps while we are in this world
16 we should try to make the best of it. It starts with small step-by-step
17 to our parents, our family, our friends. And then the circle of good deeds
18 acts: being positive with respect is expanded through the good deeds that
19 I have already mentioned, by volunteering for example. See how the
20 people and the children who have cancer fight for their lives. Maybe you
21 will take an example from them and understand the meaning and
22 importance of life. Maybe the time has come for you to think about
23 others also and not only your own enjoyment. Think about these things.
24 I wish you a long and fruitful life.

Example (49) comprises several components: a title (line 1), an answer to a question the boy asked in line 28 of Example (46) (lines 2–4), a reproach (lines 4–12 and 15–23), a response to the boy's argument that "In the end everybody dies, so does it matter if I die a little earlier?" (lines 12–15), an alternative that focuses on helping the distressed (lines 8–12 and 16–19) and a concluding wish for a good life (line 24).

In the title, answerer B positions herself in relation to the adolescent's message by focusing on the meaning of life, a concept the adolescent attempts to define unsuccessfully in his first discursive conspiracy (Example (46), lines 7–8: "But still I can't find my place in this world"). Then, the answerer relates to the boy's question (Example (46), line 28: "Is he crazy?"). She reaffirms that the boy is sane, and thereupon provides her interpretation of the boy's adolescent self. She also foregrounds his sensitivity and his attempt to test the limits of things (line 4), adding new dimensions to the list of "gifts" compiled by answerer A.

Positioning herself in relation to a boy who, as our analysis has shown, probably seeks instant solutions (Green 2003b), this answerer prefers to focus on the process of "looking for", a process verb she repeats three times. Compared with answerer A's empathetic message that lists the gifts the boy has, this reproachful message foregrounds

116   *Cyber multilogues*

the domain of "doing" rather than that of "having" (Rand 1993) in a world full of people who are crying out for help because they are so ill. In conclusion, focusing on what the boy has, and what he can do, answerers A and B offer alternative perspectives to the suicidal plan formulated in Example (46). Example (50) shows how the adolescent responds to the two messages:

Example (50) The boy

1 Life, is it that important?
2 I've read your answers. In two messages you wrote that the gift of life is
3 the greatest gift one can get.
4 Basically, I agree, but what would you say if I'm not happy about the
5 gift that was given to me?
6 I agree that my life is OK now. I don't have any serious problems or
7 anything like that. But what am I doing with my life?
8 I live in this world but I am not contributing to its progress.
9 I as an individual can't exert my influence over the really important
10 matters, so why should I be a part of something that influences me,
11 when I can't influence it? So why is it good to be alive?
12 If everything I do I do for myself?
13 And I don't give anything of myself to anybody else, or influence the
14 course of events taking place around me.

The message can be divided into the following: title (line 1) and an answer to the previous messages (lines 2–14). Having read the two answers, the boy opens his second message with an interrogative title that weighs the importance of life and does not present death as the only possible solution, as it was in his first message (see Example (46), line 1). This interrogative title positions the boy in two worlds: in relation to the virtual others in the world of the present, and in relation to significant others in the narrated past world.

Then, the adolescent relates to the gifts foregrounded in answerer A's message, and recycled in answerer B's message in terms of the good deeds that such a gifted boy can do (Example (50), lines 2–5), emphasizing that he is not pleased with the gifts because he cannot use them to contribute to others (lines 7–8 and 9–11). Compared with Example (46), the change in the boy's perspective is striking. Having heard from the two answerers, the boy shifts from an egocentric domain where he has failed to find meaning so far (see Example (46)) to an altruistic and public domain of doing, where he wonders why he does not contribute to the community. Questions – a salient evaluative device used in this message (lines 4–5, 7, and 10–12) – establish a tone of uncertainty.

In conclusion, the second message written by the boy in response to the first two answerers indicates a shift from an egocentric perspective on life in which he cannot find meaning and which he wants to end, to a focus on life in which he can contribute to the living. The central themes foregrounded in the message cohere with (i.e., are related to) themes emphasized by the first and second answerers, respectively (i.e., life is a gift and one should do things for others and not think only about oneself). They contradict the boy's first message, in which he did not accept the alternative of life.

The cyber multilogue does not terminate at this point, however. The boy then receives an answer from the hotline volunteer who may have sensed that the time had come to move the philosophical trilogue to more practical grounds of coping. He recommends that the boy read and talk with other people about his problem. The boy responds in a short message entitled "I spoke, but it didn't really help", emphasizing that his girlfriend, the only person, in his opinion, who can understand him, threatens that she will also commit suicide. In response to this, answerer A writes a short message entitled "Finding the taste of life" in which she recycles the ideas of "having" and "doing" foregrounded by answerer B and herself in messages (48) and (49) (i.e., the boy has gifts and can therefore help others). She also reiterates the volunteer's practical advice, advising the boy to consult with the school counselor. The next message is also written by the volunteer, who once again advises the boy to seek professional help. In Example (51), the boy relates to the practical advice showered on him in several messages:

Example (51) The boy

1   Absolutely not, the person who is testing the limits does not know them.
2   I don't think I'm testing my limits. The last thing I want to do is hurt
3   others through my dying.
4   But, as I said, I don't think that I am important enough to really influ-
5   ence the life of someone else. So this isn't relevant.
6   I'm trying to live in the way that is best for me, but as I said, I don't
7   know what's suitable for me. Perhaps what's best for me has not been
8   shown to me. That's why I'm asking these questions.

In Example (51), the boy relates to a trope produced by Answerer B in Example (49), line 4: "a boy looking for something, testing the limits of things." In Example (49), the idea of "testing the limits of things" expressed in the context of a reproachful message had a negative meaning of waste. However, in Example (51), the boy protests that he does not wish to hurt others, and then he adds somewhat contradictorily that he is not that important to others (lines 4–5): "But as I said, I don't think that I am important enough to really influence the life of someone else. So this isn't relevant."

Then, the boy produces an affirmative clause that is very different from his suicidal message in Example (46) and his dubitative statements in Example (50): "I'm trying to live in the way that is best for me, but as I said, I don't know what's suitable for me. Perhaps what's best for me has not been shown to me. That's why I'm asking these questions" (lines 6–8). These sentences suggest that the boy has changed his basic attitude and that he is ready now to explore the ways of the living, but that he still needs help.

Upon receiving this message, the volunteer sends a short message showing empathy for the boy's difficulties, and saying that he (i.e., the volunteer) too has availed himself of professional help. He advises the boy to call up the hotline and provides him with telephone numbers. Examples (52) and (53) are the final messages sent to the forum by the boy:

Example (52) The boy

1 Shabbat shalom.[88]
2 Thank you for the telephone numbers. I think that the responses have
3 really helped me. I still don't know what I will do, but at least now I
4 have a different perspective than before. I will probably call ERAN,
5 because I don't think I'll feel comfortable discussing it with anyone face
6 to face. So I think that the phone numbers you have given me will be
7 most helpful. Thanks.

Example (53) The boy

1 Hi.
2 I've had these feelings for a year and a half, but only now have I found
3 my inner courage and shared my thoughts with other people.
4 And I'm afraid to see the school counselor because she might send me to
5 a psychologist or something like that, and at a time like this I don't think
6 that's what I need. That's why I wrote to this site because it is probably
7 the only place where I can speak about it without being afraid that
8 some action will be taken against me.

In Example (52), the boy affirms that he has changed (lines 3–4). Then, relating to the advice to consult with a professional, he emphasizes that he prefers to use telephone communication (lines 4–7). In Example (53), he expresses his fear of meeting with a counselor or a psychologist (lines 4–5) and stressess the advantages of the cyber forum (lines 6–8).

In conclusion, the multilogue conducted in response to the adolescent's suicidal message can be divided into two stages. In the first, answerers A and B foreground the dimensions of "having" and "doing" in the boy's life, respectively, in their attempt to persuade him that life is worth living (Examples (48) and (49)). The boy's response in Example (50) coheres with these answers, and indicates a cognitive shift from egocentric death-oriented thinking to a focus on the alternative of life.

The second operation of the virtual rescue team is opened by the volunteer's practical recommendation to read and talk with other people. The texts in the second stage are shorter and interrelated, as our analysis has shown. It is evident in this stage that following the volunteer's example, answerers A and B also emphasize the importance of professional help, to which the boy responds positively in his last two messages.

The striking change in the boy's perspective on life and his acceptance of the advice via the virtual rescue team may be interpreted discursively by a close examination of how the participants' tropes cohere. The adolescent produces several remarkable figurative constructions: A title: "The only way to be released from the jaws of life"; a figurative conspiracy that summarizes the reasons for his problem: "But still I can't find my place in this world"; and a cluster of tropes by means of which he attempts to express his perspective on life: "I see life from a different perspective than most kids my age. I think that life is only one phase and death is another. I don't believe in life after death, but I believe that life has to end sometime. So let's say that I don't feel comfortable now. *Why not be ahead of my time and move on to the next phase?*" The last tropes are, in our opinion, organizing devices that both summarize his perspective on his life and foreground a solution.

Answerer A relates to the first figurative conspiracy, but modifies it carefully by saying "You may have found the solution on your own". In addition, she offers a cluster of tropes of her own that will be recycled by the boy and by answerer B: "See all the gifts that God gave you and understand that there is much more to life than throwing it away at such a young age."

Answerer B defines the boy's suicidal intentions by producing her own trope: "Testing the limits of things". She also relates to the boy's figurative conspiracy ("I can't find my place in the world"), replacing the lexical item "find my place" with "look for" and "give" ("Look for ways to give something meaningful to life"). The boy's response to A and B relates to the metaphorical gifts emphasized by A: "But what would you say if I'm not happy about the gift that was given to me?" In addition, he relates to B's metaphorical directive by complaining that "I don't give anything of myself to anybody else." These tropes indicate a cognitive shift from a world where the boy cannot find meaning to a focus on life and the contribution he can make to the living.

The volunteer's message marks a discursive turn in the multilogue, as our analysis shows. He advises the boy to seek professional help, an idea that is emphasized by all the answerers in the ensuing short messages where direct non-figurative language replaces tropes and results in a remarkable change in the boy's perspective and state of mind.

Bearing in mind the four-world model we presented in the introduction and have elaborated on in the course of this book, we have seen in subsection 1.1 how a virtual rescue team attempts to shift the focus of the discussion from the troubled past world in which the adolescent plans to put an end to his life to a future world of possibilities and hope.

1.2. "I was the best source of light on the market"

"I was the best source of light on the market" – the second digital writer – does not provide any clear contextualizing biographical details and hides behind tropes. In this respect, she resembles "Like you're the world's only sucker" – the hotline caller presented in Chapter 3. Therefore, it is very difficult for the answerers to understand what the caller's problem is. Five answerers respond to the first message. In Examples (54–57), we present the problem-message and the first three answers. The last two answers are summarized.

Unlike *Why not be ahead of my time?* – the adolescent digital sufferer presented in subsection 1.2 – "I was the best source of light on the market" writes a problem-message, but does not relate to the answerers' messages. Therefore, it is impossible to tell to what extent the answerers were able to help this troubled sufferer. In Example (54), this person describes her problem. Although the writer's gender is feminine as marked in the original Hebrew version by adjectival and nominal forms, it is not a conclusive piece of discursive evidence because in cyberspace it is easy to mask one's identity. In the ensuing discussion, however, we will use the feminine pronoun *she* to refer to this person:

Example (54) "I was the best source of light on the market"

1 I was in the light, at the center, the brightest section, like the center of a
2 bulb that radiates heat. I was so full of light that it overflowed out of me
3 to the outside, in every possible direction, indiscriminately. I have never
4 known what suffering is. I have never understood why people are sad or
5 nervous. What? Don't they know that things tend to work out on their
6 own? And they called me an angel because when they got close to me
7 they inhaled the light that I radiated. It was not under control. Light has
8 its own soul and it [the light] was determined to flow out of me to the
9 outside. Although it spread indiscriminately, I had enough because in
10 the place where I was there is an infinite quantity of light that penetrated
11 me forcefully and then went out of me to the others day by day, day
12 after day. I have become light, because it used to walk close to me, it
13 never let go of me. I was the best light on the market. Imagine a
14 medicine you don't have to swallow, just get close to it in order to
15 recover. I enjoyed illuminating others. I drew life from the ability to
16 illuminate. I thought I was special, unique, talented. I thought I had an
17 innate ability to make others happy. I thought I knew what to say, how
18 to say it, to illuminate the souls of others. The truth is that it was only
19 the light that illuminated those close to me. I had nothing to do with the
20 phenomenon. I was the messenger of light, talentless, devoid of unique
21 therapeutic ability, as it turned out. I was a nothing who was lucky
22 enough to get a good location where she could stay in the center of the
23 light. And today when the light is gone, I am unable to illuminate.
24 Because from the beginning it did the job. When I ceased to illuminate,
25 those who once used to come to me to get the light were gone. I can't
26 even think of one person that was once close to me that really remained
27 here. I think that I don't even have one true friend. There is no one to
28 illuminate me, and my soul is so dark that I can't see what there is inside
29 it. I am not special without the light. Today I understand the meaning of

30 suffering. I have met depression and anger face to face. I know why
31 people aren't happy. They don't walk along the highway. Away from
32 the center of the light. I have become one of them, waiting for someone
33 to give me some light. Once I didn't understand why people wish to die.
34 Today I wonder why I should go on living. Why do people drag on day
35 after day after day? What? Do you think that the meaning of life will
36 suddenly dawn on you? It's a fantasy, not reality. And by the way,
37 things don't work out on their own, as the light people think. They have
38 to be taken care of. And if it's impossible? Surely one can't see well
39 without light. Can one arrange things if there's no light? And generally
40 speaking, if one is devoid of the ability to illuminate, then there's no
41 meaning.

Who is the digital writer who wrote the message presented in Example (54)? How old is this person? Why is she in trouble? It is very difficult to answer these questions. What the message does show is that the person writing it uses "light" and "dark" as central organizing tropes. Accordingly, from her perspective in the present darkness, this troubled person refers to two stages in her life. In the first stage of euphoria, she positions herself in relation to others as a superior source of "light" that illuminated others (lines 1–16). Then, she comments on the illusion she lived in when she thought she was a source of light (lines 16–23). Finally, the digital writer describes her state of mind at the present (lines 23–41) "when the light is gone" (line 23).

This problem-message is not contextualized in a detailed narrative format. In a former telephone interaction in Chapter 3 initiated by "Like you're the world's only sucker" – another sufferer who refused to narrate a personal story – there are a lot of self-building paralinguistic features indicating that the caller is a woman and that she is depressed. In the written digital problem-message presented in Example (54), it is very difficult to decide conclusively who this troubled person is.

We suggest three possible selves that may have composed this message and sent it to the forum. Perhaps the person was a poet who wrote a carefully planned text, just like *Amputating the cancerous leg* in Chapter 3. Following this line of thought, we can further say that this aloof poet wants to express elevated ideas that are epitomized via two central tropes: "light" and "darkness".

Another possibility that we would like to entertain is that this person is a proponent of one of the New Age groups, and accordingly has adopted its characteristic jargon, which usually comprises light concepts such as "inner light", "source of light", "central light", "blinding light", "victory of light", "light we share", "ocean of light", "bridge of light", etc. (Thaler, Singer, and Lalich 1995).

A third possibility could be that the person who wrote the message may suffer from a thinking disorder – a process that includes delusions, abstract thinking and disturbances in concept formation (Kaplan and Sadock 1988). It is also possible to say that all three selves – the poetic, the New Age and the mentally ill (Green 1986) – constituted dimensions of the digital writer's self. In Example (55), we present the laconic but thought-provoking seven-word message of answerer A, who relates to two of the three selves that we propose: the insane and the poetic:

Example (55) Answerer A

A crazy trigger ... and also a talent.

Following the determinative self-defining seven-word message presented in Example (55), the hotline volunteer hastens to write a carefully worded mitigative answer that does not define who "I was the best source of light on the market" is, as answerer A did, but attempts to provide her with help:

Example (56) Answerer B: A hotline volunteer

1 I understand that there have been different times in your life. A time
2 when you radiated light all around you, and now, it's a time when you
3 feel how you have lost the light and you have a heavy load to carry. I
4 don't know how old you are, and how much experience you have gained
5 in the course of your life, but it seems that like any other person, you too
6 have changing feelings, and the joy and rejoicing are replaced by
7 sadness. You seem very clever, and I'm sure that you'll be able to find
8 out if what is taking place in your life now is a temporary crisis that may
9 pass or if you have entered a long and tiresome state of being in the
10 dark. You can make up your own mind whether you have the strength to
11 bring the light back to you, and I'm hopeful that this is exactly what will
12 happen, or whether you are in a state in which you need the help of
13 professionals. At any rate, it seems to me that you should not give in.
14 You should do anything to make your life full and rich. I'm keeping my
15 fingers crossed and hoping you'll be able to find the way to cope with
16 everything and once again be the center of overflowing light.
17 Yours Nati.

124   *Cyber multilogues*

The male volunteer's answer can be divided into several parts. In lines 1–3, he summarizes the contents of the problem-message, taking the precaution not to attach any self-defining tags to the problem-message sender. Accordingly, in lines 3–6, the volunteer does not focus on unique features displayed in the problem-message, but rather emphasizes that the digital writer is like other people whose feelings change from time to time. Referring to other people, the volunteer probably attempts to mitigate the effect of the former message that depicted self-portraits of the insane and the poetic.

Then, the responsible volunteer compliments "I was the best source of light on the market's" cleverness, an asset that, in his opinion, will enable the problem-writer to find out whether the present state of darkness is temporary or enduring (lines 7–10). Always careful not to be offensive, the volunteer adds that the problem-writer has to find out whether she can solve the crisis on her own or whether perhaps she needs professional help (lines 10–13). At the end of the message, the volunteer writes empathetic and encouraging comments (lines 14–16) and signs the message with the polite and amiable complimentary "Yours".

Example (57) was written by an answerer who summarizes several issues that should concern the problem-writer:

Example (57) Answerer C

1   Who turned the light off?
2   You describe two extreme situations.
3   An exceptional situation where you are the star in the kingdom of light
4   and people gather around you.
5   A state of gloom and loneliness, depression and suicidal thoughts.
6   And in the middle there is nothing???
7   Who turned the light off?
8   How come all of a sudden there's no light and no people around you?
9   What happened to the enormous amount of energy you radiated?

The third answerer's message, which is succinct and thought-provoking, comprises two components. The first is an accurate and clear description of the two extreme states the writer describes (lines 2–5). The second is questions – four probing questions that are indicated by interrogative pronouns (lines 1, 7, 8, and 9) and one intonation question (line 6). The questions are addressed to the writer and their cumulative effect in this short but very eloquent message is the construction of a forceful demand for the writer to find answers to the questions.

The questions urging the writer to unfold a specific story may be related to two of the six components described by Labov (1972). Thus, "Who turned the light off?" twice repeated in lines 1 and 7, and "How come all of a sudden there's no light and no people around you?" (line 8) require that the problem-message provide the problem-causing chain of events – an obligatory component in any personal story.[89] Other questions seem to urge "I was the best source of light on the market" to provide evaluation, another important component of personal stories. This is expressed in the intonation question "And in the middle there is nothing???" (line 6) and the *wh*-question "What happened to the enormous amount of energy you radiated?" (lines 9).

The fourth answerer is another hotline volunteer, who relates to the powerful questions illustrated in Example (57) and emphasizes that the writer should try to answer these questions not necessarily in the forum, but for herself, so that she can change direction. Finally, the fifth answerer relates to the "light" metaphor, stressing that the light is within the writer and therefore she has to find it. He also suggests that the writer seek professional mental help, engage in sports, or seek some kind of spiritual guidance.

To recapitulate: The self-distancing storyless problem-message presented in Example (54) may have been written by a poet, a New Age proponent or a mentally ill person. The first answerer carelessly orients himself to the first and the last possible selves, an infelicitous and irresponsible discursive move that cyberspace makes possible. The hotline volunteer, the next answerer, hastens to mitigate the harsh effect that the first answerer's message may have exerted on "I was the best source of light on the market" and discreetly advises her to seek professional help, if necessary. The next thought-provoking answer demands that the caller provide the contextualizing narrative format, either to the forum participants or to herself, in order to shed light on the incoherent message. The fourth answerer is another hotline volunteer who relates to a former message and suggests that the troubled writer try to answer the unanswered questions. Finally, following the discursive footsteps of the first volunteer, the fifth lay answerer makes several practical recommendations including professional mental help, sports or some kind of spiritual guidance. It seems that the multilogue, which is ignited by "light" – a storyless trope – does not move in the direction of any definite destination and remains in the realm of general advice. Who is "I was the best source of light on the market"? What happened to her as a result of the cyber multilogue that she herself initiated? We will never know for sure.

2. Summary

In Chapter 6, we explore how troubled selves fare in a hotline cyber forum by analyzing two virtual dramas. The first cyber sufferer is a suicidal adolescent we named *Why not be ahead of my time?* The second cyber sufferer, like "The world's only sucker", the hotline caller presented in Chapter 3, refuses to tell a contextualizing personal story. As a result, we are unable to define which contents in the digital writer's tortured past world the trope "I was the best source of light on the market" actually summarizes.

In response to the first detailed problem message presented by *Why not be ahead of my time?*, a virtual rescue team collaborates in a coherent two-stage multilogue. In the first stage, these anonymous but sensitive and responsible forum participants somehow manage to relate to the painful figurative versions of the adolescent's past world in a perfectly orchestrated multilogue. This virtual rescue team finally succeeds in shifting the emphasis of the boy's figurative arguments from the tormented past world to a future world where life is worth living. In the second stage, the hotline volunteer directs the discussion to more practical grounds of coping, where figurative language is replaced by non-figurative directives. At the end of the sequence of messages, a striking change in the boy's perspective on life is evident.

The second cyber sufferer refuses to contextualize her message. Therefore, the multilogical discussion is conducted incoherently and aimlessly without any overt discursive goals or results. We will never be able to tell who wrote the self-distancing storyless problem-message presented by a digital writer we named "I was the best source of light on the market". Was this sufferer a poet? Or may be this person was a New Age proponent? We also suggested that perhaps this suffering self was a mentally ill person. Supervised by the responsible hotline volunteers, the answerers attempt to relate to these virtual selves, but their collabora tive efforts are unsuccessful because they communicate in an abstract domain that is not grounded in actual experience.

It is important to note that in both sequences of messages presented in Chapter 6, the hotline volunteers constitute professional anchors of empathy and emotional support who attempt to move the discussion to more practical grounds of coping in the first example, and mitigate the unleashed and careless criticism of one cyber answerer in the second.

Finally, Chapter 6 provides additional discursive evidence that supports one of our conclusions formulated at the end of Chapter 3. We show that succinct figurative versions of the self enhance interpersonal communication when they are produced within detailed narrative formats. In the absence of a contextualizing story, the tropes fail to refer to anything and do not contribute to the multilogue.

Part 3
The discursive construction of control

Chapter 7
Negotiating the right to advertise the self

Our interpretive interface of the radio corpora analyzed in Part 2, Chapters 3 and 4, shows that only some media-worthy lay participants manage to present their troubled experience via detailed and succinct discursive self-portraits and negotiate better future worlds with the radio team. Other suffering souls are hastily banished from the public arena by the representatives of the institution, who are eager to pinpoint more rating-oriented callers.

We also discover that even when callers make relevant presentations of their problems, the psychologists cannot or do not always want to explore the complexities of the narrators' past, opting instead for instant future-directed solutions. As a result, at certain discursive junctions, lay callers and professionals have to negotiate what the focus of the interaction is. The hotline telephone discourse explored in Chapter 5 is free from the dictates of the overhearing audience. Consequently, the troubled callers presented in that chapter are able to produce self-displaying narrative and figurative formats that are noticed and profitably used by the volunteers in order to help the callers. Then, in Chapter 6 we show that cyber interactions are open to any troubled soul who wishes to voice his or her opinion.

In Part 3, we explore "Night birds talk", a radio program that offers callers a site where they can narrate exceptional stories to the overhearing audience without offering mental help. Each of the callers presented in Chapters 7 and 8 discursively constructs issues of control and loss of control in one way or another. The callers whose stories are unfolded in sections 1 and 2 are a healer and a gay woman. Both make an attempt to present and advertise their selves in public. In Section 3, we summarize the chapter.

1. The healer: "I produce a new mechanism that controls the addictive behavior"

The first caller claims he is a healer who treats various addictions. The

132   *Negotiating the right to advertise the self*

caller commences by exposing his full identity, and, despite the tight question–answer interview format that the program host imposes, makes an individual narrative contribution consisting of generic and specific stories. These focus on how he discovered his exceptional ability, how he understood and controlled it, and finally how he uses it at present to help the addicted. Out of the 21 troubled selves presented in this book, the healer is the only one who is not troubled, but actually proposes to help others, just like the psychologists and para-professional volunteers we met in previous chapters. Example (58) shows how the caller discovers that he was endowed with an exceptional ability that he can use in order to help heavy smokers:

Example (58) "The wave used to penetrate my body"

```
 1  C:  I discovered I am endowed with an ability that I can use to help
 2      cigarette addicts and all sorts of other addictions like overeating.
 3  H:  What are these powers you are talking about?
 4  C:  When I was a child I used to feel all sorts of sensations. For example,
 5      I used to walk about in the neighborhood, my hands stretched out on
 6      both sides, and people asked me: "What are you doing?" I said: "I
 7      feel the tickling in the air." Yes, I used to feel certain sensations in
 8      my hands when I was close to plants and trees, people and animals.
 9      At a certain stage, I suddenly realized that there was something
10      unique about me and other people did not have the same experience.
11      I would experience a kind of a shock, like a wave that would
12      hold my head and pull my skull backward. My whole head would
13      stretch so much sometimes. The wave used to penetrate my body
14      through my head and my hands and would leave through my
15      legs.
```

At first, it seems that the caller is aligning himself with the host's agenda to present exceptional stories. The caller constructs the meaning of exceptional early experiences when he felt how natural energies forcefully penetrated his body. Using generic stories (lines 4–15), the articulate caller produces vivid and detailed descriptions of exceptional childhood experiences during which he discovered that he was able to absorb natural energies, control them and use them for healing.[90] The fluent verbalization of the generic stories indicates that the caller must have narrated and edited these generic stories repeatedly over the years. In this way, they have become his professional self-portrait.

However, it soon becomes evident that the caller aspires to make his exceptional stories sound as trustworthy as possible. To accomplish this discursive task, he uses two evaluative devices. First, in response to the host's probing question about his powers (line 3), the caller prefers to use his own idiosyncratic terminology – lexical items that enable him to define his childhood experiences. Accordingly, he produces the following nouns: "ability" (line 1), "sensations" (lines 4 and 7), "tickling" (line 7), "something unique" (lines 9–10), "shock" (line 11), and "wave" (lines 11 and 13).

Constructed dialogue (lines 6 and 7), another evaluative device employed by the caller, enhances the trustworthiness of the stories. Thus, the caller recycles, as it were, meaningful excerpts from conversations that he held with other people. It is interesting to note that the adult narrator chooses to describe an early stage in his life when he did not control the energies that penetrated him but was a mere pawn[91] used by the energies, very low on the agency scale that we discussed in former chapters. Low-level agency is discursively constructed in lines 11–15 via transitive utterances in which the narrator places himself in an object position: "a wave that would hold my head and pull my skull backward. My whole head would stretch so much sometimes. The wave used to penetrate my body through my head and my hands and would leave through my legs."[92]

In Example (59), the caller continues to construct his professional self and further resists the host's attempts to participate in the construction of the meaning of the caller's unique experiences:

Example (59) "Were you scared when you discovered such a power?"

1   H: And your parents? Were they worried?
2   C: No. They didn't pay attention to it. I was an ordinary kid, very
3   naughty, except for this ability. There was no special symptom.
4   H: Which means that you had very unique and different sensations,
5   C: Very clear.
6   H: And also very frightening?
7   C: It didn't frighten me. It simply made me very very curious at a very
8   very young age. This may be one of the things that drove me to fol
9   low this direction, curiosity and my very strong urge to really
10   understand what was happening.
11 H: Were you scared when you discovered such a power?
12 C: No. I wasn't scared. I asked myself: "What's going on here?"

In response to the caller's presentation of a healing ability, the rating-oriented host repeatedly attempts to foreground the awesome and inexplicable features of the narrator's story. The latter, guided by his own need to advertise his abilities in the media, tries to rectify this perspective by presenting a self-portrait of an ordinary child who became a curious grown-up and then subjected an unusual phenomenon to scrupulous scrutiny in the quest for a plausible explanation of his ability (lines 7–10, 12).

To accomplish their opposing discursive tasks, the host and the caller use different discursive resources. The host asks evaluative questions (lines 1 and 11) and produces evaluative adjectives (lines 4, 6, and 11) in order to shift the interaction to the domain of the mysterious and the inexplicable. The healer, on the other hand, insistently answers the host's questions negatively (lines 2, 7, and 12) and uses everyday lexical items (lines 2–3 and 5) to establish that what happened to him can be accounted for within the domain of ordinary experience.

To position his story within a domain of phenomena that can be explained scientifically, the caller even formulates a question that calls for a trustworthy answer (line 12) that he provides, as we shall see later on in Example (61). In Example (60), the unrelenting host directs the caller to give an example of a strange experience:

Example (60) "Give us an example of a strange experience"

```
1   H: Give us an example of a strange experience.
2   C: One day, I was going home from school and I saw a pigeon that was
3      dying, really dying. I put my hand over it, and that was really the fi-
4      nal stage of its life. It was really dying. And at that moment blood
5      came out of its nose, it choked and died. Now at that moment when
6      my hand was going down over it, I suddenly felt a strong tickling in
7      my hand, and it was clear to me that something had left its body,
8      because then I was already very very skilled in my sensations, it was
9      clear that something had left its body at that moment and simply
10     went out,
11  H: So what is really happening? How do you define this power? How
12     can you help people?
```

In response to the host's directive to tell a strange story (line 1), the caller unfolds an exceptional experience that is packaged in a narrative format (lines 2–10). The vivid and detailed narration includes a description of energy transfer from the body of a dead pigeon into the healer. Adapting Labov's structural elements to interactional problem discourse, we see that the abstract summarizing the gist of the story is produced by the host in line 1. The contextualizing orientation is verbalized in lines 2–3. The complicating action that often results in an unexpected situation is produced in line 3, 4–5, and 6–7: "I put my hand over it", "And at that moment blood came out of its nose, it choked and died" and "I suddenly felt a strong tickling in my hand".

However, the host breaks in and bombards the narrator with a chain of questions that shift the interaction from the past to the present (lines 11–12). The latter uses repetition and the adverbial "really" to emphasize that what he is saying is true: "and saw a pigeon that was dying, really dying. I put my hand over it, and that was really the final stage of its life. It was really dying" (lines 2–4). Then, in line 6, the eloquent narrator uses the adverbial "suddenly" to mark the time point when the energy transfer begins. In Example (61), the caller provides an answer to the host's questions and his own research question formulated in Example (59), line 11: "So what is really happening?":

Example (61) *I produce a new mechanism that controls the addictive behavior*

1 C: Today I actually use it [the ability] to cure heavy smokers,
2 H: What do you do? A cigarette addict comes to you and you touch his
3   hand,
4 C: No. I don't touch him. I use the electromagnetic field that surrounds
5   him,
6 H: What? What? What do you do?
7 C: Actually, I use this ability that I'm endowed with to produce a proc-
8   ess that is very similar, that can be related to say, a tape cassette. *I*
9   *produce a new mechanism that really controls the addictive*
10   *behavior*. It's a process that ((unclear)) that means it operates on all
11   the levels, from the physical to the psychological.

The generic story that the adult narrator unfolds purports to provide a scientific explanation via a model that he developed to use the energies absorbed from the environment to cure heavy smokers (lines 7–10). The healer believes that he is able to use the electromagnetic fields surrounding his patients in order to implant his hypnotic instruc-

136 *Negotiating the right to advertise the self*

tions (Erickson, Rossi, and Ross 1976) – figuratively described in terms of a tape cassette – in the minds of his clients. In this way, he controls their addiction. The experienced host verbalizes his surprise, and allows the articulate narrator to accomplish his task without interference. It is interesting to note that the adult healer displays a high level of syntactic agency (lines 1, 4–5, 7 and 8–10) that contrasts with the helpless pawn controlled by the energies presented in Example (58).

In conclusion, we suggest that the healer's verbal behavior exhibits skilful use of evaluative devices, comprising agency markers and figurative language and results in a discursive portrayal of a professional who is able to heal addicts by controlling their lack of control. In addition, the eloquent caller's pseudo-scientific orientation reflected in his narrative and figurative contribution suggests that he uses public territory to advertise his healing ability, although he does not say so explicitly.

2. The lesbian: "That person didn't have horns and didn't have a beard"

The caller is a lesbian in her early thirties. She avows her identity in public territory. Subsequently, she makes a twofold missionary attempt to demystify stereotypes related to homosexuals and lesbians and help members of this community come out of the closet. In Example (62), she describes self-discovery and self-acceptance processes in adolescence (Green 2004):

Example (62) "We don't have sexual drives that are uncontrollable"

1 C: I didn't know whether I should call you tonight, because the name of
2   the program is "Drives and Instincts", a title that has very negative
3   connotations, especially for a lesbian, because it's immediately
4   related to sexual drives that are uncontrollable. It's very important for
5   me to say that homosexuals and lesbians, and I'm lesbian, we don't
6   have sexual drives that are uncontrollable or that control us. They are
7   simply directed at,
8 H: So let's change the title.

Example (62) shows how the caller accomplishes two tasks. She commences her self-presentation by establishing her social affiliation within the homosexual and lesbian community. To do so, she uses the pronouns "I" and "we", discursive markers that indicate how the caller wishes to present herself (Malone 1997): an individual member of a larger gay community (lines 4–6). Self-presentation is connected to another task: publicizing the fact that gay men and women are in control of their "Drives and Instincts" – the title of the program on that particular evening (lines 1–4). In the face of such a missionary introduction, the host humorously suggests changing the title of the program (line 8). In Example (63) the caller and the host engage in a tight question–answer format:

Example (63) "When did you discover for the first time that boys don't interest you?"

1   H: When did you discover for the first time that boys don't interest you?
2   C: When I was 15 I had a boyfriend, and at that time I also had a good
3   girlfriend, a classmate. And little by little I saw that I enjoyed being
4   with her more than with him, although we did not have sex. It was a
5   platonic friendship and my boyfriend was gradually neglected. He
6   was gradually neglected. I felt he was less interesting.
7   H: And then you became a close friend of your girlfriend?
8   C: Yes. Nothing happened at first. We didn't have sex. We were friends
9   for a long time, but it's very difficult for a young girl who doesn't
10   really understand what's happening,
11 H: You still didn't understand?
12 C: No. For a long time I didn't understand, and when one begins to
13   understand, one has very sad feelings,
14 H: When did you discover, when did you say to yourself for the first
15   time "I'm a lesbian"?
16 C: At the age of 16, about 16.
17 H: Was there a specific event that,
18 C: No. Little by little one becomes aware of it. That it's simply, little by
19   little one accepts it more and more. It takes time because for so many
20   years we were told all the time that it's bad, that it's not good, that
21   it's negative, things like that.

The caller is confronted by the host's insistent questions that require that she make a personal revelation rather than continue her convincing preaching. He demands that she reveal to the overhearing audience the exact time point when she discovered her gay self (lines 1, 7, 14–

15, and 17). She complies with his request to make a personal rather than a collective contribution, but insists on narrating a gradual and painful self-discovery process in adolescence.

Her self-discovery process is discursively constructed by the juxtaposition of perception and cognition verbs (e.g., "see", "understand", "become aware of", and "accept", lines 3, 10, 18, and 19) and process adverbial (e.g., "little by little", "gradually", and "for a long time", lines 3, 5, 9, and 12) that are repeated several times and co-construct a gradual process of awareness-raising. Torn between an ongoing process of self-discovery, on the one hand, and social stereotypes on the other, the adult caller describes how her early adolescent self experienced feelings of fear of rejection and abandonment that are characteristic of adolescents during their developmental process (Green 2004), but are particularly acute in her case (lines 12–13 and 19–21) (see Kahn 1991 for a description of the factors affecting the coming out process for lesbians).

The caller positions her growing awareness as an adolescent vis-à-vis the dictates of a hostile, unenlightened society that condemned the young adolescent's newly discovered self. This discursive task is accomplished via a chain of subordinate utterances in which repetition of the lexical items "bad", "not good", and "negative" emphasizes the powerful social dictates (lines 20–21).

In Example (64), the caller further describes how difficult it was for her to keep her gay self in the closet:

Example (64) *That person didn't have horns and didn't have a beard*

1　H: Didn't you want to speak to your parents?
2　C: I was very afraid, very afraid ((pause)) of people who are close to me
3　　 who would say bad things, that I would not be loved anymore. It's
4　　 very difficult. At that age, if I had seen a person on TV who had said:
5　　 "I'm a lesbian and I'm happy." If I had seen such a person saying
6　　 those things, if I had seen that *that person didn't have horns and*
7　　 *didn't have a beard*, I would have felt much better, if this person had
8　　 said: "It's good [to be gay]. One can live with it. It's wonderful." It
9　　 would have made a difference.

In response to the host's question, the caller explains that she did not share what was then a secret with anyone, including her parents, because she was afraid that they would not love her (lines 2–3). Then, she narrates a hypothetical personal story that could have happened in the past but did not (lines 4–9). Because the personal story did not actually take place in the past, it is narrated via conditional utterances.

Two self-displaying evaluative resources are used by the caller in these hypothetical stories: constructed dialogue emphasizing that it is good to be gay (lines 5 and 8) and an organizing trope (lines 6–7). When narrators use constructed dialogue, they usually create an effect of nearness, as we have seen in former chapters. However, in Example (64), the repeated speech representations embedded in hypothetical utterances conspire to distance the past voices.

The hypothetical story is summarized via two negative utterances coordinated by the conjunction "and" (line 6). Each utterance comprises a synecdoche, a figurative form in which a part is put for the whole: "that person didn't have horns and didn't have a beard." The two parts – the "horns" and the "beard" – evoke a persecuted stereotypical male evil-doer. The fact that the coordinated utterances are in negative forms emphasizes that the caller does not associate this stereotypical figure with her self-portrait anymore. In other words, using an organizing trope, the caller publicly announces that lesbians and homosexuals are ordinary people who are in control of their lives and are not persecuted anymore.

In conclusion, the gay caller makes an attempt to emphasize that homosexuals and lesbians are men and women in control of their "drives and instincts". The host persistently demands that she reveal personal details about her gay self. She complies with his request and unfolds a gradual and painful self-discovery process in adolescence within an unenlightened, hostile society that condemned the young adolescent's newly discovered self. The caller summarizes her narrative contribution via an organizing trope that constructs her individual and collective selves.

3. Summary

The interactions presented in Chapter 7 show that "Night birds talk" differs from the previous sites explored in Chapters 3–6 because it does not offer mental help. Once the gatekeeping operators attach a classificatory tag that reads: "This caller's story is worth listening to," the callers gain access to the workshop rooms where they can weave the meaning of their past experiences via narrative discourse.

The interactions presented in Chapter 7 show that the turn-taking design of this program differs from that of "The two of us together and each of us alone", the program presented in Chapters 3 and 4. The program host of "Night birds talk" is very keen on participating in the meaning-making processes of the callers' past worlds that he has never visited. Therefore, he asks evaluative questions and continually makes evaluative comments, often interrupting the callers in the middle of the utterance.

However, both *I produce a new mechanism that controls the addictive behavior* and *That person didn't have horns and didn't have a beard*, the callers presented in Chapter 7, overpower the hegemony of the representatives of the institution, and manage to use the media to attain their own goals. The two callers, who are so different from each other, relate to and display issues of control in their respective narrative and figurative contributions.

It is also possible that these callers manage to overpower the host's hegemony because the latter wanted to be overpowered. He must have understood that these media-worthy narrators can help him attain his goals as well. In other words, it seems that the host relaxes his authoritative grip on the turn-taking willingly and lets the callers unfold their interesting rating-oriented stories.

In order to advertise his healing powers, the eloquent healer presents his pseudo scientific explanations and overcomes the host's persistent efforts to direct the interaction toward the inexplicable. Accordingly, the healer uses various discursive resources that are summatively organized by means of a figurative self-portrait of a professional who is able to control heavy smokers' lack of control: *I produce a new mechanism that controls the addictive behavior*.

The gay woman adopts a missionary goal as well. She attempts to demystify stereotypes related to homosexuals and lesbians by showing that gay men and women are in control of their "instincts and drives". She complies with the host's persistent demands and reveals personal details about her gay self. However, she does not abandon her goal. The caller summarizes her narrative contribution via an organizing trope that shows that she and the community she represents are not persecuted anymore: *That person didn't have horns and didn't have a beard*.

Chapter 8
The construction of addictive disorders in discourse

In Chapter 7, we presented interactions from "Night birds talk", a radio program that offers callers a site where they can narrate exceptional stories to the overhearing audience. We also emphasized that in the telephone and cyber sites described and analyzed in Chapters 3–6 problems are presented and attempts are made to negotiate solutions. The radio site presented in Chapters 7 and 8 focuses mainly on the presentation of callers' breath-taking stories.

The two callers we hosted in Chapter 7 gain access to this site to advertise their selves. They continually reject the host's unrelenting attempts to participate in the meaning construction processes when they feel that his agenda does not promote their ends. In Chapter 8, we explore six more interactions from our "Night birds talk" corpus,[93] in which callers' discursive contributions display addictive behaviors.

We are able to identify such discursive patterns in the stories of a love addict, a compulsive eater, a sex addict, an abstinent gambler as well as stories of codependent callers such as an abstinent alcoholic's wife, a gambler's girlfriend and an anorexic's mother.[94] These are spotted by the authors among other callers who do not display any discursive characteristics of addictive behaviors, such as those presented in Chapter 7.

A previous discourse study focuses on agoraphobia – a psychological disorder defined as "a fear of being anyplace where one might feel alone and vulnerable to fear and panic" (Capps and Ochs 1995: 3). In that case study, several discursive features entitled "the grammar of helplessness" and characteristic of this pathological condition are identified in the personal stories of an agoraphobic. This woman unfolds personal stories in which she often puts herself in non-agentive roles by using irrealis forms such as hypothetical past forms, negation, modality of necessity and *try*-constructions.

In section 1, we provide a definition of addictive behaviors, a macro-theoretical framework that we subsequently relate to in our interpretive and interfacing comments. In section 2, we present six addicted and codependent selves, and in section 3, we summarize the chapter.

1. Addictive behaviors and codependency

Addiction and codependency are related pathological behaviors that are frequently considered to be mirror images of each other. A broad definition of addiction (Thombs 1999) includes object-oriented addictive behaviors such as abuse of legal and illegal psychoactive substances (e.g., drugs, alcohol, caffeine, and nicotine), eating disorders, pathological gambling and computer addiction (Green 1993).

Excessive sexuality, work, shopping, spending, exercise, and love (Peele and Brodsky 1976, 1991) are also regarded as addictive behaviors, although they lack a clearly defined object. Because addictive behaviors are recursive, they have been associated with Obsessive Compulsive Disorder (see American Psychiatric Association, DSM IV, 1994). The most salient symptom of this disorder is an urge to repeat certain actions, thoughts or words (Munitz 1997).

Schaef (1987: 18) defines addiction as "any process over which we are powerless. It takes control of us, causing us to do and think things that are inconsistent with our personal values and leading us to become progressively more compulsive and obsessive." There are other salient emotional, behavioral, and cognitive characteristics that facilitate the definition of addictive behaviors. "A sure sign of addiction is the sudden need to deceive ourselves and others – to lie, deny and cover up. Addiction is anything we feel *tempted* (emphasis in the original) to lie about" (ibid.).

Addicts often report that the addictive experience is highly rewarding (Green 1995), that it effects a change in their mood and sensations (Peele 1985) and alters their ordinary state of consciousness and perception of the world (Weil 1986). Tart (1974: 43) defines an altered state of consciousness (ASC) in the following words: "An ASC may be defined as a qualitative alteration in the overall pattern of mental functioning, such that the experiencer feels his consciousness is radically different from the way it functions ordinarily." Addicts also report a feeling of omnipotence (Freud 1920) based on their conviction that their thoughts and imagination possess unlimited powers. Accordingly, they often believe that because they initiated the addictive process, they are capable of controlling and stopping it of their own free will at any time.

Addictive behaviors are also associated with loss of control. Locus (or location) of control (Rotter 1973) is a central multidimensional personality construct extensively researched in the last three decades of the twentieth century (Chubb, Fertman, and Ross 1997; Lefcourt and Davidson-Katz 1991). Internal locus of control is defined as the extent to which the individual believes that his behavior is controlled by factors inside of him, such as ability and personality traits. External locus of control is related to factors outside of the individual, such as luck, fate, and powerful others. The definition of one's locus of control as internal or external is not dichotomous, but varies situationally (Chubb, Fertman, and Ross 1997).

Because they are not in control, addicts are intolerant of delay in attaining the effect of the object of their addiction, and that is what enhances the compulsive aspects of addiction. This is manifested in sensations of arousal, physiological changes, or relaxation and detachment from the world (Green 1995). Consequently, addicts' time conceptualization differs from that of non-addicts. Attempts to discontinue the behavior frequently result in psychobiological disturbances, which in turn often result in relapse and continuation of addictive patterns (American Psychiatric Association, DSM IV, 1994).

Codependency (Beattie 1987; Schaef 1987; Wright and Wright 1999) is defined as the process by which the family or parts of it adapts to the addict's compulsive behavior, and during which that behavior also becomes the family's problem. Codependent persons can be family members such as parents, spouses, children, siblings, and cousins who are affected by the addict's behavior and who are often obsessed with the need to stop or control it. In some cases, codependents can also be significant others, such as friends or caretakers.

Schaef (1987: 30) describes the family's pathological involvement in the following words: "Codependents frequently have feelings of low self-worth and find meaning in making themselves indispensable to others ... Codependents are sufferers – Good Christian Martyrs. Their goodness is directly related to their suffering and the rewards they expect (and receive) because they are willing to sacrifice so much ... Codependents are selfless to the point of hurting themselves."

2. Addicted and codependent selves

2.1. The love addict: "Everything simply started snowballing"

The caller is a 36-year-old Jewish divorcée who reflects on her past relationship with a Druze. The Druze are members of a Middle Eastern religious ethnic minority that forbids conversion and intermarriage (Webster 1989). In Example (65), she portrays an addictive love that made her break two taboos – the man was married and he was a Druze – and ultimately ruin her life:

Example (65) *Everything simply started snowballing*[95]

```
 1  C: ((sighs)) My story actually begins about nine years ago. Well, I met a
 2     guy at work, a non-Jewish guy, a Druze.
 3  H: Yes.
 4  C: We were strongly attracted to each other.
 5  H: Did you know he wasn't Jewish?
 6  C  Yes, there was this thing, something that can't be explained, some
 7     thing that happened, and it couldn't be stopped.
 8  H: Why was it necessary to stop it? When one loves,
 9  C: Yes, but ((sighs)) the man wasn't Jewish, and he's a Druze. His
10     tradition. The man was married,
11  H: So you say that there are two problems. First, the man is not Jewish,
12     and second he is married,
13  C: Married, and this was something that had to be stopped. And it was
14     as if it went out of control completely.
15  H: What was it in him that made you want him when you also knew that
16     he, that he meant trouble? After all, a married man. Why did you
17     continue this relationship?
18  C: I don't know how to explain it.
19  H: Mm,
20  C: I definitely don't know how to explain it ((sighs)). Even today when I
21     am in a state of,
22  H: But we haven't reached that state yet. We're following the sequence
23     of events.
24  C: OK. Even today, I say I simply don't know how to explain what
25     happened.
26  H: So let's continue. You and him. You love each other. You're at
27     tracted to each other. What happens then?
28  C: There was, we felt that it was the two of us, and nothing else mat
29     tered. And when the decision was made, everything started rolling
```

```
30       along. He left the village. Yes, he left the village. Yes.
31   H:  His wife, and his wife?
32   C:  And his wife, and the children, and his religion, and the community
33       and everything. *Everything simply started snowballing.* I became
34       pregnant. He was still married, and efforts were made to bring him
35       back to the village. It didn't work, and I gave birth to, a daughter was
36       born. A year later, he divorced his legal wife, and lived with me, and
37       the whole thing sort of started, started going round in a cycle of [96]
38       births, pregnancies and births. Every year,
39   H:  What?
40   C:  Every year.
41   H:  Every year you had a child?
42   C:  Every year for seven years I had a child. After eight years, he simply
43       decided that he's having an identity crisis. That's the term. He can't
44       go on. He wants to get out of here,
45   H:  What did your parents, family, friends, people at work say?
46   C:  Let me tell you. At the beginning it didn't bother me so much,
47       because I loved him. There was love here, that is, this union, this
48       desire to be together. It was above everything, and everything else
49   H:  was dwarfed. How do you react when the man in your life is going to
50       abandon you? Those must have been very sad moments.
51   C:  ((sighs)) It's hard to define it. It was simply something that, you
52       remain hanging in the air. You, you crash suddenly. I'm trying to
53       come down from the dream to reality. That man ruined my life. He
54       simply ruined my life. He simply dragged me down with seven
55       babies. Today I'm at the lowest point. I'm homeless. I have no
56       financial resources. I'm appealing to everyone, to any authority that
57       can save me. I want people to pull me up.[97]
```

Figurative forms are a salient feature of Example (65). They display and construct the gist of the caller's painful narrated world. In response to the host's evaluative questions (lines 8, 15–17, 26–27, 31, 41, and 49–50) and comments (lines 22–23 and 26–27) that call for a chronologically ordered and logical (line 22) explanation, the caller emphasizes that it is difficult for her to explain her addictive behavior (lines 6–7. See also lines 18, 20–21, 24–25, and 51), and thereupon resorts to a metaphoric description that facilitates the description of her relationship. Using tropes, the caller compares the relationship to something that couldn't be stopped (line 7). The idea of an undefined and uncontrolled moving entity is further elaborated on in lines 13–14, 29–30, 33, and 37–38).

The caller also uses tropes when the host urges her to describe how she reacted when her lover decided to leave. She responds that it is difficult to define what happened (line 51), and once again produces a metaphoric description of her fall from a high point of happiness to a low point of despair (lines 51–53). Furthermore, she uses figurative language to foreground the unreal dimensions of the relationship – a "dream" (line 53) that took place at a high altitude (lines 48 and 52–53).

Some of the tropes the caller produces are figurative conspiracies. She verbalizes these complex structures to describe her addictive love (lines 7, 13–14, 29, 33, and 37–38) and her abandonment (lines 42–44 and 53–54). Structurally, these tropes comprise two or more evaluative devices intertwined in one structure. Semantically, they conspire to create a discursive portrait of loss of control in the description of the addictive love, and helplessness and victimhood in the description of the separation.

The conspiracies constructing the meaning of the caller's love (lines 7, 13–14, 29–30, 33, and 37–38) illuminate different dimensions of the caller's behavior. Figurative language depicts an undefined movement of a non-human external force (McReynolds 1990)(e.g., "and it couldn't be stopped"). Following Malone (1997: 52), who emphasizes that "pronouns can be studied as a concrete example of just how interactants signal their involvement", we think that indefinite pronouns such as "it", "something", and "everything" indicate a low level of agency (see Harré 1995). Irrealis forms such as modality, negation, and passive foreground the unreal dimensions of the caller's behavior (i.e, "couldn't be stopped" and "had to be stopped"). In "and it couldn't be stopped" (line 7), five evaluative devices are used in the same utterance: figurative language, an indefinite pronoun, modality, negation and passive.

In lines 42–44 and 53–55, the caller verbalizes the traumatic separation experience. She begins to narrate the story and is interrupted by the host's evaluative question that attempts to direct her personal story to an interpersonal domain that interests him (line 45, "What did your parents, family, friends, people at work say?"). The caller does not comply with the institutional directive, and elaborates figuratively on the meaning of her love before the separation (lines 46–48). Thereupon, the host asks a second evaluative question (lines 49–50,

"How do you react when the man in your life is going to abandon you? Those must have been very sad moments.").

In her attempt to construct the meaning of the separation, the caller uses figurative conspiracies that display her feelings of helplessness and victimhood: "After eight years, he simply decided that he's having an identity crisis. That's the term. He can't go on. He wants to get out of here" (lines 42–43). The first conspiracy ("He can't go on") combines an agentive subject ("he"), tense shift, negation, and a trope ("can't go on"). The second ("He wants to get out of here") comprises an agentive subject ("he"), tense shift ("wants"), a trope ("get out"), and a deictic adverb of place ("here"). The erasure of the caller from the narration serves to foreground her helplessness vis-à-vis the determined behavior of the abandoning lover.

In lines 51–53, she reintroduces and situates her abandoned self in relation to her lover, and in lines 53–55 produces another sequence of figurative conspiracies: "That man ruined my life. He simply ruined my life. He simply dragged me down with seven babies." These figurative conspiracies comprise repetitive syntactic structures in which the caller positions herself as a helpless victimized recipient of the controlling agent, the syntactic subject of these utterances ("That man", "he"). In addition, the caller uses several figurative verbs that intensify her helplessness and victimhood ("ruin" and "drag down").

Using a figurative conspiracy, the caller also appeals to the over-hearing audience for help (lines 56–57, "I want people to pull me up."). She employs an utterance in which figurative language (i.e., the caller is down) and low level of agency indicated by the syntactic position in which she places herself in the embedded utterance ("people to pull me up") conspire once again to construct her helplessness and despair.[98] How can we explain these complex figurative forms? It is possible to assume that in order to verbalize the complexity of the emotionally charged past world, the narrator has to use more complex discursive resources, such as figurative conspiracies. This is a tempting idea that we have explored in Chapters 5 and 6.

The caller's eloquence must have amazed the experienced host, who responds to the exceptional events by relaxing his control over the turn-taking system, and simply completing the caller's utterances (line 31) or verbalizing his amazement (lines 39 and 41). We suggest that

Everything simply started snowballing is the organizing figurative conspiracy that summarizes the caller's perspective on her addictive love with the inevitable tragic ending.

In conclusion, our analysis of the caller's discursive contribution shows that she uses figurative conspiracies to construct emotional, cognitive, and behavioral dimensions of the formation and disintegration of her addictive relationship in the narrated past. One of the conspiracies (i.e., *Everything simply started snowballing*) both summarizes the gist of her addictive experience and foresees the inevitable tragic ending. These are oriented to the host as well as the overhearing audience who are expected to rescue the caller who has not been able to help herself. However, the decision to call this conspiracy a story-internal organizing trope is based on our interpretation only and is not validated by interactional empirical evidence.

The conspiracies described in subsection 2.1 are verbalized at discursive junctions when the caller explains that it is very difficult for her to express her addictive love, loss of control, low level of agency as well as helplessness, and possibly even anger after the separation. The experienced host relaxes his control over the turn-taking system, and enables the caller to verbalize her amazing story.

2.2. The obese eater: "I'm like a blender"

The caller in Example (66) is a 39-year-old female food addict. She is married, has two children, weighs 146 kilos (322 pounds), and suffers from severe health problems induced by obesity:

Example (66) *I'm like a blender*

```
1   H: What is the daily routine of an eater like you? You get up in the
2       morning,
3   C: I get up in the morning and send the kids to school. Afterwards I
4       have plenty of time for the kitchen ((laughs)) for food ((laughs)).
5       I make myself a cup of coffee with two pittas [an Oriental flat hollow
6       unleavened bread that contains about 210 calories] and yellow cheese
7       and ((pause)) if I go to town, then I also eat a sandwich, you know,
8       a baguette with tuna, and then I visit a friend ((pause)) and there's
9       plenty of food,
10  H: Does your friend eat too?
11  C: Oh, not always. When they see me eat, they're not hungry ((sighs)).
```

12   Yes? Afterwards I go to my sister's. And I also eat there. In short,
13   wherever there's food, I eat,
14 H: But now it's lunchtime. We've come to lunch. What do,
15 C: I have no lunch. I have no morning. I have no night. I have no, I have
16   no meals. All day, wherever there's food, I eat. I have no hour,
17 H: All the time? Non-stop?
18 C: Yes. Yes. My mouth is actually, I scarcely ever sleep, because *I'm*
19   *like a blender*. I grind. I eat, eat, eat a lot, and I weigh 146 kilos.
20 H: What does your family say?
21 C: The family? They don't, They call me "kolboynik" [a dish placed on
22   dining tables in Israeli communal settlements for the disposal of
23   leftovers]. What can I tell you? A blender. I can't help it. What can I
24   do? I ((pause)) visit my sister on Saturday. I, I, I eat all the leftovers.
25   The children leave food. I eat. I don't feel anything. I don't,
26 H: What do they say? Do they laugh at you? Make fun of you? Are they
27   sad?
28 C: No. No. They pity me. I feel that they pity me. My sister says, they
29   say: "Eat a little. Don't overdo it."
30 H: But do you say to yourself: "That's enough"? Are there moments
31   when you manage to overcome the need?
32 C: ((sighs)) For an hour, two hours ((laughs)). It doesn't, it doesn't
33   work. It doesn't work. I simply ask, like this girl[99] ((pause)) this
34   anorexic girl to close me up. I love food. I love food. I need food.
35 H: So what do you expect? What type of miracle medicine?
36 C: I should be closed up. That's the medicine. They should give me only
37   the doses [of food] that I'm entitled to get,
38 H: ((laughs)) What does it mean, close you up? Do you want to be in
39 C: jail?Yes, as simple as that. Why not? As long as I live. For a period
40   of three months, or at least at the beginning they should teach me
41   how to eat. You know. They should close up my intestines. I believe
42   my intestines are 400 inches wide. What can I say to you ? I don't
43   know what to say to you. I'm neither hungry, Gideon, nor full. It's a
44   problem.

Several salient discursive features characterize the obese eater's narrative contribution: food-oriented generic stories in the present tense, obsessive repetition of lexical items connected with eating, and tropes including an organizing simile. The food-oriented generic stories (lines 3–9, 11–13, 15–16, and 24–25) focus on the eater's daily routines and comprise transitive utterances indicating a high level of agency (i.e., the caller is an active agent). However, in the context of the generic stories, the high level of agency is food-oriented, and constructs a portrait of a compulsive eater and loss of control.

Other discursive features further enhance the description of loss of control. The narrator obsessively repeats utterances related to eating, and lists food items. In our opinion, these repetitions are hierarchically organized by the *blender* simile, summatively disclosing a self that has no internal control, like a machine.[100] Like the abstinent gambler presented in Example (68) below, she also constructs discursively the meaning of an altered state of consciousness (line 25, "I eat. I don't feel anything. I don't").

In response to the host's incomplete question (line 14), which is probably inspired by a common daily script (Schank and Abelson 1977), the caller provides her idiosyncratic definition of the concept of time (lines 15–16). The obese eater, like the sex addict and the abstinent gambler in Examples (67) and (68), repeatedly emphasizes that her family does not understand her (lines 21 and 28–29).

The family's perspective is organized metaphorically by means of the "kolboynik" metaphor (line 21). Elsewhere in the interaction in sections that are not presented in the book, she compares her husband to "a bird". The dimensions of the bird become preposterously minuscule in comparison with the gigantic dimensions of the caller (lines 41-42).

Like *Everything simply started snowballing* in Example (65) and the anorexic's mother presented in Example (70), the caller repeatedly expects to get help (33–34, 36–37, and 41). This plea is repeated ten times in the entire interaction in utterances that are low on the agency scale (e.g., "they should close up my intestines", line 41). Repetition of the plea to "be closed up" and the description of the gigantic intestines in lines 41–42 conspire to portray a huge hole in the body, a metaphor frequently used by excessive eaters in the clinical setting.

In conclusion, the obese narrator disregards the host's questions and makes a very unique contribution via salient discursive features such as food-oriented generic stories, obsessive repetition of lexical items connected with eating and metaphors. These are summatively organized by the *blender* simile that discloses a self that has no internal control. The narrator also expresses her definitions of the concepts of time and altered states of consciousness. It is evident that like *Everything simply started snowballing*, *I'm like a blender* is constantly aware of the hidden participant, the overhearing audience, and expects that it will somehow save her.

2.3. The sex addict: "But sex was always something strong inside"

The caller in Example (67) is a 36-year-old male divorcé who tells the host that he grew up in the U.S.A. and discovered in adolescence that he was obsessively preoccupied with sex. At a later stage in his life, he worked as a male prostitute:

Example (67) *But sex was always something strong inside*

```
1   H: What is the drive that invaded your life?...
2   C: Sex. Since I was 15, or 16. It has always been ((pause)) inside, for a
3      long time. Twenty-four hours on my mind. Sex has always been on
4      my mind, all the time. It's a thing that can't be taken out. I grew up in
5      the U.S.A., in Los Angeles, and it has always been on my mind. Why
6      is it that you suddenly feel like having sex in the middle of the day?
7   H: What else did you do? A human being has to do other things?
8   C: We played football, went to school, but sex was always something
9      strong, very strong inside. Today it's even stronger. The older you
10     are, the more difficult it is to live without it.
11  H: Have you been married?
12  C: Yes. For seven years. I had sex only with my wife. We had sex
13     almost every day. Sex is something ((sighs, hums)). One goes to
14     work, one gets up in the morning, works the whole day, but at night
15     when the children go to bed, or when it's all over, you must have sex.
16  H: Isn't it difficult for you to deal with it all the time? Isn't it difficult?
17  C: I love it. I love it. It's not a job. It doesn't come by force. It comes
18     naturally.
19  H: And the girls, the women, your friends, do they know you are what
20     you are?
21  C: Oh, I wouldn't admit it at first, but when a girl is with me, she knows
22     that sex is an important thing, and the truth is that I had a relationship
23     with a girl for a long time, for two years, something like that.
24  H: So you had a steady girl friend?
25  C: I used to. She was so jealous. That's why I divorced my wife. You
26     can't smother a man with jealousy, but sex is always better with a
27     person who you've been with for a long time. If it's good, you do it
28     again. You eat a piece of steak, one bite, if it's good, you go back to
29     the same restaurant.
```

152 *The construction of addictive disorders in discourse*

The sex addict's narrative contribution brings to mind salient features identified in the stories of other addicts presented in this chapter: addiction-oriented generic stories, organizing tropes that summarize the essence of the addict's story, and repetitive reference to codependents. Sex-oriented generic stories (lines 5–6, 8–9, 12–15, and 26–29) depict daily routines listed one after the other, culminating in the satisfaction derived from sex, an activity that is discursively distinguished from other daily activities by means of "but", a coordinator of contrast (Quirk et al. 1985) (lines 8, 14, and 21) and vocal sounds like sighing and humming (line 13).

Like the abstinent gambler in Example (68), the sex addict defines the inexplicable through body-internal metaphors (lines 2–4 and 8–9) summatively organized in *But sex was always something strong inside*. Subsequently, in lines 25–26, the caller uses a figurative statement referring to his wife: "You can't smother a man with jealousy", drawing a collective profile of jealous codependent women such as his ex-wife and his girlfriends. Unlike the abstinent gambler in Example (68), who views gambling as an illness, the sex addict expresses an ego-syntonic (i.e., behaviors and wishes that are compatible with the addict's ideals or conceptions of himself) attitude towards the disorder (lines 17–18) (Rycroft 1972).

2.4. The abstinent gambler: "I'm not there today"

The caller is a 39-year-old married male who describes how he became addicted, the years of addiction, the abstinence process and his codependent "naive" wife who does not understand him.[101] Subsequently, the gambler seeks help in a self help group, and quits gambling. Repetitive reference to the help provided by the self-help group, including terminology characteristic of the jargon of such groups (e.g., addiction as an illness), suggests that, like the healer and the lesbian presented in Chapter 7, this caller must have had a missionary purpose for calling in. In Example (68), the abstinent gambler portrays his life before and after the abstinence process:

Example (68) *I'm not there today*

1   H: It means that your life, your social life was involved, was connected
2   to,

Addicted and codependent selves 153

3   C: But gambling was the center because this thing simply doesn't leave
4   you, the adrenaline that circulated in my body. This need of a human
5   being who feels that he's in his galaxy, not in this world, he's in his
6   galaxy. There, the adrenaline circulates in the body. You simply
7   crave for another dose, and another dose. You don't want to stop
8   playing. So you play on Sunday. If you win, then you win. If you
9   lose, then you lose everything that you have. You want more money.
10   Why? What you need is this supply of air.
11 H: I understand that you are ashamed of it.
12 C: The truth is that I'm ashamed of it, but on the other hand I'm also
13   glad that *I'm not there today*. There were days when I had to pick up
14   my son or my wife on my way home from work. So I'd drive toward
15   the building where my wife works,
16 H: Yes.
17 C: And there were days when if I had to turn right, the car would turn
18   left. I don't know how to explain it. The steering wheel simply has to
19   turn right,
20 H: Aha,
21 C: And it turns left, and the indicator also turns left.
22 H: And today? Are you happy?
23 C: Today I'm a happy man. Today my wife feels that she has a husband,
24   and a life. I must tell you a story, a very interesting story that
25   happened to me. My wife isn't Israeli. She wasn't born here, and we
26   visited her homeland. We spent the weekend in a town where her
27   sister lives. She invited us for the weekend, and there's a big casino
28   where I gambled a few times. And this time we visited this town after
29   I stopped gambling, about three months after I stopped gambling. So
30   we are inside the house, and the casino is right across the street. I
31   looked at it, and I didn't see anything because deep inside I know
32   that *I'm not there today*.

In Example (68), there are gambling-oriented generic stories (lines 8–10 and 13–15, 17–19, and 21). The generic stories in lines 13–15, 17–19, and 20) focus on driving, an everyday routine, discursively constructed by means of "would". This routine is disrupted when human agency is replaced by machine agency (lines 17–19, and 21), an indication of loss of control.

The narrator does not know how to explain his compulsive behavior (line 18). However, repetitive use of metaphors in Example (68) does display the meaning of addiction from the caller's point of view (lines 3–6 and 10). These evaluative metaphors indicate that addiction is essential for life ("What you need is this supply of air, line 10). Metaphoric language is also used to describe the caller's altered state of consciousness summatively organized in lines 4–6: "This need of a human being who feels that he's in his galaxy, not in this world, he's in his galaxy."

The caller joins a self-help group when his addictive behavior becomes intolerable, and consequently resumes responsibility for his life. The specific story (lines 25–32) presents an abstinent self that resumed control of its life, reflecting on the meaning of addiction. The new perspective is metaphorically organized and repeated twice in line 13 ("I'm not there today") and line 32 ("deep inside I know that I'm not there today").

In conclusion, our analysis shows that the trope *I'm not there today* is the caller's organizing trope. The caller's narrative contribution depicts two portraits: that of an addict obsessively verbalizing his impatient need through repetition of figurative and non-figurative language, and the abstinent gambler who *is not there today*. The two portraits suggest a behavioral shift, which in turn may be a shift in the caller's location of control from a gambling-dependent existence and externality to abstinence and a higher level of control.

2.5. An ex-alcoholic's wife: "He becomes a nervous wreck that drags you along"

The caller in Example (69) is an ex-alcoholic's wife who provides a codependent's perspective on alcoholism: the development of addiction, the suffering of the family and the help provided by an AA (Alcoholics Anonymous) self-help group (Rycroft 1972):

Example (69) *He becomes a nervous wreck that drags you along*

```
1  H: When did the crisis really begin ? When did you see that you had to
2     deal with what's called an alcoholic?
3  C: The exact moment? No, it was a chain of events. Drinking starts with
4     beer and then you add arrack[102] to the beer, or cognac or the devil
5     knows what. And then bottles, and then when the alcoholic can't hide
6     his drinking, it doesn't work anymore. This thing that I can quit
7     whenever I want. "What are you saying? It's all your fault. It's all his
```

fault. It's all their fault." Then, there's the hiding.
H: Was it obvious that your husband drinks? Does he function as a father? As a husband?
C: He functions. He doesn't function. He doesn't function. He can't function. He tries to function. He acts as if he functions. He doesn't function. *He becomes a nervous wreck that drags you along.* I'm sorry I keep concentrating on myself. I've come to talk about the families of alcoholics, not about alcoholics. How we cope with,
H: But first of all we should know about your distress.
C: Yes, yes. They become violent physically and verbally.
H: Did he treat you violently?
C: No, but the children, especially our first-born, because he's the eldest. The others are too young. Violence, mental abuse. It's mental. This beating. It hurts for one moment, and it's over a few minutes later
H: How do you react when you see what your husband is actually doing to him, to his family and to you? What do you do?
C: I responded with my personal madness.
H: What did you do?
C: There was a point when, to stop the violence, both verbal and physical, I used violence myself although the violence was not directed at me. But because I had to protect my child, I used violence. I threatened to do something outrageous. I am really not violent.
H: What does it mean? What did you do?
C: I threatened him with a knife, and I also meant it at that very moment.
H: And he broke down?
C: He didn't, I did, looking for a way out, out of this madness, this lunacy, because I was in such a mental state that out of despair, out of, out of helplessness, simple stark helplessness. This is something that can't be described when you experience it.
H: Yes.
C: For example, what really shocked me terribly, and it made me pick myself up and seek help. I really wanted him to die, not because I hate him, and not because he is bad, and not because he is not a good husband. I joined a support group. At the first meeting I was like a corpse, which means I didn't have an opinion. I didn't, didn't know what I wanted. I didn't want anything, I just wanted, I just wanted nothing. I remember the last time he drank. It was winter and the guy was flat out on the bed. The windows in the house are wide open, yes it was the end of December, and it's raining cats and dogs outside.

50   The bed is soaking wet. The guy is fast asleep, totally unconscious,
51   and it was the first time that I simply let him lie like that and die in
52   the rain, yes, let him catch cold.

Example (69) can be divided into two parts. In lines 1–40, the host attempts to be actively involved in the co-construction of the caller's co-dependent world. In line 40, he relaxes his control, and allows the caller to verbalize how she felt, what she thought and how she coped when she could not take it any longer (lines 41–52). In the first part, the caller rejects the host's authoritative directive to specify a time point indicating when the crisis began (lines 1–2). She prefers to unfold a gradual process depicting how controlled alcohol consumption turns into alcoholism (lines 3–8) (Steinglas 1996).

The process is discursively constructed via generic stories in which lexical items of various alcoholic beverages are embedded. Repetition is summatively intensified by the formulaic phrase "the devil knows what", and repetitive use of "and then", a concatenation of "and", a co-ordinator, and "then", a temporal conjunct. Constructed dialogue in lines 7–8 may be an indication that the caller was reliving the unpleasant experiences when she heard her husband's discursive attempts to deny and conceal his addiction.

In response to the host's chain of questions that attempts to focus on the father's addictive behavior (lines 9–10), the caller gropes for words (lines 11–13), and then produces an organizing figurative conspiracy that summarizes the meaning of codependency: *He becomes a nervous wreck that drags you along* (line 13). It consists of a figurative head noun (i.e., *a nervous wreck*) and a defining figurative relative clause (i.e., *that drags you along*) that refer to the addict and his family, respectively. Thus, the whole noun phrase (i.e., *a nervous wreck that drags you along*) constructs the meaning of codependency, displaying the family's loss of control in the struggle against the addicted husband.

Subsequently, the caller attempts to direct the conversation to a less personal domain, exposing her missionary goal in public (lines 14–15). However, she complies with the host's request to focus on her personal agony (lines 16–17). The family agony is narrated through generic and specific stories showing how, under the influence of alcohol, the friendly, loving, and interesting husband and father is transformed into a violent, abusive man (lines 17 and 20–22).

The caller also emphasizes her personal suffering by syntactic and lexical repetition that foregrounds her emotional (lines 36–39) and cognitive (lines 45–46) state of mind. In her attempt to explain her perspective on her husband's addiction, she gropes for words once again and utters contradictory utterances that may reflect loss of judgment and confusion in the narrated world (lines 45–47). The figurative conspiracy "I did (i.e., break down), looking for a way out" (line 36) comprises two utterances. The main utterance ("I broke down") and a subordinate utterance ("looking for a way out") display interrelated affective and cognitive dimensions of the caller's self.

However, even in moments of crisis, the caller's behavior, displayed in transitive utterances (lines 28–31, and 33), indicates that she attempts to control the situation by defending her eldest son from the violent father, joining a support group and leaving the addict to resume control of his life. The use of a simile (lines 44–45, "I was like a corpse") rather than a metaphoric equation (i.e., "I was a corpse") further supports this interpretation.

Furthermore, we think that the caller's narrative contribution shows that this codependent woman is endowed with an internal locus of control. This trait enables her to break the web of codependent relations, seek help, and ultimately save her husband and her family. In the end, she verbalizes a turning-point story describing how her husband quit drinking (lines 47–52). Tense shift indicates that the caller is probably reliving the experience as she is narrating it (Pillemer, Desrochers, and Ebanks 1998; Schiffrin 1981): "The windows in the house are wide open, yes it was the end of December, and it's raining cats and dogs outside. The bed is soaking wet. The guy is fast asleep, totally unconscious" (lines 48–50). The description of this strong woman provides an interesting example showing the relevance of micro discourse analysis that enabled us to shy away from generalizing universal descriptions and foreground the local particular features of one exceptional woman.

In conclusion, like other lay callers who participated in "Night birds talk", *He becomes a nervous wreck that drags you along* rejects the host's continual attempt to participate in the meaning construction process and instead unfolds a gradual process. This process depicts how controlled alcohol consumption turns into alcoholism. At times, under the weight of her overwhelming emotions, this eloquent caller gropes for words, and then resorts to figurative conspiracies to express

158   *The construction of addictive disorders in discourse*

her lot. The caller's narrative discourse indicates that she is probably endowed with an internal locus of control that enables her to save her husband and her family.

2.6. The anorexic's mother: "We live in daily hell"

Example (70) provides excerpts from an interaction between an anorexic's mother and the host. The anorexic is in her late twenties. In response to the host's chronologically oriented questions, the caller describes how she discovered that her daughter suffers from anorexia nervosa and how she has attempted to help her daughter:

Example (70) *She is condemned to slow and painful extinction and we live in daily hell*

```
1   C: Last year her condition deteriorated. She weighs as I said at the
2      beginning 32 kilos [70 pounds].
3   H: Oh. How tall is she?
4   C: One meter sixty-four [5 feet 5 inches]
5   H: Oh,
6   C: And she lives on about 300 calories a day.
7   H: Oh,
8   C: And it's clear that it's impossible to stay alive,
9   H: A walking skeleton,
10  C: True. Her condition is so critical that the doctor said she can die any
11     day,
12  H: What are you saying?
13  C: Because her life has been in danger for the last six months,
14  H: It's impossible. Forgive me for saying harsh things, but perhaps
15     forced hospitalization is a solution,
16  C: Oh, well, I will also get to it ((strange laughing tone)). Anyway, they
17     think it's a hopeless case. And in addition she is over 18 and
18     hospitalization can't be forced on her,
19  H: Oh, I understand.
20  C: Because there are no closed wards or special hospitals for adult
21     anorexics. They're hospitalized in mental hospitals. And this isn't a
22     suitable place for the treatment of this illness. I simply think that in
23     psychiatric hospitals, as have been told, there are patients whose
24     conditions deteriorate because of what they see around them.
25  H: When you get close to her and say to her: "My child, ((inhales)) you
26     must do something." When you talk to her, how does she respond?
```

27   What does she say?
28 C: Sometimes she's fed up. She's fed up, and she just runs away. She
29   just leaves the house. She doesn't agree to be hospitalized, of her
30   own free will. No way. And if one mentions forced hospitalization,
31   she threatens that she'll commit suicide. I don't know. I'm helpless,
32   and the social worker said to me that it's tragic that in this country
33   they don't know what to do in such severe cases. *She is simply*
34   *condemned,condemned to slow and painful extinction.* Right now, I
35   have to save my daughter's life,
36 H: Which means, if one can't force a treatment on a person in her
37   condition ((sighs)), after all, it's, it's I dare say a mental illness, isn't
38   it?
39 C: Because the doctors don't know in such cases, they simply
40   hospitalize them in mental hospitals, and this isn't the appropriate
41   place because in these hospitals they don't know what to do. I'm
42   begging for help, please help my daughter, because it's hard for me
43   to accept that I'm losing her because there isn't an appropriate
44   facility. *We live in a daily hell* and don't know what else can be done.

Example (70) provides a codependent's description of an anorexic's process of dying. She admits that her daughter suffers from a mental illness, describes her unsuccessful attempts to help her daughter, and appeals to the overhearing audience for help. It is evident that the mother fully understands her daughter's condition (lines 1–2, 6, 8, 10–11, 13, 16–18, and 39–41). In response to the description of the dying daughter, the host produces evaluative and exclamatory utterances (lines 3, 5, 7, 9, 12, and 36–38) that are summatively organized by means of "A walking skeleton" (line 9) – the host's figurative perspective on the process of dying. Subsequently, he also offers a practical solution in lines 14–15 for the problem (i.e., forced hospitalization).

The mother devises different arguments against hospitalization (lines 16–18, 20–24, and 29–31). Thereupon, she concludes with two organizing metaphors presenting her perspective on her daughter's life and her own condition. The daughter *is condemned to slow and painful extinction* (lines 33–34) and *we live in daily hell* (line 44). Like *He becomes a nervous wreck that drags you along* presented in Example (69), *She is condemned to slow and painful extinction* and *we live in daily hell* – the tropes produced by the anorexic's mother – encapsulate the codependent's helplessness vis-à-vis the unfolding tragedy.

We interpret the mother's response to the host's solution as an indication that although she has known for several years how severe the situation is, she chooses not to hospitalize her daughter in a mental health institution, and opts instead for an odd alternative in these dire circumstances: an appeal to the overhearing audience for help (lines 41–43). It is possible that the codependent's refusal to hospitalize her daughter and the arguments she presents to explain her irrational decision are generated by unconscious pathological motives to keep the daughter sick. Perhaps the mother is also motivated by what others would say.

In conclusion, Example (70) provides a codependent's description of an anorexic's process of dying. The mother puts forward different arguments against hospitalization and produces two organizing metaphors presenting her perspective on her daughter's life and her own condition: *She is condemned to slow and painful extinction and we live in daily hell.*

3. Summary

Located in our fourth world, we can now summarize the characteristic features of the gallery of callers presented in Part 3 (Chapters 7 and 8) in our analyses of the "Night birds talk" corpus. Aware of the public nature of the radio program, these callers are oriented toward the overhearing audience. Some callers expect to be rescued, whereas others attempt to advertise services or people who helped them cope with the addiction and resume control of their lives.

It seems plausible to assume that these callers easily gained access to the public arena because their detailed and painful stories of control and loss of control were deemed media-worthy and entertaining by the gatekeeping station operators. The non-addicted callers described in Chapter 7 overpower the panoptical hegemony of the host – the representative of the institution – and manage to use the media to attain their own goals.

What are the characteristic features of the interactions presented in Chapter 8? Four addicted callers and two codependents are given the floor to voice their painful detailed stories and succinct tropes. Addiction- and co-dependency-displaying discursive features identified in these stories constitute the main discovery of the chapter. Our analyses show that other media-worthy callers (e.g., the healer and the gay woman presented in Chapter 7) do not use such resources.

In their attempt to express the inter- and intrapersonal dimensions of their addictive and codependent behaviors in the past, these callers often grope for words and then resort to figurative resources such as organizing tropes and figurative conspiracies as well as addiction-oriented generic stories. Tropes constitute succinct self-portraits of addictive behaviors presenting the meaning of pain, loss of control, the formation process of altered states of consciousness, and the callers' conceptualization of time and abstinence. In addition, the callers we hosted in Chapter 8 used generic stories that depict the routines characteristic of the addicted and codependent.

The figurative forms these callers produce offer a viable perspective on cognitive, affective, and behavioral dimensions of these sufferers. For example, the love addict and compulsive eater conceptualize loss of control in terms of *a snowball* and *a blender*, respectively. The compulsive eater defines the concept of time from the addict's perspective by saying "I have no morning, I have no night." The abstinent gambler summarizes addiction and abstinence by saying *I'm not there today*. In addition, he also defines the meaning of being in an altered state of consciousness as being *in his galaxy*. Another caller, a sex addict, defines the complexities of his past experience through body-internal tropes summatively organized in *but sex has always been something strong inside*.

Perhaps there were other addicted selves tuned in to the program "Night birds talk" the night it was broadcast. The four addicted and abstinent selves that gain access to the program do not deny that they have a problem and are willing to make a public confession. The addicts' tropes can be profitably arranged along a continuum showing where they are. Both *I'm like a blender* and *But sex has always been something strong inside* are still in the world of the addicted as the tenses they use indicate. *Everything simply started snowballing* and *I'm not there today* – the other two – avow that they have managed to or, as in the case of *Everything simply started snowballing*, were forced to quit.

The abstinent alcoholic's wife and the codependent anorexic's mother succinctly define the meaning of codependency by means of figurative constructions when they say *he becomes a nervous wreck that drags you along* and *she is condemned to slow and painful extinction* and *we live in daily hell,* respectively. As we have already shown, the former's narrative and figurative contributions indicate that she must have broken the web of codependent relations, and ultimately saved herself, her husband, and her family. The latter, on the other hand, still lives *in daily hell*, as she confesses.

In Chapters 7 and 8, our decisions to define certain tropes as organizing are based on our analyses of the data. In neither chapter were we able to find evidence of "next-turn validation" (see Chapter 2 and empirical evidence in Chapters 3, 5, and 6 showing how professional participants indicate that they have noticed what the callers say). Does it mean that the host, psychologists, and volunteers who notice the succinct tropes in Chapters 3, 5, and 6 are more attuned to what the callers are saying than the host presented in Chapters 7 and 8? We believe that they are, since the goal of the sites presented in these chapters is not mere presentation of exceptional stories, but also the negotiation of possible solutions to the callers' problems.

In their attempt to verbalize their addictive and codependent behaviors, the callers presented in Chapter 8, like the hotline and cyber sufferers explored in Chapters 5 and 6, also resort to succinct figurative conspiracies that facilitate the encapsulation of their perspectives on the multidimensional complexities of their worlds. Structurally, these tropes comprise two or more evaluative devices intertwined in one structure. Semantically, they conspire to create discursive portraits of the processes of loss and regaining of control. The conspiracies are verbalized at discursive junctions when the callers say that it is very difficult for them to express their affliction.

The repetitive construction of addictive behaviors viewed from the addict's or codependent's perspectives constitutes a third salient discursive feature explored in Chapter 8. This is accomplished via generic stories and pertinent lexical items that are conducive to the construction of the caller's daily routines, altered state of consciousness, and at times their pleas for help addressed to the overhearing community.

Using evaluative questions and comments, the host overlooking the workshop room where these callers are trying to express the meaning of their tortured past experience continually attempts to participate in the process. However, the addicted and codependent selves presented in Chapter 8 and the healer and lesbian in Chapter 7 often reject his panoptical interests and insist on expressing their opinions. Elsewhere we argue (Green and Kupferberg 2000: 318) that "the 'strength' of these lay callers is derived from their urgent need to address the overhearing audience on the one hand, and the lenient attitude of the host who was ready to give in as long as an exceptional story was produced."

Part 4
Redefining the boundaries of problem discourse

Chapter 9
Theoretical conclusions and action-oriented implications

This book set out to explore how participants in problem discourse – sufferers who visit the actual and virtual sites described in this book, and professional, para-professional, and lay others – accomplish complicated discursive undertakings of problem presentation and negotiation of possible solutions. In Chapters 1 and 2, we situate our four-world model of discourse analysis vis-à-vis a contemporary theoretical landscape that lies between Foucault's macro perspective on institutional discourse and micro-analytic conversation analysis.

Accordingly, at the end of Chapter 1, we formulate a general question that is subdivided into two specific questions. The three questions are presented once again below: (1) How is meaning constructed by professional and lay participants visiting the telephone and cyberspace sites explored in this book? (2) To which discursive resources do participants in telephone and cyberspace problem discourse resort in order to accomplish their complicated tasks of problem presentation? (3) To what extent are these resources related to the interactional and meaningful construction of problems and solutions?

In Chapters 3–8, we study participants' world-making, moving between micro and macro levels of analysis and summarizing our findings in interpretive comments. In Chapter 9, Section 1, we answer the questions formulated in Chapter 1, and elaborate on the theoretical implications of our findings. In subsection 1.1, we relate to our first question and suggest that the boundaries we establish in the introductory Chapters 1 and 2 should be redefined. In subsection 1.2, we answer the second and the third questions and focus on the theoretical significance of these answers. First, we elaborate on the summative and multilogical functions of organizing figurative language identified and described in the book. Then, we show that these central tropes are sometimes, but not always, conducive to the interactional and meaningful construction of the problem-causing narrated world as well as future worlds where the problems can be solved.

168 *Theoretical conclusions and action-oriented implications*

In subsection 1.2, we also relate to the theoretical implications of the connection between narrative discourse, organizing figurative language and global coherence presented in Chapter 2 and repeatedly referred to and elaborated upon in the chapters of the book. Finally, we explain why some, but not all of the troubled selves presented in this book, are able to accomplish trans-world journeys into a better future in their attempt to solve the problems of the painful past. In Section 2, we examine the practical implications of these theoretical findings for problem discourse with examples from the clinical and educational settings.

1. Theoretical conclusions: Global figurative coherence in a multilogue

1.1. Professional and lay voices reshape the boundaries of problem discourse

Our analyses of radio, hotline, and cyber problem discourse provide us with empirical evidence that enables us to relate to the first question. In Chapters 3 and 4, we focus on individuals seeking help in a radio program open to the overhearing audience. We discover that only media-worthy callers such as *Amputating the cancerous leg, I was really like a mother to him, In a big bang* and *I don't know how to get close to my middle son* are approved by the radio gatekeepers and are allowed to present their troubled narrative and figurative contributions. We define media-worthiness as a gift comprising assertiveness, readiness to argue with the media representatives, and good story-telling skills including the ability to focus on the essence of the problem by means of figurative resources.

Always under the panoptical institutional eye, and often constrained by time limitations characteristic of radio programs, these callers manage to produce story-internal organizing tropes – summative versions of the narrated worlds. *Amputating the cancerous leg* and *I was really like a mother to him* make their self-presentations in the reception phase of the call. The former feels that it is right to do so, whereas the latter is instructed to do so by the collaborative host. The psychologists notice the callers' succinct self-portraits and make efficient therapeutic use of them. Thus, these tropes enhance the interactional negotiation of effective solutions that can be implemented by the callers in the future.

As for *In a big bang* and *I don't know how to get close to my middle son* – the externally-directed callers presented in Chapter 4 – in the time-bounded and overhearing-audience oriented program, the psychologists cannot or do not want to explore the complexities of the callers' past experience. Instead they opt for instant future-oriented solutions that enable them to display their knowledge, but are not anchored in the troubled past worlds that the callers present.

Other suffering souls like *Life is like a jail* and "One can talk about all kinds of subjects" have evidently entered the wrong site. In the public arena of radio discourse whose goal is the entertainment of the overhearing audience rather than healing, their tedious and incoherent self-constructions are rejected by the media representatives, who banish them in an eager quest for more rating-worthy callers. Finally, "This puzzle – I have to find the missing part" does not manage to solve her problems for other reasons that illuminate and reinforce the successes of *Amputating the cancerous leg*, and *I was really like a mother to him*. She wastes precious time on complimenting the media representatives and therefore fails to present her own problem in the reception phase.

These effective and ineffective interactions show that radio problem discourse is multilogical – a multiparticipant situation in which the overhearing audience, the unseen participant, rather than the welfare of the callers is constantly on the minds of the institutional representatives. At some discursive junctions, these gatekeepers relax the tight inspection of the workshop rooms and let the callers' take over. For example, although *Amputating the cancerous leg*'s determined request to present her self via a planned poetic text undermines the host's authority, he finally complies with it. Another dramatic moment when the clear boundaries between the institution and the lay callers are blurred takes place when *In a big bang* is instructed by the authoritative male psychologist to hate her deceased mother. This move creates an unprecedented media drama in which the host and the female psychologist desert their posts at the panoptical tower, and enter the more democratic workshop room in order to support the caller who was obliged to confront the domineering psychologist.

In Part 3, we analyze "Night birds talk" – a radio program that focuses on the narration of exceptional stories – and identify a multifarious gallery of troubled lay selves who, once they are approved by the gatekeeping operators, undermine the host's efforts to participate in the construction of their idiosyncratic past experience and manage to use the media for their own ends.

The healer and the lesbian attempt to advertise their selves, displaying self-portraits of people in control. The healer positions himself among other professionals, such as the radio psychologists, as a person who does not seek help, but can provide help to the troubled others. In this respect, he is an exception in the gallery of the 21 sufferers presented in this book. Likewise, motivated by urgent needs to address the overhearing audience, the addicted and codependent selves presented in Chapter 8 often reject the host's panoptical moves and signal their pressing need to construct their self-perceived portraits. As they talk, these callers present glimpses of their altered states of consciousness and their conceptualization of time and withdrawal processes – individual expressions of their troubled experience that are often alien to the host's discursive agenda.

The three hotline callers presented in Chapter 5 are not obliged to undergo any kind of inspection. They easily gain access to the hotline site where their story-internal past-building organizing tropes that are noticed by the volunteers enhance the interactional negotiation of solutions. However, in the case of *Am I their floor rag?* the presence of her mother – an unexpected overhearing visitor – undermines the caller's credibility and obliges the volunteer to assume the role of a judge. The cyber site presented in Chapter 6 is the most democratic, albeit insecure, site where anything can be said. Accordingly, the volunteers function as gatekeepers in an attempt to prevent the abuse of sufferers' by irresponsible anonymous answerers.

We see, then, that the speech events presented in Chapters 3, 4, 7, and 8, and in the hotline cyber discourse in Chapter 6, the negotiation of problems is shaped, to some extent, by the overhearing or overreading communities. These unseen participants influence the discursive processes of meaning making. In fact, these speech events constitute multilogues of voices that are sometimes in conflict and sometimes work in tandem, but are always tuned to the unseen others. At times, we can even say that the boundaries between the panoptical institution and the workshop rooms are suddenly blurred, and then redefined when professional and lay participants change their positioning due to unexpected emerging circumstances.

Theoretical conclusions: Global figurative coherence in a multilogue   171

In view of the determination and ability of some troubled selves to present themselves despite the limitations characteristic of the sites they visit – an ability we dub media-worthiness – we divide the telephone and cyber selves we hosted in this book into three groups: The presenters and negotiators (PN), the presenters (P), and the non-presenters and non-negotiators (NPNN). The first group comprises media-worthy callers who, having gained access to a site, manage to accomplish the tasks of problem presentation and negotiation. The second group comprises sufferers who only succeed in presenting their problem, but do not fulfill the second task of problem negotiation. The third group comprises selves that do not accomplish either of the tasks.

The groups are presented below. Each includes the figurative or non-figurative titles given to the troubled selves. Out of the 21 callers and digital writers presented in this book, eight manage to present and negotiate their problems. The presenters and negotiators (PN) are as follows: *Amputating the cancerous leg, I was really like a mother to him, In a big bang, I don't know how to get close to my middle son, Am I their floor rag?, The lion and the snake, My life is a story in a book* and *Why not be ahead of my time?*

Nine callers succeed in presenting themselves, but do not carry out the second task. *Life is like a jail* is banished from the interaction by the institutional representatives, while the others (i.e., *I produce a new mechanism that controls the addictive behavior, That person didn't have horns and didn't have a beard, Everything simply started snowballing, I'm like a blender, But sex was always something strong inside, I'm not there today, He becomes a nervous wreck that drags you along* and *She is condemned to slow extinction and we live in a daily hell*) participate in a program that focuses mainly on problem presentation. Therefore, they are not allowed to negotiate possible solutions.

Four sufferers do not manage to accomplish any of the tasks. The non-presenters and non-negotiators (NPNN) are as follows: "This puzzle – I have to find the missing part", "One can talk about all kinds of subjects", "Like you're the world's only sucker" and "I was the best source of light on the market". The first and the second do not present their problems coherently at the beginning of the call. Therefore, even if their problems are noticed by the psychologists, the latter have no time to probe these problems any further. The third and the fourth suf-

1.2. Figurative trans-world journeys

In this subsection, we will answer the second and third research questions that we formulated in Chapter 1, and elaborate on the significance of our findings. The analyses in Chapters 3–8 provide us with answers to the questions. They show that story-internal figurative language has summative and multilogical functions that – in some cases but not all, as we have shown in 1.1 – enhance interactional and multiactional communication. In other words, some troubled callers and digital writers manage to express the meaning of their experience via detailed personal stories as well as succinct story-internal organizing figurative constructions. These succinct formats are sometimes noticed by other participants, who relate to them and use them interactionally while they are accomplishing the second discursive task of problem talk: problem negotiation.

We also find out that the organizing tropes gleaned from our corpora display gender issues, some of which were probably on the mind of the troubled selves' when they entered the problem talk sites, and others that we uncover in our interpretive comments. Are organizing tropes indicative of gender differences? Do men and women produce different organizing tropes? Following our analyses, we put forward the following claim. Organizing tropes do construct various dimensions of troubled men and women including conscious and unconscious productions related to their femininity or masculinity. However, these are intermingled with other dimensions of the complex human self and cannot be explored in isolation. This claim is supported by current scholarship (Bing and Bergvall 1998; Johnson 1997) that emphasizes that research should move beyond binary thinking on gender differences and attempt to focus on the differences gender makes rather than on gender differences (Johnson 1997, citing Cameron 1992). Future research could further explore this issue.

Central figurative constructions perform several communicative tasks. First, they summarize the gist of other self-disclosing non-figurative evaluative resources that display various dimensions of the narrated experience. From the callers' point of view, organizing figurative language, then, like tense shift and constructed dialogue, functions as an evaluative device that shortens the distance between the narrated world and the present. In the drama of *Am I their floor rag?*, more than in any other speech event presented in the book, the past actually merges with the present when the family dynamics and conflicts enacted on the air are summarized by means of an organizing trope.

Moreover, producing both detailed personal stories and summative story-internal organizing tropes, the callers and digital writers present two salient versions of their troubled self to other participants in the present world of the ongoing discussion. In this way, they often prevail over the limitations characteristic of this speech situation, and sometimes enhance the multi-actional negotiations of effective solutions when other participants make use of the callers' organizing tropes. We define organizing tropes in relation to the personal story in which they occur as story-internal elements that summarize other evaluative resources and constitute succinct versions of emotional, cognitive, sociocultural, and behavioral dimensions of the troubled self.

Our analysis also shows that certain organizing tropes that we call "figurative conspiracies" share structural, discursive, and psychological complexity. Structurally, they comprise two or more self-displaying evaluative devices interwoven in the same utterance or digital sentence. From discursive and psychological points of view, conspiracies are produced at those junctions where the narration of the sufferers' problem reaches an emotional climax and when very significant or dramatic themes are unfolded.

Grounded in the empirical evidence presented, analyzed, and interpreted in this book, we claim that there are discursive junctions when troubled participants in problem discourse, and probably in any kind of talk, are obliged to use the ultimate and possibly the most succinct discursive resources at their disposal to emphasize and clarify their point. Our book provides examples showing that figurative conspiracies are often produced at these points. Examining *Am I their floor rag?* again, we see that it consists of two evaluative devices: a trope and a rhetorical question. The trope refers to biological, emotional, and interpersonal dimensions of the tortured young woman. The rhetorical question in which the trope is embedded constructs the caller's determination not to put up with the situation. Moreover, the conspiracy is produced at a very crucial discursive junction after the caller's mother has produced a contrastive narrative version, and the caller hastens to convince the volunteer that her own version is more reliable than her mother's.

Everything simply started snowballing constitutes another example. She produces a conspiracy consisting of two evaluative devices that conspire to create a discursive portrait of loss of control, but each evaluative device illuminates different dimensions of the caller's addictive behavior and state of mind. In this conspiracy, figurative language depicts an undefined movement of a non-human external force, and the indefinite pronoun indicates a low level of agency.

A third example is provided by *He becomes a nervous wreck that drags you along*. Asked by the host to describe how her husband functions as a spouse and a father, she gropes for words and then produces her figurative definition of codependency. Finally, *Why not be ahead of my time?* produces this figurative construction when he is struggling with complex definitions of the meaning of life, the very cognitive task that may have triggered suicidal thoughts in his adolescent mind in the first place.

How can we explain the discursive phenomenon we entitled figurative conspiracies? On the basis of the evidence presented in this book, we claim that the more intense the caller's emotional state is, and the more urgent he or she perceives the situation, the more complex the figurative language becomes. Urgency and emotional intensity reach their climax in the dramas unfolded in Chapters 5, 6, and 8. In these telephone and digital multilogues, the sufferers resort to figurative conspiracies to externalize and co-construct psychological complexity.

The data-driven claim that is put forward in the present book is different from the theory-driven hypotheses formulated in experimental psycholinguistic studies conducted in the 1960s to test the connection between transformational complexity and processing (Scovel 1998). As we repeatedly emphasize in the course of this book, we are first and foremost attuned to how participants in discourse actually make use of the discursive resources at their disposal. Our current research (Green and Kupferberg in preparation) provides additional enlightening empirical evidence that points to a possible link between discursive and psychological complexity.

The examples presented in our book, then, reveal a significant aspect of problem discourse: the centrality of organizing tropes – discursive vehicles that connect the world of the present with the narrated past. These tropes also constitute links connecting the present world with a future world in which the insights and awareness gained in the present can be tested in vivo.

For example, the psychologist explains to *Amputating the cancerous leg* that she is healthy and her pain is "a phantom pain" that she

Theoretical conclusions: Global figurative coherence in a multilogue 175

will not feel in a future world after her divorce. Similarly, the psychologist minimizes the responsibility and guilt displayed in *I was really like a mother to him* by offering a healthier figurative perspective on the caller's narrated world that she can adopt in the future: *You were to some extent like a mother to him*. The volunteer's figurative answer to *Am I their floor rag?* also relates to a future world where *a clean-up job is needed*.

The only way to be released from the jaws of life offers a unique example where a virtual rescue team and a teenager set out to discuss the latter's suicidal intentions figuratively and multi-actionally, and eventually co-construct a different perspective on life. Tropes mark discursive junctions, which show how the participants modified the adolescent's figurative title, *Why not be ahead of my time?* until he admits that he has changed his perspective.

The co-construction of meaning accomplished by the lay and professional participants we host in this book can be accounted for by the four-world model we presented in Chapter 2. In the context of naturally occurring problem discourse – the empirical evidence presented in this book – the following key constructs are defined and interrelated within the boundaries of the model: personal stories, organizing tropes, and global coherence. We regard these constructs as central because they encapsulate the essence of the book that shows that problem discourse is often rich in personal stories and organizing tropes. The latter are related to personal stories since they constitute succinct versions thereof. These discursive vehicles may also enhance global coherence because they lubricate the multi-actional discussion in the present moment, facilitate the reconstruction of the narrated past world within the ongoing present, and carry it further on into a future of possibilities.

There are two sufferers whose figurative language constitutes apparent exceptions that actually illuminate the figurative phenomena described in this book. "Like you're the world's only sucker" and "I was the best source of light on the market" refuse to contextualize their problems in narrative formats. In the case of "Like you're the world's only sucker" who verbalizes her troubles on the phone, we make an attempt to define her gender and emotional state of mind. As for "I was the best source of light on the market", the digital writer, we define three possible selves that could be related to this cyber sufferer. This enigmatic plural self renders the answerers' task practically impossible. Therefore, the virtual discussion wanders about aimlessly without any clear discursive goals or results.

There is one example in the book that suggests that sometimes the engine of problem discussions should be non-figurative. The volunteer's response to the suicidal adolescent in Chapter 6 shows that the volunteer understands that the time has come to move the discussion to more practical grounds of coping and therefore he resorts to the non-figurative language of directives. This example illustrates that problems are often presented via tropes, but to verbalize solutions, especially in cases of emergency, professionals who are constrained by time limits opt for non-figurative and unambiguous language.

2. Action-oriented implications

The transition from micro- to macro-worlds is a circular process in an action-oriented book such as ours where the findings are subsequently implemented in practice. The time has come to list the practical implications gleaned from our interpretive analyses of problem discourse and answer another question that has been implicit in the pages of this book: Is telephone and digital problem discourse conducive to problem solving?

Analyses of the multilogues presented in this book show that the extent to which professional and lay voices and teams of voices are able to help the sufferers who have already gained access to the site is limited because there is no time to open the world-building figurative constructions, unearth their unconscious layers and co-construct global coherence.

However, the insights gained from the interactions presented in the chapters of this book can be applied in order to enhance telephone, cyber and psychotherapeutic problem discourse. Especially pertinent is the discovery that tropes may constitute discursive vehicles that shorten processes and make them more effective. Below we list several recommendations for professional and lay participants in problem discourse, but we also believe that these can enhance other institutional and non-institutional interactions and multi-actions.

Professionals and para-professionals should encourage sufferers to package their problems in narrative formats and organizing resources.

They should be attuned to these evaluative devices – discursive resources that can provide invaluable information about the narrators' self.In addition, they should make use of the narrators' figurative contributions in their responses. If constrained by time, professionals should ask narrators to place succinct and figurative versions of their troubled self on the negotiating table as soon as possible.

We will briefly present two examples that show how the organizing tropes produced by clients in the clinical setting were conducive to therapeutic processes. The selected figurative constructions were verbalized within a narrative format of turning-point moments. The first client is a 24-year-old homosexual, an outstanding, intelligent, and articulate university student. He decided to come out of the closet and disclose his sexual orientation to his parents.

Having narrated how he made this disclosure to his father, the young man summatively organized the experience in the following words: "When I told my father, he accepted it and that night there was a turning point concerning my self image. *For the first time, I felt I was one piece. My hands and my legs were connected to my body. Before that night, I had been like a Picasso painting.* Suddenly there was a feeling of coherence". The figurative language produced by the young man was noticed by the therapist. After the young man felt he was connected to himself, the goal of therapy was to help him establish a mature and stable relationship with a male friend.

Another client is a 26-year-old student who had experienced traumas and losses in childhood, had become addicted to marijuana, and was a frequent abuser (i.e., used the drug several times a day). As an adult, he suffered from adaptation problems in various domains of life (e.g., occupation, university studies, and family). He also produced an organizing trope that encapsulated an emotional encounter with a significant family member: "When I don't smoke, I am exposed to everything. After I used marijuana, *I had a protective filter. I was protected from the outside and the inside.*" Following this turning point, therapy focused on the question of whether the young man could go on living without using a fragile artificial filter. The two examples show how story-internal organizing tropes exposed the problem and provided the therapist with a key for the ensuing therapeutic interventions.

Our discoveries of the expressive and dialogical functions of tropes in Chapter 3 and the contribution of titles to the interactions in Chapter

4 inspired us to design face-to-face and cyber programs for interpersonal communication in a college of education (Kupferberg in press; Kupferberg and Ben-Peretz 2004; Kupferberg and Gilat 2002). The programs are based on the following assumption: Student teachers' professional development from novicehood to professionalism often takes place at turning-point moments (Denzin 1999) whose significance can be co-constructed with more experienced others. Accordingly, we designed models of face-to-face and cyber communication that were adapted to teacher education.

The face-to-face and cyber models comprise the following components: (1) Student teachers are encouraged to provide a title to their problems. (2) Students unfold their problems. (3) Participants (i.e., student teachers and professional teachers) negotiate the meaning of the problems. (4) Participants focus on the contribution of the interaction. Analyses of the corpora (Kupferberg in press; Kupferberg and Ben-Peretz 2004; Kupferberg and Gilat 2002) show that face-to-face and cyber interactions that were based on the model were conducive to the construction of insights, awareness, behavioral change and professional development.

Epilogue

The 21 troubled selves we hosted in this book were eager to air their troubles in a problem-discussion site, but gaining access to such sites was quite a demanding task, especially in the case of sufferers who chose the therapy-style talk shows. Only media-worthy callers were approved by the radio gatekeepers who seemed determined to satisfy the insatiable appetite of the sensation-seeking audience at home with breathtaking stories.

What motivated lay callers to make persistent efforts to be on the air in reality radio programs, aware of the fact that time limit might undermine the efficiency and the depth of the therapy-like interactions (Raviv and Abuhav 2003) and that they would be expected to publicize their most intimate secrets (Macdonald 2003)? It is possible that they contacted these sites in order to seek help. Perhaps they had other motives, such as "remedying misleading stereotypes and correcting the stigma attached to marginalized groups; achieving the legendary '15 minutes of fame'; taking revenge; and seeking promotion for some achievement that they wanted to sell" (Priest 1995, as cited in Macdonald 2003: 87). The hotline callers presented in our book reached the telephone and cyber sites with no difficulty. There, their troubled world was readily explored by the para-professional volunteers who attempted to provide help and prevented the abuse of cyber sufferers' by irresponsible anonymous answerers.

Our analyses show that therapeutic achievement was almost impossible in the sites visited in this book. At best, callers and cyber sufferers were provided with some behavioral instructions and awareness raising advice. However, we know that in their attempts to make sense of their troubled world, the selves we hosted provided us with *a real treasure* comprising *figurative gems* such as organizing tropes, figurative conspiracies and clusters of tropes that reflected and constructed cognitive and emotional processes and lubricated the multilogue. Having shown how effective these tropes are, we hope that their functions will be further explored in naturally occurring discourse in domains where problems are negotiated (e.g., law, medicine, social work, politics, and education).

Epilogue

Other institutional eyes that have been vigilant throughout the chapters of this book are ours. Located in the fourth world proposed by us, we constantly related to the participants' discursive undertakings from our perspective – one stance out of many possible others that can explore problem discourse. We are hopeful that additional scholarly eyes will examine our interpretive interface from different theoretical and methodological stances and will shed more light on problem discourse in various institutional and non-institutional settings and on organizing figurative phenomena – the heart of the multilogue.

Notes

1. The terms *self* and *identity* are interconnected in Western culture (Edgar and Sedgwick 2003: 346–350). Following Rowan and Cooper (1999), Sehulster (2001), and Duranti (2001), we use the term *self* as a generic term that comprises the social interpersonal term *identity* – "or membership in one or more social groups or categories" (Duranti 2001: 106), as well as the intrapersonal conscious and unconscious dimensions. Thus self is "the composite of all these identities and roles, as well as perhaps that which holds the package together and prevents fragmentation" (Sehulster 2001: 201).
2. In this preliminary section of the book where we introduce human beings who attempt to solve their problems in actual and virtual sites, we use the more general modifier *contemporary* rather than *postmodern*. See Section 2 of this chapter and footnotes 12 and 14.
3. Gubrium and Holstein (2001) describe various institutional sites. Other studies focus on clinical therapy (Anderson 1997; Buttny and Jensen 1995; Frie 2003; Rowan and Cooper 1999; White and Epston 1990), counseling (Silverman 1997), support groups (Denzin 1993), hotline (Gilat, Lobel, and Gil 1998; Kupferberg, Green, and Gilat 2002; Latzer and Gilat 2000), radio problem discourse (Green and Kupferberg 2000; Kupferberg and Green 1998, 2003; Raviv and Abuhav 2003), confession (Shuy 1998), and cyberspace (Gackenbach 1998; Wallace 1999). Raviv and Abuhav (2003) provide an overview of historical and current ethical aspects related to the psychologizing of the media.
4. The troubled selves described and interpreted in this book are given names that they themselves produce. Some of the names are figurative. See "List of the troubled selves" at the front of this book.
5. Throughout this book, we show that the building blocks of problem discourse are different narrative genres.
6. The book is based on several studies conducted between 1995 and 2002 in which the authors explored hotline, radio, and cyber problem discourse. Partial findings of these studies were published in journals (Green and Kupferberg 2000; Kupferberg and Green 1998, 2003; Kupferberg, Green, and Gilat 2002).
7. Following Labov and Fanshel (1977), Buttny and Jensen (1995) propose the term *problem-talk* for talk where lay participants communicate with psychologists about their problems. Another commonly used term is *troubles talk* (ten Have 2001). In this book the terms *problem*

discourse and *problem talk* are used interchangeably when reference is made to spoken telephone interactions and written cyber interactions.

8. Following Drew and Heritage (1992), several publications focused on institutional discourse. See Gubrium and Holstein (2001), Gunnarsson, Linell, and Nordberg (1997), Heritage (1997), and Sarangi and Roberts (1999a).

9. In radio and cyber problem discourse, there are other powerful, albeit unseen participants. These are the overhearing audience and the virtual community.

10. We avoided the more idiomatic English phrases "pluck up" or "muster one's courage" and provided the literal translation of what the boy said.

11. Smith (1997) lists four recurring approaches in the history of thought on meaning: (1) The referential approach, which identifies what an expression refers to in context; (2) The mentalist approach, which identifies meaning with mental contents such as images, concepts and prepositional contents; (3) The contextualist approach, which locates the search for meaning in complex relations between the language use and the language user's context; (4) The dissolutionist approach, which shows that meanings do not exist.

12. Following Hartley (2002), we distinguish between the terms *modernity/postmodernity* and *modernism/postmodernism*. Like *antiquity*, the former terms refer to social epochs that took place in human history, whereas the latter are theoretical concepts that attempt to define the major characteristics of these epochs.

13. A paradigm is a collection of ideas that guide scientific inquiry. Paradigm shifts, according to Kuhn (1970), take place in abrupt revolutions rather than in gradual processes of transformation.

14. Postmodernism is defined in founding texts produced in a variety of domains ranging from philosophy, sociology, history, psychology, and literature to art history, architecture, legal studies, and geography (Taylor and Winquist 1998). For postmodern approaches to problem discourse see Anderson (1997), Frie (2003), and Rowan and Cooper (1999). For overviews of the postmodern self, see Holstein and Gubrium (2000) and Rowan and Cooper (1999).

15. It is not easy to define the term *discourse* because there are many approaches to discourse as the following publications show: Jaworski and Coupland (1999), Schiffrin (1994), Schiffrin, Tannen, and Hamilton (2001) and van Dijk (1997). Schiffrin (1994) distinguishes between structural and functional approaches to language and discourse. See also Cumming and Ono (1997). The structural approaches describe language as a closed system that is not related to the context in which

it functions, but whose components (e.g., syntax, morphology, semantics, and phonology) are interrelated. Functional approaches to language that take context into consideration deal with discourse, not with language as a closed system.

16. For a description of the narrative turn in social science, see Chamberlayne, Bornat, and Wengraf (2000).
17. *Talk at Work* is the title of Drew and Heritage's (1992) influential book on institutional discourse.
18. See Hutton (1988) for an overview of Foucault's works. Following Drew and Heritage (1992), there have been several publications that have focused on institutional talk from a conversation analytic perspective. Below we list some of them: Gubrium and Holstein (2001), Gunnarsson, Linell, and Nordberg (1997), Hester and Francis (2000), Sarangi and Roberts (1999a) and Thornborrow (2002).
19. See Martin, Gutman, and Hutton (1988). The interview was conducted in a faculty seminar on "technologies of the self" presented at the University of Vermont in the fall of 1982.
20. The panopticon was designed by Jeremy Bentham (1748–1832), an English philosopher, economist, and theoretical jurist.
21. See Fairclough and Wodak's (1997), Thornborrow's (2002) and van Dijk's (2001) overviews of CDA and other social theories such as those of Habermas, Bourdieu, and Giddens, which inspired CDA.
22. See Holstein and Gubrium (1994) and Holstein and Gubrium (2000). Phenomenology is based on the assumption that "phenomena are the building blocks of human science and the basis for all knowledge" (Moustakas 1994). Ethnomethodology was pioneered by Garfinkel (1967), a student and critic of Parsons (1951), who advanced a model of "social order built on the contingent, embodied, ongoing, interpretive work of ordinary members of society" (Holstein and Gubrium 2000: 87). Garfinkel's model does not assume the existence of a prescribed social order, but examines how it is constructed in real-time interaction. Following in Garfinkel's footsteps and focusing primarily on naturally occurring interactional discourse, sociologists like Sacks (1992) and Sacks, Schegloff, and Jefferson (1974) set out to explore how social order is actually unfolded in moment-by-moment conversational interaction. For overviews, see Lynch (2000) and Psathas (1995).
23. Thornborrow (2002) emphasizes that the very term *institutional talk* is problematic because much of the talk that takes place in institutional settings is often a continuation of conversation in ordinary life.
24. The following sources relate to narrative genres in problem discourse: Anderson (1997), Brockmeier and Carbaugh (2001), Ferrara (1994),

Green and Kupferberg (2000), Kupferberg and Ben-Peretz (2004), Kupferberg and Gilat (2002), Kupferberg and Green (1998, 2003) and Kupferberg, Green, and Gilat (2002).
25. The following scholars advocate the construction of an interface between micro- and macro-analyses: Bamberg (2001), Gee (1999), Heller (2001), Holstein and Gubrium (2000), Linell (1998), Miller (1997), Scollon and Scollon (2001), Thornborrow (2002), and van Dijk (2001).
26. "A linguistic loom" (Hoffman 1997) and "a workshop room" are constructivist metaphors (Spivey 1997). The idea that language is a sociocultural tool was initiated in Vygotsky's work (1978, 1986), elaborated on in Wertsch (1998) and adopted by functional discourse analysts whose perspectives are sociological, anthropological, and psychological (Edwards 1997; Schegloff, Ochs, and Thompson 1996).
27. For overviews that describe the relationship between narrative discourse and self-construction, see Brockmeier and Carbaugh (2001) and Holstein and Gubrium (2000).
28. Psathas (1995) provides an overview of telephone interactions.
29. The example is taken from our radio corpus presented in Chapter 2.
30. In Chapter 1 we emphasize that ICA does not advocate an a priori approach that views every institutional interaction as asymmetrical. It emphasizes that only turn-by-turn micro-analysis can show what actually takes place in the interaction (Drew and Sorjonen 1997; Thornborrow 2002). These sources also emphasize that the boundaries between talk at work and non-institutional discourse are not always clear and that participants sometimes cross the boundaries.
31. Brockmeier (2001) uses the term *gestalt* to describe the complexity of narrative discourse. As for the constructivist component apparent in this view, see Bamberg (1997d) and Bruner (1986, 1990).
32. Bruner (1986, 2001) relates to Goodman's (1984) idea of world-making.
33. See our analyses in Chapters 3–8. See also Cortazzi (1993) and Cortazzi and Jin (2000).
34. A detailed analysis of the interaction is presented in Chapter 3.
35. This definition of the relationship between discourse and context is bidirectional. Foucault's unidirectional definition views the voices of participants in problem discourse as being objectified by the powerful and dominating technologies of the self.
36. Georgakopoulou and Goutsos (2000) offer a critical overview beyond genre, but argue that the term is "useful at describing contextual fit of texts" (ibid.: 77).
37. Hymes (1972) lists features of context that researchers should relate to

in their analyses: setting, scene, participants, ends, act sequence, key, instrumentalities, norms of interaction, and genre.
38. Breuer and Freud as cited in Berman (2002: 10) claim that the term was coined by Anna O., Breuer's patient.
39. For an overview of the concept of time in Western civilization and how it is related to narrative discourse, see Brockmeier (2000, 2001).
40. Among these are Adler (1929), Erikson (1964), Fromm (1962), Hartmann (1964), Horney (1939), Kernberg (1980), Kohut (1964), and Lacan (1988). Lacan's theory of speech and language in psychoanalysis is a meeting point between linguistics, philosophy, and psychoanalysis (Evans 1996).
41. See overview in Bublitz (1999). *Cohesion* is a text-dependent concept, first defined by Halliday and Hasan (1976) and accepted by the scholarly community as a well-defined and useful term beyond the sentence boundary.
42. For overviews of the connection between storytelling and storage in autobiographical memory, see Conway and Rubin (1993), Nelson (1993), Schank and Abelson (1995), Thompson et al. (1998) and Wyer (1995).
43. Brockmeier and Carbaugh (2001) provide a multidisciplinary overview of the meaning of the narrative turn. Brockmeier and Harré (2001) emphasize that this turn took place in the 1980s in various disciplines, and list the names of scholars associated with it: Bakhtin (1981, 1986), Bauman (1986), Britton and Pellegrini (1990), Bruner (1986, 1990), Mitchell (1981), Nelson (1989), Ricœur (1981, 1984, 1985, 1991), Sarbin (1986), and Schafer (1989).
44. The following sources relate to narrative genres in problem discourse: Anderson (1997), Brockmeier and Carbaugh (2001), and Lieblich, Tuval-Mashiach, and Zilber (1998). Other sources relate to the contribution of tropes to problem discourse: McMullen (1996), McMullen and Conway (1994, 1996), and Siegleman (1990). Barker (1996) and Ferrara (1994) discuss both, but do not focus on the connection between the two.
45. A special issue of *The Journal of Narrative and Life History*, edited by Bamberg (1997a), offers a critical overview of Labov's contribution. See also Cortazzi and Jin 2000.
46. Labov's structural elements were defined on the basis of data elicited in interviews. In naturally occurring problem discourse, participants often co-construct some of the components as our analyses in Chapters 3–8 show.
47. The data of Capps and Ochs (1995) comprise the recording of dinnertime interactions and interviews of agoraphobic sufferers. The authors

186 Notes

do not use the term *evaluative devices* but their study focuses on self-revealing grammatical structures.
48. For a different approach and different classifications of evaluative devices, see Segal (2001). Cortazzi and Jin's (2000) critical overview of the Labovian evaluation emphasizes that Labov focused on the narrator's evaluation *in* the narrative text. Labov (1972) did not relate to the response of the audience (i.e., *evaluation of the narrative)* nor did Labov relate to the researcher's comments (i.e., *evaluation through the narrative*). Our four-world model presented below captures these distinctions.
49. Fleischman (1990) distinguishes between *realis* or the discourse of experience, grammaticalized via present and past tenses, *and irrealis*, or the discourse of the unreal and hypothetical which is grammaticalized via future tense, conditionals, wish and negative forms, etc.
50. Our definition of world-making is inspired by Bamberg (1997b), Brockmeier (2001), Bruner (1986, 2001), Goodman (1984), and Ochs (1994). Bamberg's (1997b) three-level analysis of narrative positioning was particularly useful. We prefer to use the term *world* rather than *level* because the former term displays and constructs the multidimensional and multidirectional complexities of problem discourse. Our four-world model consists of the participants' present, past, and future worlds and the researchers' world. Brockmeier (2001), Bruner (2001), Chafe (1994), Harré (1996), and Ochs (1994) also discuss the meaning of the present and its relationship to the past and the future. Ochs cites Heidegger (1962) and Ricœur (1984, 1985, 1991), who indicate that "anticipation of the future drives human thoughts and action" (Ochs 1994: 125).
51. Since antiquity, philosophers have shown that time is an elusive concept (Brockmeier 2000, 2001; Klein 1994;). Following Brockmeier (2000, 2001) and Ricœur (1984, 1985, 1991), we argue that narrative time constructed linguistically in problem discourse differs from chronological time. Brockmeier (2000, 2001), Comrie (1976, 1985), Klein (1994), and Kupferberg (1999) focus on how language encodes time.
52. The complete analysis is presented in Chapter 4.
53. The complete analysis is presented in Chapter 8.
54. Positioning was first defined in Davies and Harré (1990). See overview in Harré and Langenhove (1999).
55. In light of the abundance of theories that attempt to explain trope interpretation, Gibbs (2001) emphasizes that "figurative language scholars have always experienced an identity crisis" (ibid.: 317). To solve the crisis of identity, Leezenberg (2001) proposes formulating a theory of

figurative language that is sensitive to contextual factors. Although Leezenberg emphasizes the preeminence of context and language use, his approach to figurative language is grounded in an abstract domain where humans are mere *cognitive agents* whose discourse consists of invented declarative sentences in possible or decontextualized contexts.

56. See critical overview in Leezenberg (2001).
57. Conceptual metaphors are often indicated by upper-case italicized small capitals.
58. In conversations conducted in July, 2002, the hosts participating in the programs analyzed in this book also admitted that they were constantly aware of the overhearing audience and oriented themselves to it.
59. The terms *reception* and *dismissal* are adopted from Liddicoat et al. (1994). The term *problem presentation* is taken from Buttny and Jensen's (1995) discussion of therapeutic discourse in the clinical setting. Time means of the calls and the three phases were computed: a call lasts 16 minutes, the reception phase – 5 minutes, the problem discussion – 10.5 minutes and the dismissal phase – 30 seconds.
60. See overview of cyberspace discourse (Crystal 2001) and Herring (2001). Gackenbach (1998), Raviv and Abuhav (2003), and Wallace (1999) explore cyber psychology.
61. We prefer to use the *term multilogue*, rather *than dialogue* because there are more than two participants.
62. Crystal prefers to use the term *chatgroup* as "a generic term for any multi-participant electronic discourse, whether in real time or not" (Crystal 2001: 129), including forums.
63. For a comparison between phenomenology and hermeneutics see Shlaski and Arieli (2001). Holstein and Gubrium (1994) and Gubrium and Holstein (2000) define the phenomenological sources of conversation analysis. In their quest for meaning, phenomenologists emphasize that "first is experience; language and thought follow" (Pinar et al. 2000: 404), whereas conversation analysts focus on language.
64. Chafe (1994: 29) describes how what is said is located in peripheral consciousness, a "periphery of semiactive information that provides context for the locus of ongoing, constantly changing discourse" and then this *cotext* is relocated and used again.
65. Some of the examples presented in Chapter 3 were published in Kupferberg and Green (1998).
66. Berman and Slobin (1994: 520–522) show how high, mid, and low degrees of narrative agency are constructed in narrative discourse by means of evaluative syntactic devices. A high level of agency is effected when an agent is in subject position of an active sentence; a me-

dium level – when the subject agent is "demoted" (Biber 1988) to a prepositional phrase; a low level – a when the agent is embedded in a prepositional phrase and functions as a source adverbial. For further discussion of agency, see Givon (1990), Green and Kupferberg (2000), Harré (1995), and Harré and Gillet (1994).
67. See Malone's (1997) overview of the function of pronouns.
68. Repetition, as we show in Chapter 3 and passim, is a self-builder that establishes importance. See Buttny and Jensen (1995). See also Green and Kupferberg (2000), Kupferberg and Gilat (2001), and Kupferberg and Green (1998, 2001, 2003) for empirical evidence on repetition in interviewing and telephone interactions.
69. Following Robinson (1995), we define the noticing of discrete figurative language forms as detection and rehearsal in short-term memory prior to encoding in long-term memory and following the allocation of attention to certain input features. Kupferberg (1995, 1999) and Kupferberg and Olshtain (1996) show how salient linguistic features can enhance noticing. Giora (2003) defines salience on the basis of context-free criteria (i.e., conventionality, frequency, familiarity, and prototypicality). The tropes produced by the troubled caller in this naturally occurring interaction and in other examples presented in the book are not necessarily conventional, frequent, familiar or prototypical. We argue that what makes the psychologist notice these tropes is their idiosyncratic use within the more detailed narrative format. Thus, salience is created by the production of two versions of the troubled self that work in tandem: the detailed personal story and the organizing trope.
70. For other factors undermining telephone problem discourse see Chapters 1 and 2 and passim. See also Kupferberg and Green (1998) and Raviv and Abuhav (2003).
71. Labov's (1972) structural definition of personal stories includes orientation, where the narrator provides contextualizing details that illuminate the complicating action or the problem-causing chain of events.
72. The literal translation of the caller's organizing trope is "even I was like a mother to him." The caller used *afilu* 'even', an emphatic Hebrew conjunction that shows the extremity or intensity of the situation in comparison with other situations (Avnion 1997). In the English translation, we used the stance adverbial 'really' (Biber et al. 1999) as an emphatic marker. It is noteworthy that the caller does not say "he was like a son to me", but rather *I was really like a mother to him*, emphasizing her perspective on the relationship.
73. The salience of the organizing trope *I was really like a mother to him*

meets the criteria set by Giora (2003) and described in Chapter 2. However, it is very difficult to explain the salience of this trope in the context of a naturally occurring interaction only by the criteria that Giora puts forward. The salience of this trope can be accounted for mainly in terms of the detailed emotionally-charged narrative format that the troubled caller unfolds and then summarizes figuratively.

74. The psychologist uses two Hebrew stance adverbials – *kimat* 'almost', and *ktsat* 'a little' to minimize or downtone the intensity expressed in the caller's simile. The literal translation of the Hebrew utterance is "you were almost a little like a mother".
75. Quirk et al. (1985: 825) define rhetorical questions in the following words: "The rhetorical question is an interrogative in structure, but has the force of a strong assertion. It generally does not expect an answer." Biber et al. (1999: 206) add: "By choosing an interrogative form, the speaker appears to let the addressee be the judge, but no overt response is expected."
76. The young woman told the radio team that she is religious. Ultra-Orthodox Jewish women do not use contraceptives. This explains her successive pregnancies.
77. The caller producing this trope used the Hebrew words *smartut rizpa* 'floor rag'. In Israel, *smartut rizpa* is used for washing floors. It also means a "person who is humiliated and degraded". We preferred to use the literal translation, "floor rag", rather than the more adequate English compound "doormat", because the volunteer relates to the issue of cleaning in her answer. See Example (40), line 15.
78. The examples presented in Chapter 5 were published in Kupferberg, Green, and Gilat (2002).
79. The average length of ERAN calls is 18 minutes. This was brought to our attention by Izhak Gilat, ERAN's professional coordinator, in a personal communication.
80. See Example (24) and comments in Chapter 4, Capps and Ochs (1995) and Green and Kupferberg (2000) for other examples of self-disclosing negative forms.
81. When the caller's first version is unfolded, the volunteer does not seem fully convinced that the caller is telling the truth. This is reflected in comments such as "according to what you say" and "you claim that".
82. Tropes are context- and culture-dependent. In another study (Bar-Kol and Kupferberg 2001) we explored the organizing tropes of men and women who made the transition from teaching to principalship. One of the Arab female principals organizes her transition story by describing herself as a queen: "I was *a queen*. Nobody touched me. Nobody took me seriously" (ibid.: 313). She also describes her own mother as *a*

queen when she depicts how her father treated her mother. Both metaphorical queens are created in the context of the Arab tradition where the queen is first and foremost the almighty king's wife. The queen has no rights, but she is treated with honor.

83. In the third stage of the call, when the caller attempts to convince the volunteer that her version of the story is true, she produces 44 turns in which there are 18 rhetorical questions.

84. We preferred the term *interpersonal utterance* instead of *interpersonal clause* – the unit used by Halliday (1985).

85. Telic verbs denote an action viewed as completed as in: "I found the book." Atelic verbs such as "look for" relate to a process as in: "I am looking for the book" (Hopper and Thompson 1980). The adolescent uses the telic verb "find", whereas the answerer uses the atelic verb "look for".

86. Adolescents' feelings of aloneness are often intensified by conflicts with their parents that sometimes lead to suicide (Maltsberger 1998).

87. In Hebrew, gender is grammatically encoded in the verbal system and therefore it is easy to see that the answerer is a female, or at least chooses to present herself as such.

88. The boy begins the message with the Hebrew greeting uttered before the Sabbath.

89. According to Labov (1972), other components like the abstract and the coda are not obligatory.

90. Parapsychological phenomena such as energy transfer, telepathy, clairvoyance, precognition or other forms of extrasensory perception (ESP) are currently unexplained in terms of known physical or biological mechanisms (Bem and Honorton 1994).

91. McReynolds (1990) lists conceptual figurative formulas that guide Western thinking on issues of control. Following McReynolds, we can say that when the caller describes his childhood experiences, he chooses THE CONTROLLING POWERS AND THE PERSONS ARE PAWNS formula and positions himself as a pawn in relation to these powers.

92. The "wave" metaphor produced in lines 11 and 13 could be regarded as an organizing trope that summarizes the unusual *generic stories* described by the caller. We do not define it as an organizing trope for two reasons. First, it is not produced within a specific past-tense story like other organizing tropes discussed in previous chapters. In addition, the host does not relate to the "wave" metaphor in his response to the caller, but chooses the more general term *power* (see Examples (59) and (60)). Can we say that organizing tropes summarize the meaning of generic stories, as well? This is a question that future research could explore in the future.

93. Some of the examples presented in Chapter 8 are published in Green and Kupferberg (2000).
94. *Anorexia nervosa*, or refusal to maintain body weight at or above a minimally normal weight for age and height (American Psychiatric Association, DSM IV, 1994), is considered an addictive behavior (Bulik 1987). See also Minuchin, Rosman, and Baker (1978).
95. The caller uses the Hebrew noun *kadur sheleg* 'snowball'.
96. The caller used the Hebrew word *ketzev* 'rhythm'.
97. Such tropes are often used in Western civilization to define states of despair. The metaphor can be described as an instance of UNHAPPINESS IS DOWN, which is a conceptual metaphor (Lakoff and Johnson 1980).
98. Bamberg (1997c, d) describes how emotions are constructed via syntactic structures. See other examples in Chapter 5 and passim.
99. See Example (70) below in which the anorexic's mother unfolds her codependent's story. When the program was broadcast, the anorexic's mother's call preceded the obese eater's call.
100. McReynolds' (1990) conceptual trope INNER FORCES OR PERSONS ARE MACHINES is probably the concept underlying what the caller says, if one adheres to a conceptualist approach to figurative language.
101. Abbot, Cramer, and Sherrets (1995) focus on the family's inability to identify the emerging pathological addictive pattern.
102. An Asian rum-like alcoholic beverage that is distilled from a fermented mash of malted rice with toddy or molasses (Webster 1989).

References

Abbot, D. A., S. Cramer, and S. Sherrets
    1995   Pathological gambling and the family: Practice implications. *Families in Society* 76, 213–219.

Adler, A.
    1929   *Problems of Neurosis*. London: Kegan Paul.

American Psychiatric Association
    1994   *Diagnostic and Statistical Manual of Mental Disorders* (4th ed.). Washington, D.C.: American Psychiatric Association.

Anderson, H.
    1997   *Conversation, Language and Possibilities. A Postmodern Approach to Therapy*. New York: Basic Books.

Avnion, E. (ed.)
    1997   *Sapir Dictionary. A Hebrew–Hebrew Dictionary*. Jerusalem: Hed Arzi and Itaav.

Bakhtin, M. M.
    1981   Discourse in the novel. In Holoquist, M. (ed.), *The Dialogic Imagination*. Translated by C. Emerson and M. Holoquist. Austin, TX: University of Texas Press, 259–422.
    1986   Speech genres and other late essays. In Emerson, C. and M. Holoquist (eds.), Austin, TX: University of Texas Press.

Bamberg, M. (ed.)
    1997a   Oral versions of personal experience: Three decades of narrative analysis. Special issue of *Journal of Narrative and Life History* 7.
    1997b   Positioning between structure and performance. *Journal of Narrative and Life History* 7, 335–342.
    1997c   Emotion talk(s): The role of perspective in the construction of emotions. In Niemeier, S. and R. Dirven (eds.), *The Language of Emotions: Conceptualization, Expression, and Theoretical Foundation*. Amsterdam: John Benjamins, 209–225.
    1997d   A constructivist approach to narrative development. In Bamberg, M. (ed.), *Narrative Development: Six Approaches*. Hillsdale, NJ: Lawrence Erlbaum, 89–132.
    1999   Is there anything behind discourse? Narrative and local accomplishments of identities. In Maiers, W., B. Bayer, B. D. Esgalhado, R. Jorna, and E. Schraube (eds.), *Challenges to Theoretical Psychology*. North York, Ontario: Captus University Publications, 220–227.

Barak, A.
2001 Locally and culturally constructing otherness. Paper presented at the Eliot Mishler Narrative Group, Clark University, May.

Barak, A.
2000 Internet and suicides: Another expression of the two faces of the Internet. *Haye'utz Hachinuchi* 9, 111–128.

Barker, P.
1996 *Psychotherapeutic Metaphors: A Guide to Theory and Practice*. Bristol, PA: Brunner/Mazel.

Bar-Kol, R. and I. Kupferberg
2001 From teaching to principalship under the male umbrella: Transition stories of men and women in the Arab sector. *Studies in Educational Administration and Organization* 25, 121–143.

Bauman, R.
1986 *Story, Performance, and Event: Contextual Studies of Oral Narrative*. Cambridge: Cambridge University Press.

Beattie, M.
1987 *Codependent No More*. Center City, MN: Hazelden Educational Materials.

Beck, A. T.
1976 *Cognitive Therapy and the Emotional Disorders*. New York: Meridian.

Beebe, B. and F. M. Lachmann
2002 *Infant Research and Adult Treatment: Coconstructing Interactions*. Hillsdale, NJ: Analytic Press.

Bell, A.
1992 *The Language of News Media*. Oxford, U.K.: Blackwell.

Bem, D. J. and C. Honorton
1994 Does Psi exist? Replicable evidence for an anomalous process of information transfer. *Psychological Bulletin* 115, 4–18.

Bergman, M. S.
2000 *The Hartman Era*. New York: Other Press.

Berman, A. R. and D. I. Slobin
1994 *Relating Events in Narrative: A Crosslinguistic Developmental Study*. Hillsdale, NJ: Lawrence Erlbaum.

Berman, E.
2002 The long voyage. In Berman, E. (ed.), *Psychoanalytic Treatment*. Petach Tikva, Israel: Am Oved, 7–47

Biber, D. S.
1988 *Variation across Speech and Writing*. Cambridge: Cambridge University Press.

Biber, D., S. Johansson, G. Leech, S. Conrad, and E. Finegan (eds.)
1999 *Longman Grammar of Spoken and Written English*. Harlow, U.K.: Longman.

Bing, J. M. and Bergvall, V. L.
  1998   The question of questions: Beyond binary thinking. In Coates, J. (ed.), *Language and Gender: A Reader*. Malden, MA: Blackwell, 495–510.

Bowlby, J.
  1973   *Separation Anxiety and Anger*. London: Hogarth Press.

Brewer, W. F.
  1988   What is autobiographical memory? In Rubin, D. C. (ed.), *Autobiographical Memory*. Cambridge: Cambridge University Press, 25–49.

Britton, B. K. and A. D. Pellegrini (eds.)
  1990   *Narrative Thought and Narrative Language*. Hillsdale, NJ: Lawrence Erlbaum.

Brockmeier, J.
  2000   Autobiographical time. *Narrative Inquiry* 10, 51–73.
  2001   From the end to the beginning: Retrospective teleology in autobiography. In Brockmeier, J. and D. Carbaugh (eds.), *Narrative and Identity: Stories in Autobiography, Self and Culture*. Amsterdam: John Benjamins, 247–280.

Brockmeier, J. and D. Carbaugh
  2001   Introduction. In Brockmeier, J. and D. Carbaugh (eds.), *Narrative and Identity: Stories in Autobiography, Self and Culture*. Amsterdam: John Benjamins, 1–37.

Brockmeier, J. and R. Harré
  2001   Narrative: Problems and promises of an alternative paradigm. In Brockmeier, J. and D. Carbaugh (eds.), *Narrative and Identity: Stories in Autobiography, Self and Culture*. Amsterdam: John Benjamins, 39–58.

Bruner, J. S.
  1986   *Actual Minds, Possible Worlds*. Cambridge, MA and London: Harvard University Press.
  1990   *Acts of Meaning*. Cambridge, MA and London: Harvard University Press.
  1997   A narrative model of self-construction. In J. Snodgrass and R. L. Thompson (eds.), *The Self across Psychology. Annals of the New York Academy of Sciences* 818, 144–161.
  2001   Self-making and world-making. In Brockmeier, J. and D. Carbaugh (eds.), *Narrative and Identity: Stories in Autobiography, Self and Culture*. Amsterdam: John Benjamins, 25–37.

Bublitz, W.
  1999   Introduction: Views of coherence. In Bublitz, W., U. Lenk, and E. Ventola (eds.), *Coherence in Spoken and Written Discourse:*

How to Create it and How to Describe It. Amsterdam: John Benjamins, 1–7.

Budick, S. and W. Iser
   1991   Introduction. In Budick, S. and W. Iser, *Languages of the Unsayable: The Play of Negativity in Literature and Literary Text.* New York: Columbia University Press.

Bulik, C. M.
   1987   Drug and alcohol abuse by bulimic women and their families. *American Journal of Psychiatry* 144, 1604–1606.

Buttny, R. and A. D. Jensen
   1995   Telling problems in an initial family therapy session: The hierarchical organization of problem talk. In Morris, G. H. and R. J. Chenail (eds.), *Talk of the Clinic: Explorations in the Analysis of Medical and Therapeutic Discourse.* Hillsdale, NJ: Lawrence Erlbaum, 19–47.

Capps, L. and E. Ochs
   1995   *Constructing Panic. The Discourse of Agoraphobia.* Cambridge, MA: Harvard University Press.

Cameron, D.
   1992   Not gender difference but the difference gender makes-explanation in research on sex and language. *International Journal of the Sociology of Language* 94, 13–26.

Chafe, W.
   1994   *Discourse, Consciousness, and Time.* London: The University of Chicago Press.

Chamberlayne, P., J. Bornat, and T. Wengraf (eds.)
   2000   *The Turn to Biographical Methods in Social Science: Comparative Issues and Examples.* London: Routledge.

Chiappe, D. L. and M. J. Kennedy
   2001   Literal bases for metaphor and simile. *Metaphor and Symbol* 16, 249–276.

Chubb, N. H., C. L. Fertman, and J. L. Ross
   1997   Self-esteem in adolescence. *Adolescence* 32, 113–129.

Coates, J.
   1995   The negotiation of coherence in face-to-face interaction: Some examples from the extreme bounds. In Gernsbacher, M. A. and T. Givon (eds.), *Coherence in Spontaneous Text.* Amsterdam: John Benjamins, 41–58.

Comrie, B.
   1976   *Aspect. An Introduction to the Study of Verbal Aspect and Related Problems.* New York: Cambridge University Press.
   1985   *Tense.* New York: Cambridge University Press.

Conger, J. J.
  1997   *Adolescence and Youth: Psychological Development in a Changing World.* New York: Harper and Row.
Conway, M. A. and D. C. Rubin
  1993   The structure of autobiographical memory. In Collins, A. F., S. E. Gathercole, M. A. Conway, and P. E. Morris (eds.), *Theories of Memory.* Hillsdale, NJ: Lawrence Erlbaum, 103–137.
Cooley, C. H.
  1964[1902] *Human Nature and the Social Order.* New York: Scribner's.
Cooper, M. and J. Rowan (eds.)
  1999   Introduction: Self plurality – the one and the many. In Rowan, J. and M. Cooper (eds.), *The Plural Self: Multiplicity in Everyday Life.* London: Sage, 1–9.
Cortazzi, M.
  1993   *Narrative Analysis.* London: The Falmer Press.
Cortazzi, M., and L. Jin
  2000   Evaluating evaluation in narrative. In Hunston, S. and G. Thompson (eds.), *Evaluation in Text.* New York: Oxford University Press, 102–141.
Craib, I.
  1998   *Experiencing Identity.* London: Sage.
Crystal, D.
  2001   *Language and the Internet.* Cambridge, U.K.: Cambridge University Press.
Cumming, S. and T. Ono
  1997   Discourse and grammar. In van Dijk, T. A. (ed.), *Discourse Studies: A Multidisciplinary Introduction. Discourse as Structure and Process*, vol. 1. London: Sage, 112–137.
Davies, B. and R. Harré
  1990   Positioning: The discursive production of selves. *Journal for the Theory of Social Behavior* 20, 43–63.
Denzin, N. K.
  1993   *The Alcoholic Society: Addiction and Recovery of the Self.* New Brunswick, NJ: Transaction Publishers.
  1999   Biographical research methods. In Keeves, J. P. and G. Lakomski (eds.), *Issues in Educational Research.* Amsterdam: Pergamon, 92–102.
Douglas, J. D.
  1976   *Investigative Social Research.* Beverly Hills, CA: Sage.
Drew, P. and J. Heritage
  1992   Analyzing talk at work. In Drew, P. and J. Heritage (eds.), *Talk at Work. Interaction in Institutional Settings.* New York: Cambridge University Press, 1–65.

Drew, P. and M. L. Sorjonen
  1997　　Institutional dialogue. In van Dijk, T. A. (ed.), *Discourse Studies: A Multidisciplinary Introduction. Discourse as Social Interaction*, vol. 2. London: Sage, 92–119.
Duranti, A.
  1997　　*Linguistic Anthropology*. New York: Cambridge University Press.
Duranti, A. (ed.)
  2001　　*Key Terms in Language and Culture*. Oxford, U.K.: Blackwell.
Edgar, A. and P. Sedgwick (eds.)
  2003　　*Cultural Theory: The Key Concepts*. London: Routledge.
Edwards, D.
  1997　　*Discourse and Cognition*. London: Sage.
Eggins, S. and D. Slade
  1997　　*Analysing Casual Conversation*. London: Cassell.
Erickson, M. H.
  1983　　Healing in hypnosis, vol.1. *The Seminars, Workshops and Lectures of M. H. Erickson*. New York: Irvington Publishers.
Erickson, M. H., E. L. Rossi, and S. Ross
  1976　　*Hypnotic Realities. The Induction of Clinical Hypnosis and Forms of Indirect Suggestion*. New York: Irvington.
Erikson, E.
  1964　　*Insight and Responsibility*. New York: W. W. Norton.
Evans, D.
  1996　　*Introductory Dictionary of Lacanian Psychoanalysis*. London: Routledge.
Fairclough, N.
  1992　　*Discourse and Social Change*. Cambridge: Polity Press.
Fairclough, N. and R. Wodak
  1997　　Critical discourse analysis. In van Dijk, T. A. (ed.), *Discourse Studies: A Multidisciplinary Introduction*. London: Sage, 258–282.
Ferrara, K. W.
  1994　　*Therapeutic Ways with Words*. New York: Oxford University Press.
Fleischman, S.
  1990　　*Tense and Narrativity. From Medieval Performance to Modern Fiction*. London: Routledge.
Foa, E. B., T. Keane, and M. Friedman (eds.)
  2000　　*Effective Treatment for PTSD*. New York: Guilford Press.
Foucault, M.
  1977　　*Discipline and Punish: The Birth of the Prison*. New York: Vintage.

1988 Technologies of the self. In Martin, L. H., G. Huck, and P. H. Hutton (eds.), *Technologies of the Self: A Seminar with Michael Foucault*. London: Tavistock Publications, 16–49.

Freud, S.
[1920] Mourning and melancholia. *Complete Works*, vol. 14. Standard
1953 English Edition. London: Hogarth Press.
1920 *Beyond the Pleasure Principle*. London: Hogarth.

Frie, R.
2003 *Understanding Experience: Psychotherapy and Postmodernism*. Hove, U.K.: Routledge.

Fromm, E.
1962 *Beyond the Chains of Illusion*. New York: Simon and Schuster.

Gackenbach, J. (ed.)
1998 *Psychology and the Internet: Intrapersonal, Interpersonal, and Transpersonal Implications*. San Diego, CA: Academic Press.

Garfinkel, H.
1967 *Studies in Ethnomethodology*. Englewood Cliffs, NJ: Prentice Hall.

Gee, J. P.
1999 *An Introduction to Discourse Analysis: Theory and Method*. London: Routledge.

Georgakopoulou, A.
1994 Modern Greek oral narratives in context: Cultural constraints and evaluative ways of telling. *Text* 14, 371–399.
1997 *Narrative Performance. A Study of Modern Greek Story Telling*. Amsterdam: John Benjamins.

Georgakopoulou, A. and D. Goutsos
2000 Revisiting discourse boundaries: The narrative and non-narrative modes. *Text* 20, 63–82.

Gergen, K. J.
1991 *The Saturated Self: Dilemmas of Identity in Contemporary Life*. New York: Basic.

Gergen, M. M.
1994 Free will and psychotherapy: Complaints of the draughtman's daughters. *Journal of Theoretical and Philosophical Psychology* 14, 87–95.

Gernsbacher, M. A. and T. Givon
1995 Introduction: Coherence as a mental activity. In Gernsbacher, M. A. and T. Givon (eds.), *Coherence in Spontaneous Text*. Amsterdam: John Benjamins.

Gibbs, R.
1994 *The Poetics of the Mind: Figurative Thought, Language and Understanding*. New York: Cambridge University Press.

2001 Evaluating contemporary models of figurative language understanding. *Metaphor and Symbol* 16, 317–333.

Gilat, I, and Y. Latzer
i.p. Calls to the Israeli hotline during the Intifada. *Megamot.*

Gilat, I., T. Lobel and T. E. Gil
1998 Characteristics of calls to the Israeli hotlines during the Gulf War. *American Journal of Community Psychology* 26, 697–704.

Giora, R.
2003 *On Our Mind: Salience, Context and Figurative Language.* New York: Oxford University Press.

Givon, T.
1990 *Syntax: A Functional Typological Introduction*, vol. 2. Amsterdam: John Benjamins.

Glucksberg, S. and B. Keysar
1993 How metaphors work. In Orteny, A. (ed.), *Metaphor and Thought* (2nd ed.). Cambridge, U.K.: Cambridge University Press, 401–424.

Goffman, E.
1959 *The Presentation of Self in Everyday Life.* New York: Doubleday.

Goodman, N.
1984 *Mind and Other Matters.* Cambridge, MA: Harvard University Press.

Green, D.
1985 Cognitive Strategies in Secular and Religious Widows' Answers to their Children's Questions, and Their Influence on Orphans' Death Conceptualization. Unpublished doctoral dissertation, Tel Aviv University, Tel Aviv.
1986 Involuntary converts? The cult phenomenon in the Western world and in Israel. *Psychology and Counseling* 4, 113–139.
1992 Personality and addiction. Paper presented at The 4th Ibero-American Conference On Addiction. Mexico City, Mexico, July.
2002 Adolescents in an uninhabited space. *Panim, Quarterly for Society, Culture and Education* 19, 93–104.
2003a Adolescents' identity formation through the Internet. Paper presented at the First Convention: Internet for Handicapped Adolescents. The Center for Educational Technology. Tel Aviv University, Israel, May.
2003b Developmental aspects of drug-abuse adolescents. In Aharoni, M. (ed.), *Childrens' Advocates.* Tel Aviv: The Buchman Faculty of Law, Tel Aviv University, 12–20.

2004 Counseling during the process of adolescents' sexual identity crystallization. In Klingman, A. and R. Erhard (eds.), *School Counselling in a Changing Society*. Tel Aviv: Ramot, 181–210.

Green, D. (ed.)
1995 *Drugs: Facts, Questions and Problems*. Tel Aviv: The Ministry of Defense Press.

Green, D. and I. Kupferberg
2000 Detailed and succinct self-portraits of addicts in broadcast stories. *Discourse Studies* 2, 305–322.
n.d. *The Discursive Construction of Trauma*. Manuscript.

Gubrium, J. F. and J. A. Holstein (eds.)
2000 Analyzing interpretive practice. In Denzin, N. K. and Y. S. Lincoln (eds.), *Handbook of Qualitative Research* (2nd ed.). Thousand Oaks, CA: Sage, 487–508.
2001 *Institutional Selves*. New York: Oxford University Press.

Gunnarsson, B., P. Linell, and B. Nordberg (eds.)
1997 *The Construction of Professional Discourse*. New York: Longman.

Halliday, M. A. K.
1985 *An Introduction to Functional Grammar*. London: Edward Arnold.

Halliday, M. A. K. and R. Hasan
1976 *Cohesion in English*. London: Longman.

Harré, R.
1995 Agentive discourse. In Harré, R. and P. Stearns (eds.), *Discursive Psychology in Practice*. Thousand Oaks, CA: Sage, 120–136.
1996 There is no time like the present. In Copeland, B. J. (ed.), *Logic and Reality*. Oxford: U.K.: Clarendon Press, 389–409.

Harré, R. and G. Gillett
1994 *The Discursive Mind*. Thousand Oaks, CA: Sage.

Harré, R. and van L. Langenhove (eds.)
1999 *Positioning Theory: Moral Contexts of Intentional Action*. Oxford, U.K.: Blackwell.

Hartley, J.
2002 *Communication, Cultural and Media Studies: The Key Concepts*. London: Routledge.

Hartmann, H.
1964 *Essays in Ego Psychology*. New York: International University Press.

Heidegger, M.
1962 *Being and Time*. New York: Harper and Row.

Heller, M.
2001 Discourse and interaction. In Schiffrin, D., D. Tannen, and H. E. Hamilton (eds.), *The Handbook of Discourse Analysis*. Oxford: Blackwell, 250–264.

Heritage, J.
1997 Conversation analysis and institutional talk: Analyzing data. In Silverman, D. (ed.), *Qualitative Research: Theory, Method and Practice*. London: Sage, 161–182.

Heritage, J. and D. Greatbatch
1992 On the institutional character of institutional talk: The case of news interviewers. In Boden, D. and D. Zimmerman (eds.), *Talk and Social Structure*. Oxford, U.K.: Polity Press, 93–137.

Herring, S. C.
2001 Computer-mediated discourse. In Schiffrin, D., D. Tannen, and H. E. Hamilton (eds), *The Handbook of Discourse Analysis*. Oxford: Blackwell, 250–264.

Hester, S. and D. Francis
2000 Ethnomethodology, conversation analysis, and 'institutional talk'. *Text* 20, 391–413.

Hoffman, L.
1997 Foreword. In H. Anderson, *Conversation, Language and Possibilities. A Postmodern Approach to Therapy*. New York: Basic Books, XI–XVI.

Holstein, J. A. and J. F. Gubrium
1994 Phenomenology, ethnomethodology, and interpretive practice. In Denzin, N. and Y. S. Lincoln (eds.), *Handbook of Qualitative Research*. Thousand Oaks, CA: Sage, 262–272.
2000 *The Self We Live By: Narrative Identity in a Postmodern World*. New York: Oxford University Press.

Honeck, R. P.
1997 *A Proverb in Mind: The Cognitive Science of Proverbial Wit and Wisdom*. Hillsdale, NJ: Lawrence Erlbaum.

Honeck, R. P. and J. G. Temple
1992 Metaphor, expertise and *pest*. *Metaphor and Symbolic Activity* 7, 237–252.

Hopper, P. and S. Thompson
1980 Transitivity in grammar and discourse. *Language* 56, 251–299.

Horney, K.
1939 *Ways in Psychoanalysis*. New York: Norton.

Hutchby, I.
1995 Aspects of recipient design in expert advice-giving on call-in radio. *Discourse Processes* 19, 219–238.

Hutton, P. H.
  1988   Foucault, Freud, and the technologies of the self. In Martin, L. H., G. Huck, and P. H. Hutton (eds.), *Technologies of the Self: A Seminar with Michael Foucault.* London: Tavistock Publications, 121–144.

Hymes, D.
  1972   Models of the interaction of language and social life. In Gumperz, J. and D. Hymes (eds.), *Directions in Sociolinguistics: The Ethnography of Communication.* New York: Holt, Rinehart and Winston, 35–71.
  1974   *Foundations in Sociolinguistics.* Philadelphia, PA: University of Pennsylvania Press.

Ingram, D.
  1994   Poststructuralist interpretation of the psychoanalytic relationship. *Journal of the American Academy of Psychoanalysis* 22, 175–193.

James, W.
  1961[1892]   *Psychology: The Briefer Course.* New York: Harper and Brothers.

Jaworski, A. and N. Coupland (eds.)
  1999   *The Discourse Reader.* London: Routledge.

Johnson, M.
  1987   *The Body in the Mind: The Bodily Basis of Meaning, Imagination and Reason.* Chicago: University of Chicago Press.

Johnson, S
  1997   Theorizing language masculinity: A feminist perspective. In Johnson, S. and U. H. Meinhof (eds.), *Language and Masculinity.* Oxford: Blackwell, 8–26.

Jung, C. G.
  1959   *The Archetypes and the Collective Unconscious.* New York: Pantheon Books.

Kahn, M. J.
  1991   Factors affecting the coming out process for lesbians. *Journal of Homosexuality* 21, 47–70.

Kaplan, H. I. and B. J. Sadock
  1988   *Clinical Psychiatry.* London: Williams and Wilkins.

Katriel, T.
  1998   Constructing distress narratives on Israeli talk radio. Paper presented at the Twelfth Sociolinguistic Symposium, London.

Kennedy, M. J. and D. L. Chiappe
  1998   What makes a metaphor stronger than a simile? *Metaphor and Symbol* 14, 63–69.

Kernberg, O. F.
1980   *Internal World and External Reality.* New York: Sason Aronson.

Klein, W.
1994   *Time in Language.* London: Routledge.

Kohut, H.
1964   Some problems of a meta-psychological formulation of fantasy. *The International Journal of Psychoanalysis* 45, 199–202.

Korolija, N.
1998   Recycling co-text: The impact of prior conversation on the emergence of episodes in a multiparty radio talk show. *Discourse Processes* 25, 99–125.

Kövecses, Z.
1990   *Emotion Concepts.* New York: Springer Verlag.
1998   Are there any emotion-specific metaphors? In Athanasiadou, A. and E. Tabakowska (eds.), *Speaking of Emotions: Conceptualization and Expression.* Berlin: Mouton de Gruyer, 131–151.

Kuhn, T. S.
1970   *The Structure of Scientific Revolutions.* Chicago: University of Chicago Press.

Kupferberg, I.
1995   Contrastive Linguistic Input and the Acquisition of Grammar in the Additional Language Classroom. Unpublished doctoral dissertation, Tel Aviv University, Tel Aviv.
1999   The cognitive turn of contrastive analysis: Empirical evidence. *Language Awareness* 8, 210–222.
2004   Exploring the professional self via narrative positioning. *Mahalahim* 5, 79–102.
i.p.   The emerging professional self in problem discourse: A case study. In Lidor, R., B. Fresko, and M. Ben-Peretz (eds.), *Methodological Considerations: Studies in Instruction and Learning.* Tel Aviv: The MOFET Institute.

Kupferberg, I. and M. Ben-Peretz
2004   Emerging and experienced professional selves in cyber discourse. In Vrasidas, C. and G. V. Glass (eds.), *Online Professional Development for Teachers.* Connecticut: Information Age Publishing, 105–120.

Kupferberg, I. and I. Gilat
2001   Detailed and succinct versions of an emerging professional self. In Ariav, T., A. Keinan, and R. Zuzovsky (eds.), *The Ongoing Development of Teacher Education: Exchange of Ideas.* Tel Aviv: The MOFET Institute, 342–359.

2002 *Metaphorical-Narrative Bridges in Interpersonal Communication: The Personal Story as a Tool for Teacher Education.* Tel Aviv: The MOFET Institute.

Kupferberg, I., I. Gilat, and D. Green
2000 Figurative language as a self-portrait of a student community in time of stress. Can we evaluate stress through the use of figurative language? *CD-ROM of articles from the 12th World Congress of Applied Linguistics.* Tokyo, August.

Kupferberg, I. and D. Green
1998 Metaphors enhance radio problem-discussions. *Metaphor and Symbol* 13, 103–123.
2001 Exploring the professional self via figurative positioning: A qualitative research method (in Hebrew). *SCRIPT* 2, 149–165.
2003 Figurative coherence in radio problem discourse. In Toury, G. and R. Ben Shahar (eds.), *Hebrew – A Living Language, III: Studies on the Language in Its Social and Cultural Contexts.* Tel Aviv University: Porter Institute.

Kupferberg, I., D. Green and I. Gilat
2002 Figurative positioning in hotline stories. *Narrative Inquiry* 11, 1–26.

Kupferberg, I. and E. Olshtain
1996 Explicit contrastive instruction facilitates the acquisition of difficult L2 forms. Special issue: Cross-linguistic approaches to language awareness. *Language Awareness* 5, 149–165.

Labov, W.
1972 *Language in the Inner City: Studies in the Black English Vernacular.* Philadelphia: University of Pennsylvania Press

Labov, W. and D. Fanshel
1977 *Therapeutic Discourse: Psychotherapy as Conversation.* New York: Academic Press.

Labov, W. and J. Waletzky
1967 Narrative analysis: Oral versions of personal experience. In Helm, J. (ed.), *Essays on the Verbal and Visual Arts.* Seattle, WA: University of Washington Press, 12–44.

Lacan, J.
1988 *Ego in Freud's Theory and in the Technique of Psychoanalysis.* Cambridge: Cambridge University Press.

Lakoff, G.
1987 *Women, Fire and Dangerous Things: What Categories Reveal about the Mind.* Chicago: University of Chicago Press.

Lakoff, G. and M. Johnson
1980 *Metaphors We Live By.* Chicago: University of Chicago Press.

Langenhove, L. van and R. Harré
1999   Introducing positioning theory. In Harré, R. and L. van Langenhove (eds.), *Positioning Theory: Moral Contexts of Intentional Action*. Oxford: Blackwell, 14–31.

Lather, P.
1994   Staying dumb? Feminist research and pedagogy in the postmodern. In Simons, H. W. and M. Billig (eds.), *After Postmodernism: Reconstructing Ideology Critique*. London: Sage, 101–132.

Latzer, Y. and I. Gilat
2000   Calls to the Israeli hotline from individuals who suffer from eating disorders: An epidemiological study. *Eating Disorders* 8, 31–42.

Leezenberg, M.
2001   *Contexts of Metaphor*. Oxford, U.K.: Elsevier.

Lefcourt, H. M. and K. Davidson-Katz
1991   Locus of control and health. In Snyder, C. R. and D. R. Forsyth (eds.), *Handbook of Social and Clinical Psychology*. New York: Pergamon Press, 246–266.

Liddicoat, A., S. Dopke, K. Love, and A. Brown
1994   Presenting a point of view: Callers' contributions to talkback radio in Australia. *Journal of Pragmatics* 22, 139–156.

Lieblich, A., R. Tuval-Mashiach, and T. Zilber
1998   *Narrative Research: Reading Analysis and Interpretation*. Thousand Oaks, CA: Sage.

Lincoln, Y. S and E. G. Guba
1998   Paradigmatic controversies, contradictions and emerging confluences. In Denzin, N. K and Y. S. Lincoln (eds), *Handbook of qualitative research*. Thousand Oaks, CA: Sage, 163–188.

Linde, C.
1993   *Life Stories: The Creation of Coherence*. New York: Oxford University Press.

Linell, P.
1998   *Approaching Dialogue: Talk, Interaction and Context in Dialogical Perspectives*. Amsterdam: John Benjamins.

Linell, P. and N. Korolija
1997   Coherence in multi-party conversation. Episodes and contexts in interaction. In Givon, T. (ed.), *Conversation: Cognitive, Communicative and Social Perspectives*. Amsterdam: John Benjamins.

Lynch, M.
2000   The ethnomethodological foundations of conversation analysis. *Text* 20, 517–532.

Macdonald, M.
2003 *Exploring Media Discourse.* Cornwall, U.K.: Arnold.
Mahler, M. S.
1963 Thoughts about development and individuation. *The Psychoanalytic Study of the Child* 18, 307–324.
Malone, M. J.
1997 *Worlds of Talk: The Presentation of Self in Everyday Conversation.* Cambridge, U.K.: Polity Press.
Maltsberger, J. T.
1998 The psychodynamic understanding of suicide. In Jacobs, D. (ed.), *Harvard Medical School Guide to Assessment and Intervention in Suicide.* San Francisco: Jossey Bass, 72–82.
Martin, L. H., H. Gutman, and P. H. Hutton (eds.)
1988 *Technologies of the Self: A Seminar with Michael Foucault.* London: Tavistock Publications.
McAdams, D. P.
1993 *Personal Myths and the Making of the Self.* New York: William Morrow and Company.
1996 Personality, modernity, and the storied self: A contemporary framework for studying persons. *Psychological Inquiry* 7, 295–321.
McMullen, L. M.
1996 Studying the use of figurative language in psychotherapy: The search for researchable questions. *Metaphor and Symbolic Activity* 11, 241–255.
McMullen, L. M. and J. B. Conway
1994 Dominance and nurturance in the figurative expressions of psychotherapy clients. *Psychotherapy Research* 4, 43–57.
1996 Conceptualizing the figurative expressions of psychotherapy clients. In Mio, J. S. and A. N. Katz (eds.), *Metaphor: Implications and Applications.* Hillsdale, NJ: Lawrence Erlbaum, 59–71.
McReynolds, P.
1990 Motives and metaphors. In Leary, D. E. (ed.), *Metaphors in the History of Psychology.* Cambridge, U.K.: Cambridge University Press, 133–172.
Mead, G. H.
1934 *Mind, Self and Society.* Chicago: University of Chicago Press.
Merriam-Webster's Collegiate Dictionary
1999 10th edition. Britannica CD.
Miller, G.
1997 Building bridges: The possibility of analytic dialogue between ethnography, conversation analysis and Foucault. In Silverman,

D. (ed.), *Qualitative Research: Theory, Method and Practice*. London: Sage, 24–44.

Minuchin, S., B. L. Rosman, and L. Baker
   1978   *Psychosomatic Families: Anorexia Nervosa in Context*. London: Harvard University Press.

Mishler, E. G.
   2000   Validation in inquiry-guided research: The role of exemplars in narrative studies. In Brizuela, B. M., J. P. Stewart, R. G. Carrillo, and J. G. Berger (eds.), *Acts of Inquiry in Qualitative Research*. Cambridge, MA: Harvard Educational Review, 119–145.

Mitchell, W. J. T. (ed.)
   1981   *On Narrative*. Chicago, IL: University of Chicago Press.

Montgomery, M.
   1991   Our tune: A study of discourse genre. In Scannell, P. (ed.), *Broadcast Talk*. London: Sage, 138–177.

Moustakas, C.
   1994   *Phenomenological Research Methods*. Thousand Oaks, CA: Sage.

Munitz, H. (ed.)
   1997   *Selected Chapters in Psychiatry*. Tel Aviv: Papyrus.

Nelson, K. (ed.)
   1989   *Narratives from the Crib*. Cambridge, MA: Harvard University Press.
   1993   The psychological and social origins of autobiographical memory. *Psychological Science* 4, 7–14.

Ochs, E.
   1979   Planned vs. unplanned discourse. In Givon, T. (ed.), *Syntax and Semantics 12: Discourse and Syntax*. New York: Academic Press, 51–80.
   1994   Stories that step into the future. In Biber, D. and E. Finegan (eds.), *Sociolinguistic Perspectives on Register*. New York: Oxford University Press, 106–135.
   1997   Narrative. In van Dijk, T. A. (ed.), Discourse Studies: A Multidisciplinary Introduction. Discourse as Structure and Process, vol. 1. London: Sage, 185–207.

Or-Bach, I.
   2000   *They Don't Want to Live*. Ramat Gan, Israel: Bar Ilan University.

Overton, W. F.
   1994   Contexts of meaning: The computational and the embodied mind. In Overton, W. F. and D. S. Palermo (eds.), *The Nature and Ontogenesis of Meaning*. Hillsdale, NJ: Erlbaum, 1–18.

Parsons, T.
1951 *The Social System*. New York: Free Press.
Peele, S.
1985 *The Meaning of Addiction: Compulsive Experience and Its Interpretation*. Lexington, MA: Lexington Books.
Peele, S. and A. Brodsky
1976 *Love and Addiction*. New York: Signet.
1991 *The Truth about Addiction and Recovery*. New York: Simon and Schuster.
Peräkylä, A.
1997 Reliability and validity in research based on tapes and transcripts. In Silverman, D. (ed.), *Qualitative Research: Theory, Method and Practice*. London: Sage, 201–220.
Pillemer, D. B., A. B. Desrochers, and C. M. Ebanks
1998 Remembering the past in the present: Verb tense shifts in autobiographical memory narratives. In Thompson, C. P., D. J. Herrmann, D. Bruce, I. D. Read, D.G. Payne, and M. Toglia (eds.), *Autobiographical Memory: Theoretical and Applied Perspectives*. Hillsdale, NJ: Lawrence Erlbaum, 145–162.
Pinar, W. F., W. M. Reynolds, P. Slattery, and P. M. Traubman
2000 Understanding curriculum as phenomenological text. In Pinar, W. F., W. M. Reynolds, P. Slattery, and P. M. Traubman, *Understanding Curriculum*. New York: Peter Lang, 404–449.
Polanyi, L.
1989 *Telling the American Story. A Structural and Cultural Analysis of Conversational Storytelling*. Cambridge, MA: MIT Press.
Power, M. and T. Dalgleish
1997 *Cognition and Emotion: From Order to Disorder*. East Sussex, U.K.: Psychology Press.
Pribram, K. H.
1990 From metaphors to models: The use of analogy. In Leary, D. E. (ed.), *Metaphors in the History of Psychology*. New York: Cambridge University Press, 79–103.
Priest, P
1995 *Public Intimacies: Talk Show Participants and Tell-all TV*. Cresskill, New Jersey: Hampton Press.
Psathas, G.
1995 *Conversation Analysis: The Study of Talk-in-Interaction*. Thousand Oaks, CA: Sage.
Quirk, R., S. Greenbaum, G. Leech, and J. Svartnik
1985 *A Comprehensive Grammar of the English Language*. New York: Longman.

Rand, Y.
- 1993 Mode of Existence (MOE): To be, to have, to do – cognitive and motivational aspects. Paper presented at the International Association for Cognitive Education. Nof Ginosar, Israel.

Raviv, A. and A. Abuhav
- 2003 Ethical issues in media counseling and therapy. In Sheffler, G., Y. Achmon, and G. Weil (eds.), *Ethical Issues in the Counseling and Mental Help Professions*, Jerusalem: Magnes, 398–409.

Reid, E.
- 1998 The self and the Internet: Variations on the illusion of one self. In Gackenbach, J. (ed.), *Psychology and the Internet: Intrapersonal, Interpersonal, and Transpersonal Implications*. San Diego, CA: Academic Press, 29–42.

Reinhart, T.
- 1995 From text to meaning: Strategies of evaluation. In Shen, Y. (ed.), *Cognitive Aspects of Narrative Structure*. Tel Aviv: Porter Institute, 4–37.

Ribiero, B. T.
- 1996 Conflict talk in a psychiatric discharge interview: Struggling between personal and official footings. In C. R. Caldas-Coulthard and M. Coulthard (eds.), *Texts and Practices: Readings in Critical Discourse Analysis*. London: Routledge, 179–192.

Ricœur, P.
- 1980 The narrative function. In Ricœur, P., *Hermeneutics and the Human Sciences*. Cambridge, U.K.: Cambridge University Press.
- 1984 *Time and Narrative*, vol. 1. Chicago, IL: University of Chicago Press.
- 1985 *Time and Narrative*, vol. 2. Chicago, IL: University of Chicago Press.
- 1991 *Time and Narrative*, vol. 3. Chicago, IL: University of Chicago Press.

Robinson, P.
- 1995 Attention, memory and the 'noticing' hypothesis. *Language Learning* 45, 283–331.

Rokeach, M., W. C. McGovney, and M. R. Denney
- 1960 Dogmatic thinking versus rigid thinking. In Rokeach, M. (ed.), *The Open and Closed Mind*. New York: Basic Books, 182–195.

Rorty, R.
- 1979 *Philosophy and the Mirror of Nature*. Princeton, NJ: Princeton University Press.

Rosen, S.
- 1980 *My Voice Will Go with You. The Teaching Tales of Milton H. Erickson*. Washington, D.C.: Norton and Co.

Rotter, J. B.
  1972   Internal-external locus of control scale. In Robinson, J. P. and A. P. Shaver (eds.), *Measures of Social Psychological Attitudes*. Ann Arbor, MI: Institute for Social Research.
Rowan, J. and M. Cooper (eds.)
  1999   *The Plural Self: Multiplicity in Everyday Life*. London: Sage.
Rycroft, C.
  1972   *A Critical Dictionary of Psychoanalysis*. Harmondsworth, U.K.: Penguin.
Sacks, H.
  1992   *Lectures on Conversation (1964–1972)*, vols. I and II (ed. G. Jefferson). Oxford: Blackwell.
Sacks, H., E. A. Schegloff, and G. Jefferson
  1972   A simplest systemics for the organization of turn taking in conversation. *Language* 50, 696–735.
Sarangi, S. and C. Roberts (eds.)
  1999a *Talk, Work and Institutional Order: Discourse in Medical, Mediation and Management Settings*. Berlin: Mouton de Gruyter.
  1999b Introduction. In Sarangi, S. and C. Roberts (eds.), *Talk, Work and Institutional Order: Discourse in Medical, Mediation and Management Settings*. Berlin: Mouton de Gruyter, 1–57.
Sarbin, T. R. (ed.)
  1986   *Narrative Psychology: The Storied Nature of Human Conduct*. New York: Praeger.
Schaef, W. A.
  1987   *When Society Becomes an Addict*. San Fransisco: Harper and Row.
Schafer, R.
  1989   *Narratives of the Self*. In Cooper, A. M., O. F. Kernberg, and E. Spector Person (eds.), *Psychoanalysis Towards the Second Century*. New Haven, CT: Yale University Press.
Schank, R. C. and R. P. Abelson
  1977   *Scripts, Plans, Goals and Understanding*. Hillsdale, NJ: Lawrence Erlbaum.
  1995   Knowledge and memory: The real story. In Wyer, R. S. Jr. (ed.), *Knowledge and Memory: The Real Story*. Hillsdale, NJ: Lawrence Erlbaum, 1–85.
Schegloff, E. A.
  1997   Whose text? Whose context? *Discourse and Society* 8, 165–187.

Schegloff, E. A., E. Ochs, and S. Thompson
   1996   Introduction. In Ochs, E., E. A. Schegloff, and S. Thompson, *Interaction and Grammar.* Cambridge, U.K.: Cambridge University Press, 1–50.

Schiffrin, D.
   1981   Tense variation in narrative. *Language* 57, 45–62.
   1994   *Approaches to Discourse.* Cambridge, MA: Blackwell.

Schiffrin, D., D. Tannen, and H. E. Hamilton (eds.)
   2001   *The Handbook of Discourse Analysis.* Oxford: Blackwell.

Scollon, R. and S. W. Scollon
   2001   Discourse and intercultural communication. In Schiffrin, D., D. Tannen, and H. E. Hamilton (eds.), *The Handbook of Discourse Analysis.* Oxford: Blackwell, 538–547.

Scovel, T.
   1998   *Psycholinguistics.* Oxford: Oxford University Press.

Segal, M.
   2001   Form–function relations in the expression of evaluation in eliciting personal experience narrative during adolescence. An unpublished doctoral dissertation, Tel Aviv University.

Sehulster, J. R.
   2001   Richard Wagner's creative vision at La Spezia. In Brockmeier, J. and D. Carbaugh (eds.), *Narrative and Identity: Stories in Autobiography, Self and Culture.* Amsterdam: John Benjamins, 187–217.

Seidman, S.
   1994   *Postmodern Turn: New Perspectives on Social Theory.* New York: Cambridge University Press.

Shlaski, S. and M. Arieli
   2001   Interpretive and postmodern approaches to educational research. In Sabar, N. (ed.), *Traditions and Trends in Qualitative Research.* Lod: Dvir, 31–76.

Shotter, J.
   1999   Life inside dialogically structured mentalities: Bakhtin's and Voloshinov's account of our mental activities out in the world between us. In Rowan, J. and M. Cooper (eds.), *The Plural Self: Multiplicity in Everyday Life.* London: Sage, 71–92.

Shuy, R. W.
   1998   *The Language of Confession, Interrogation, and Deception.* Thousand Oaks, CA: Sage.

Siegleman, E. Y.
   1990   *Metaphor and Meaning in Psychotherapy.* New York: Guilford.

Silverman, D.
- 1997 *Discourses of Counselling.* London: Sage.

Smith, L. D.
- 1997 Historical and philosophical foundations. In Mandell, C. and A. McCabe (eds.), *The Problem of Meaning: Behavioral and Cognitive Perspectives.* Amsterdam: Elsevier, 15–79.

Spivey, N. N.
- 1997 *The Constructivist Metaphor: Reading, Writing and the Making of Meaning.* San Diego, CA: Academic Press.

Steinglas, P.
- 1996 *The Alcoholic Family.* New York: Basic Books

Stewart, J. (ed.)
- 1996 *Beyond the Symbol Model.* Albany, NY: State University of New York Press.

Tart, C.
- 1974 States of consciousness and state-specific sciences. In Ornstein, R. E. (ed.), *The Nature of Human Consciousness: A Book of Readings.* New York: The Viking Press, 41– 60.

Taylor, V. E. and C. E. Winquist (eds.)
- 1998 *Postmodernism: Critical Concepts*, vols. 1–4. London: Routledge.

ten Have, P.
- 1999 *Doing Conversation Analysis: A Practical Guide.* London: Sage.
- 2001 Seconds to troubles talk: The case of radio counseling. Paper presented at Language and Therapeutic Interaction: International Conference in Discourse Analysis and Conversation Analysis, Brunel University, Uxbridge 30–31 August.

Thaler, M., M. Singer, and J. Lalich
- 1995 *Cults in our Midst: The Hidden Menace in our Everyday Life.* San Fransisco: Jossey Bass Publishers.

Thombs, D. L.
- 1999 *Introduction to Addictive Behaviors* (2nd ed.). New York: The Guilford Press.

Thompson, C. P., D. J. Herrmann, D. Bruce, J. D. Read, D. G. Payne, and M. P. Toglia (eds.)
- 1998 *Autobiographical Memory: Theoretical and Applied Perspectives.* Hillsdale, NJ: Lawrence Erlbaum.

Thornborrow, J.
- 1997 Having their say: The function of stories in talk-show discourse. Special issue: Broadcast talk. *Text* 17, 157–159.
- 2002 *Power Talk: Language and Interaction in Institutional Discourse.* London: Longman.

Titscher, S., M. Meyer, R. Wodak, and E. Vetter
    2000   *Methods of Text and Discourse Analysis*. London: Sage.
Tracy, K.
    1998   Analyzing context. *Research on Language and Social Interaction* 31, 1–28.
van Dijk, T. A.
    1997   The study of discourse. In van Dijk, T. A. (ed.), *Discourse Studies: A Multidisciplinary Introduction. Discourse as Structure and Process*, vol. 1. London: Sage, 1–34.
    2001   Critical discourse analysis. In Schiffrin, D., D. Tannen, and H. E. Hamilton (eds). *The Handbook of Discourse Analysis*. Padstow, U.K.: Blackwell, 353–371.
Vygotsky, L. S.
    1978   *Mind in Society: The development of Higher Psychological Processes* (M. Cole, V. John-Steiner, S. Scribner, and E. Souberman, editors and translators). Cambridge, MA: Harvard University Press.
    1986   *Thought and Language.* (A. Kozulin, editor and translator). Cambridge, MA: MIT Press.
Wallace, P. M.
    1999   *The Psychology of the Internet*. Cambridge, U.K.: Cambridge University Press.
Watts, R. J.
    1991   *Power in Family Discourse.* Berlin: Mouton de Gruyter.
Webster's Encyclopedic Unabridged Dictionary of the English Language.
    1989   New Jersey: Gramercy Books.
Weil, A.
    1986   *The Natural Mind*. Boston: Houghton Mifflin.
Werner, A., R. J. Campbell, S. H. Frazier, and E. M. Stone
    1984   *Psychiatric Glossary.* New York: The American Psychiatric Press.
Wertsch, J. V.
    1998   *Mind as Action.* New York: Oxford University Press.
White, M. and D. Epston
    1990   *Narrative Means to Therapeutic Ends*. New York: W. W. Norton and Company.
Wright, P. H. and K. D. Wright
    1999   The two faces of codependent Relating: a research-based perspective. *Contemporary Family Therapy* 21, 527–543.
Wyer, R. S. (ed.)
    1995   *Knowledge and Memory: The Real Story. Advances in Social Cognition*, vol. VIII. Hillsdale, NJ: Lawrence Erlbaum.

Author index

Abbot, D. A., 191
Abelson, R. P., 150, 185
Abuhav, A., 4, 41, 91, 179, 181, 187, 188
Adler, A., 185
American Psychiatric Association, 74, 142, 143, 191
Anderson, H., 8, 20, 89, 181, 182, 185
Avnion, E., 188
Baker, L., 191
Bakhtin, M. M., 19, 26, 111, 185
Bamberg, M., 27, 28, 39, 94, 184, 185, 186, 191
Barak, A., 38
Barker, P., 185
Bar-Kol, R., 22, 26, 31, 68, 189
Bauman, R., 185
Beattie, M., 143
Beck, A. T., 55
Beebe, B., 21
Bell, A., 33
Bem, D. J., 190
Ben-Peretz, M., 23, 31, 49, 178, 184
Arieli, M., 187
Bentham, J., 183
Bergman, M. S., 21
Bergvall, V. L., 172
Berman, A. R., 187
Berman, E., 185
Biber, D. S., 56, 84, 114, 188, 189
Bing, J. M., 172
Bornat, J., 183
Bowlby, J., 70
Brewer, W. F., 24, 185

Britton, B. K., 185
Brockmeier, J., 17, 20, 23, 26, 183, 184, 185, 186
Brodsky, A., 142
Bruner, J. S., 4, 15, 23, 185, 186
Bublitz, W., 21, 22, 185
Budick, S., 110
Bulik, C. M., 191
Buttny, R., 4, 181, 187, 188
Cameron, D., 172
Capps, L., 17, 24, 141, 185, 189
Carbaugh, D., 183, 184, 185
Chafe, W., 20, 65, 186, 187
Chamberlayne, P., 183
Chiappe, D. L., 32, 54, 100
Chubb, N. H, 143
Coates, J., 22
Comrie, B., 186
Conger, J. J., 111
Conway, J. B., 31, 68, 185
Conway, M. A., 31, 185
Cooley, C. H., 6
Cooper, M., 7, 8, 181, 182
Cortazzi, M., 24, 185, 186,
Coupland, N., 182
Craib, I., 20
Cramer, S., 191
Crystal, D., 38, 40, 109, 187
Cumming, S., 182
Dalgleish, T., 95, 97
Davidson-Katz, K., 143
Davies, B., 186
Denney, M. R., 57
Denzin, N. K., 31, 178, 181
Desrochers, A. B., 27, 157
Douglas, J. D., 39

Drew, P., 11, 19, 182, 183, 184
Duranti, A., 15, 181
Ebanks, C. M., 27, 157
Edgar, A., 181
Edwards, D., 20, 184
Eggins, S., 96
Epston, D., 181
ERAN, 37, 38, 103, 118, 189
Erickson, M. H., 31, 136
Erikson, E., 185
Evans, D., 185
Fairclough, N., 10, 183
Fanshel, D., 24, 181
Ferrara, K. W., 31, 32, 33, 183, 185
Fertman, C. L., 143
Fleischman, S., 24, 63, 186
Foa, E. B., 75
Foucault, M., 8, 9, 10, 11, 12, 14, 20, 42, 167, 181, 183
Francis, D., 183
Frankel, R., 109
Freud, S., 8, 20, 21, 54, 72, 142, 185
Frie, R., 8, 20, 181, 182
Friedman, M., 75
Fromm, E., 185
Gackenbach, J., 181, 187
Garfinkel, H., 183
Gee, J. P., 184
Georgakopoulou, A., 24, 26, 27, 95, 184
Gergen, K. J., 7
Gergen, M. M., 19
Gernsbacher, M. A., 22
Gibbs, R., 13, 32, 33, 186
Gil, T. E., 37, 181
Gilat, I,, 22, 28, 31, 32, 33, 37, 38, 39, 68, 178, 181, 184, 188, 189
Gillet, G., 188
Giora, R., 30, 188, 189
Givon, T., 22, 188

Glucksberg, S., 32
Goffman, E., 6
Goodman, N., 184, 186
Goutsos, D., 184
Greatbatch, D., 35
Green, D., 13, 22, 25, 28, 31, 32, 33, 35, 36, 39, 54, 57, 68, 110, 111, 112, 113, 115, 123, 136, 138, 142, 143, 163, 172, 174, 181, 184, 187, 188, 189, 191
Guba, E. G., 12, 40
Gubrium, J. F., 6, 7, 8, 9, 12, 20, 25, 181, 182, 183, 184, 187
Gunnarsson, B., 182, 183
Gutman, H., 8, 183
Halliday, M. A. K., 100, 185, 190
Hamilton, H. E., 182
Harré, R., 23, 27, 146, 185, 186, 188
Hartley, J., 182
Hartmann, H., 185
Hasan, R., 185
Heidegger, M., 186
Heller, M., 16, 184
Heritage, J., 11, 19, 35, 182, 183
Herring, S. C., 187
Hester, S., 183
Hoffman, L., 7, 184
Holstein, J. A., 6, 7, 8, 9, 12, 20, 25, 181, 182, 183, 184, 187
Honeck, R. P., 33
Honorton, C., 190
Hopper, P., 190
Horney, K., 185
Hutchby, I., 33
Hutton, P. H., 8, 9, 20, 183
Hymes, D., 15, 40, 184
Ingram, D., 31
Iser, W., 110
James, W., 6
Jaworski, A., 182
Jefferson, G., 183

Jensen, A. D., 4, 181, 187, 188
Jin, L., 184, 185, 186
Johnson, M., 29, 32, 52, 191,
Johnson, S, 29, 172,
Jung, C. G., 21
Kahn, M. J., 138
Kaplan, H. I., 123
Katriel, T., 72
Keane, T., 75
Kennedy, M. J., 29, 32, 54, 100
Kernberg, O. F., 185
Keysar, B., 32
Klein, W., 186
Kohut, H., 185
Korolija, N., 22, 39, 103
Kövecses, Z., 32
Kuhn, T. S., 182
Kupferberg, I., 13, 22, 23, 25, 26, 28, 31, 32, 33, 35, 36, 39, 49, 57, 68, 163, 174, 178, 181, 184, 186, 187, 188, 189 191
Labov, W., 18, 24, 125, 135, 181, 185, 186, 188, 190
Lacan, J., 185
Lachmann, F. M., 21
Lakoff, G., 29, 32, 52, 191
Lalich, J., 123
Langenhove, van L., 27, 186
Lather, P., 6
Latzer, Y., 37, 181
Leezenberg, M., 30, 186, 187
Lefcourt, H.M., 143
Liddicoat, A., 187
Lieblich, A., 185
Lincoln, Y. S., 12, 40
Linde, C., 22
Linell, P., 15, 19, 20, 22, 28, 183, 184
Lobel, T., 37, 181
Lynch, M., 183
Macdonald, M., 3, 4, 9, 179
Mahler, M. S., 78, 110

Malone, M. J., 94, 137, 146, 188
Maltsberger, J. T., 190
Martin, L. H., 8, 183
McAdams, D. P., 20, 22
McGovney, W. C., 57
McMullen, L. M., 23, 29, 31, 32, 68, 185
McReynolds, P., 146, 190, 191
Mead, G. H., 6
Merriam-Webster., 33
Miller, G., 25, 184
Minuchin, S., 191
Mishler, E. G., 40
Mitchell, W. J. T., 185
Montgomery, M., 35
Moustakas, C., 183
Munitz, H., 142
Nelson, K., 185
Nordberg, B., 182, 183
Ochs, E., 17, 23, 24, 26, 48, 49, 141, 184, 185, 186, 189
Olshtain, E., 188
Ono, T., 182
Or-Bach, I., 112
Overton, W. F., 6
Parsons, T., 183
Peele, S., 142
Pellegrini, A. D., 185
Peräkylä, A., 39, 47, 65, 79
Pillemer, D. B., 27, 157
Pinar, W. F., 187
Polanyi, L., 23
Power, M., 95, 97
Pribram, K. H., 33
Priest, P, 179
Psathas, G., 183, 184
Quirk, R., 96, 109, 114, 152, 189
Rand, Y., 116
Raviv, A., 4, 41, 91, 179, 181, 187, 188
Reid, E., 38
Reinhart, T., 23, 29

Ribiero, B. T., 10
Ricœur, P., 26, 185, 186
Roberts, C., 28, 182, 183
Robinson, P., 188
Rokeach, M., 57
Rorty, R., 7
Rosen, S., 50
Rosman, B. L., 191
Ross, J. L., 143
Ross, S., 136
Rossi, E. L., 136
Rotter, J. B., 143
Rowan, J., 7, 8, 181, 182
Rubin, D. C., 185
Rycroft, C., 152, 154
Sacks, H., 11, 183
Sadock, B. J., 123
Sarangi, S., 28, 183, 183
Sarbin, T. R., 185
Schaef, W. A., 142, 143
Schafer, R., 185
Schank, R. C., 150, 185
Schegloff, E. A., 15, 183, 184
Schiffrin, D., 27, 157, 182
Scollon, R., 184
Scollon, S. W., 182
Scovel, T., 174
Sedgwick, P., 181
Segal, M., 186
Sehulster, J. R., 181
Seidman, S., 6
Sherrets, S., 191
Shlaski, S., 187
Shotter, J., 20
Shuy, R. W., 181
Sieglaman, E.Y., 31, 185
Silverman, D., 181
Singer, M., 123

Slade, D., 96
Slobin, D. I., 187
Smith, L. D., 6, 182
Sorjonen, M. L., 11, 184
Spivey, N. N., 184
Steinglas, P., 156
Stewart, J., 7, 19
Tannen, D., 182
Tart, C., 142
Taylor, V. E., 182
ten Have, P., 40, 181
Thaler, M., 123
Thombs, D. L., 142
Thompson, C. P., 185
Thompson, S., 184, 190
Thornborrow, J., 10, 11, 33, 35, 183, 184
Titscher, S., 16
Tracy, K., 15
Tuval-Mashiach, R., 185
van Dijk, T.A., 10, 19, 22, 182, 183, 184
Vygotsky, L. S., 184
Waletzky, J., 24
Wallace, P. M., 181, 187
Watts, R. J., 19, 94, 98
Webster, 144, 191
Weil, A., 142
Wengraf, T., 183
Werner, A., 21
Wertsch, J. V., 20, 184
White, M., 181
Winquist, C. E., 182
Wodak, R., 183
Wright, K. D., 143
Wright, P. H., 143
Wyer, R. S., 185
Zilber, T., 185

Subject index

abstinence 152–154
addiction 35, 131–132, 136, 142–154, 156, 160–161
alcoholism 154–158
altered state of consciousness 43, 142, 150, 154, 161, 162, 170
anorexia 158–160, 191
asymmetry 11, 35
call
  discussion phase 36, 55, 67
  dismissal phase 36, 187
  effective 27, 47–56, 65, 89, 104, 168–169, 176
  ineffective 47, 56–64, 75, 169
  reception phase 36, 48, 50, 56, 59, 61, 65, 67, 69, 83, 168, 169, 187
codependency 35, 142, 143, 156, 161, 174
coherence 21–22, 177
  figurative 168–176
  global 21–22, 32, 51, 52, 64, 67, 77, 78, 168–171, 175, 176
  local 22, 60
conceptualistic approach 29
conspiracy (see trope)
context 7, 10, 15–16, 17, 19, 24, 25, 30, 53, 58, 62, 72, 73, 94, 95, 97, 98, 110, 118, 149, 182–183
constructivist paradigm 12
control 9–10, 11, 35, 43, 112, 121, 131–163, 170, 171, 173–174, 190
corpus 17, 26–27, 29, 33–38, 47, 141, 184

criteria for quality
  the next turn validation 39, 40, 51, 79
  triangulation 39, 40
  trustworthiness 40, 103, 109, 133, 134
data
  elicited 24, 33, 185
  internet 41
  naturally occurring 3, 4, 11, 12, 15, 22, 24, 29, 30, 31, 32, 33–38, 175, 179, 183, 188
data analysis
  action-oriented 3, 28, 69, 167, 176
  four-world model 13–14, 15, 25–28, 39–40, 42, 47, 64, 120, 167, 174, 186
  interpretation 5, 10, 25–28, 29, 54, 60, 78, 79, 80, 81, 87, 88, 89, 91, 101, 104, 105, 110, 114, 115, 148, 157, 186
data collection 38–41
digital writer
  adolescent 5, 33, 107–120, 121, 126, 174, 175, 176, 190
  insane 114, 123, 124
  New Age 123, 125, 126
  poetic 123, 124
  suicidal 107–120, 174, 175, 176
discourse analysis
  critical 10–11, 183
  functional approaches 15–20, 25, 29, 55, 65, 182–183
  institutional conversation analysis 8, 11–12, 13, 14, 15–18, 42

220 Subject iIndex

structural approaches 182
evaluative device 18, 22–25, 26,
    27, 28–29, 30, 31, 39, 50, 53,
    54, 57, 63, 67, 73, 75, 85, 87,
    98, 99, 102–103, 104, 110, 117,
    125, 133, 134, 136, 139, 146,
    159, 162, 174, 170–172, 174,
    177, 186, 187
  adverbial 54, 56, 85, 109, 110,
      111, 112, 114, 135, 138, 188,
      189
  constructed dialogue 17, 26–27,
      41, 75, 95, 97, 103, 111, 133,
      139, 156, 172
  figurative (see trope)
  irrealis 24, 63, 110, 141, 146,
      186
  lexical items 22, 26, 57, 85, 103,
      113, 120, 133, 134, 138, 150,
      156, 162
  modality 57, 79, 114, 141, 146
  negation 57, 74, 94, 97, 109,
      110, 112, 134, 139, 141, 146,
      147, 186, 189
  passive 146
  pronoun 17, 49, 63, 96–97, 102,
      121, 125, 137, 146, 174, 188
  question 110–111, 117, 125,
      134, 140, 145, 146, 162
  realis 184
  repetition 18, 22, 25, 49, 53, 57,
      63, 95, 96, 97, 98, 103, 110,
      112, 135, 138, 149–150, 154,
      156, 157, 188
  rhetorical question 63, 80, 85,
      96, 97, 98, 100, 112, 173,
      189, 190
  syntax 17, 22, 24, 25, 50, 63, 95,
      97, 112, 136, 147, 157, 187,
      191
  tense shift 17, 26, 27, 97, 147,
      157, 172
  transitivity 24, 49, 94, 95, 96,
      133, 149, 157
four-world model (see data
    analysis)
gender 10, 37, 98, 101, 105, 121,
    172, 175, 190
hotline (see problem discourse)
interview 8, 10, 11, 22, 24, 28,
    34–35, 36, 39, 63, 68, 73, 79,
    81–82, 91, 132, 183, 185, 188
language
  figurative 13, 23, 28–33, 39, 41,
      48, 59–60, 66, 112, 136, 146,
      147, 172–176, 177, 186–187,
      188, 191 (see also trope)
  non-figurative 30, 39, 43, 82,
      86, 120, 126, 154, 176
media-worthiness 68, 69, 168–
    169, 171, 177 (see also troubled
    caller)
modernism 6–7, 182
multilogue 38, 107–127, 168–178,
    179–180, 187
narrative
  agency 49–50, 187
  future story 49 (see also four-
      world model)
  generic story 24, 74, 135–13
  gestalt 17, 28, 39, 42, 184
  hypothetical story 23, 78
  specific personal story 23, 95–
      96, 97, 100, 102, 103, 125,
      154
noticing 188
organizing trope (see trope)
overhearing audience (see radio
    program)
panopticon 5–14, 42, 47, 64, 183
positioning
  figurative 30, 48, 54, 67, 86, 98,

99, 100, 107, 108–109
  level of 27–28, 39, 186
postmodernism 6–7, 182
problem discourse 3–4
  complexity 89, 147, 173, 174
    (see also conspiracy)
  cyber 15, 31, 38, 42, 107– 127, 168, 181
  face-to-face 8, 12, 31
  hotline 3, 4, 11, 13–14, 17, 23, 28, 33–34, 35, 37–38, 41, 43, 62–64, 67, 93–105, 107, 117–118, 120, 123, 125, 127, 131, 162, 166, 168, 170, 179, 181
  negotiation 4, 11, 56, 65, 90, 101, 103, 104, 162, 167 169, 170, 171, 172, 173
  presentation 4, 11, 13, 18, 30, 48, 50–51, 56–57, 60, 68, 69–91, 95, 100, 101, 104, 108, 132, 134, 136–137, 141–163, 167, 168–169, 171, 187
  radio 3, 16–17, 17–18, 23, 26–27, 29, 33–37, 42, 43, 47–62, 64–68, 69-91, 131–163, 168–176, 179–180, 181, 182, 184
  solution 3, 4, 5, 13, 14, 17, 30, 32, 36, 37, 39, 47–68, 69–91, 93–105, 107–127, 167–178
  volunteer 3, 11, 17, 36, 37–38, 41, 62, 63, 66, 67, 93– 105, 107, 117, 118, 119, 120, 123–124, 125–126, 127, 131, 132, 162, 170, 173, 175, 176, 179, 189, 190
radio program
  caller (see troubled caller)
  general 36, 47, 64. 69, 82–90
  host 3, 4, 11, 16, 18, 35, 36, 37, 40, 41, 42, 73–74, 79–80, 81, 82, 83, 84, 86, 90, 132, 133–135, 137, 138–139, 140, 141, 145, 146–148, 150, 151, 156, 157, 158, 159, 160, 162, 168, 169–170, 174, 187, 190
  operator 16–17, 34–35, 36, 62 64, 69, 71, 73, 84, 139–140, 160, 170
  overhearing audience 14, 16, 35, 36, 49, 65, 66, 68, 71, 83–84, 131, 137, 141, 147. 148, 150, 159, 160, 163, 168, 169, 170, 182, 187
  psychologist 3, 11, 16, 35, 36, 41, 50, 52, 53, 54, 55–56, 57–58, 59–60, 61, 62, 64, 65–66, 69, 70–71, 72, 73, 75, 76–82, 86–90, 91, 168–169, 170, 171, 174–175, 188, 189
  topic-focused 36, 47, 52–56, 69–82
salience 30, 188, 189
  self construction 5, 6–9, 10–11, 12–13, 14, 15, 17–18, 22–33, 41
  detailed and succinct formats 13, 15, 22, 31–32, 51–52, 53, 56, 67, 69, 90, 127, 131, 160, 172–176
  title 36, 38, 42, 69–91, 115, 116, 117, 136, 137, 171, 178,
    figurative 34, 42, 50–51, 78, 79, 82, 84, 85, 89, 90, 91, 108–109, 111–112, 113–114, 117, 118, 119–120, 171, 175
  trope 17, 23, 28–33, 36, 40–41
    analogy 29, 33, 48–49, 101, 104–105, 112
    bridge 13–14, 22, 42, 51, 63, 78, 167–178

cluster of 111–112, 114, 119, 120, 179
conceptual metaphor 29–30, 41, 52, 59, 69, 111, 187, 190, 191
conspiracy 63, 94–105, 109, 112, 113–114, 115, 119–120, 147, 148, 156, 157, 173–174, 179
formulaic phrase 33, 109, 112, 157
hyperbole 33, 100
metaphor 12–13, 20, 23, 30, 31, 32–33, 48, 50, 52, 54, 55, 57, 60, 63, 68, 94, 98, 100, 120, 125, 145–146, 149, 150, 152, 153–154, 157, 184, 190 (see also conceptual metaphor)
organizing 13, 36, 39–68, 70, 73, 81, 87, 90, 99, 104–105, 122, 139, 140, 148, 152, 154, 161, 168–169, 170, 172–176, 177, 179, 188–189, 190
oxymoron 33, 109
simile 23, 29, 32–33, 53–54, 55–56, 57, 58, 63, 71, 98, 100, 151, 157, 189
synecdoche 33, 139

troubled caller
  abstinent gambler 141, 150, 152–154, 161,
  addicted 25, 43, 141–154, 160–163, 170
  anonymous 5, 16–17, 36, 37, 103
  child 82–83
  codependent 43, 154–163, 170, 191
  externally-directed 42
  frequent 37, 56–59, 65, 99, 101, 104
  gay 33, 99–101, 131, 136–139, 140
  lay 4, 11, 13, 14, 35, 36, 47, 64, 65, 66, 91, 131, 157, 163, 167, 168–171, 179
  love addict 142, 144–148
  media-worthy 35, 47–56, 64, 65, 67, 68, 131, 140, 168–169, 171, 179
  obese eater 148–151, 191
  sex addict 141, 150, 151–152, 161
unit of analysis 40
virtual community 33, 107, 108, 109, 111, 112, 113, 182